ANTS
HAVE NO TASTE

by
Juliet S. Blanchard

VANTAGE PRESS
New York / Washington / Atlanta
Los Angeles / Chicago

To

Eunice, Kathy, and Marie

who brightened my way
through the Peace Corps

Contents

PREFACE

This story grew out of my experience as a Peace Corps Volunteer in the Philippines in 1962-64. The characters are fictitious composites but most of the events actually happened during the service period of our group and have been incorporated into this novel. A few, such as the fleas in chairs and double dating, have been borrowed from other volunteers. The Great Drug theme is pure fiction, but plausible.

I joined the Peace Corps to find out whether it is possible to adapt or meld dissimilar cultures without imposition or extrapolation. I found out it is a lot more difficult than I had imagined. I have tried to express the essence of what I learned through the characters in this book. It seemed that acculturation should be easier in the Philippines than in other parts of the world because English is still the language of the press, legislature, and the educated although Tagalog or "Filipino" is designated as the national language, and, it, along with dozens of dialects, is the language of home, playground, and the market. English is the medium of instruction from the third grade on. Filipinos wear American styles, are fond of American music and enjoy American jokes. When we were there, if a Filipino were asked if he had been in the U.S., he answered, "Not yet," never, "No."

Perhaps that is part of the problem. Americans and Filipinos themselves are misled by these surface similarities to expect an easier rapport. I was spared the usual "culture shock" due to previous visits in the Philippines and many other countries. Anyway differences do not come all at once as a "shock" but more as a creeping realization that the similarities are really a thin crust.

Since I know this, it is presumptuous of me to try and tell the story from the point of view of Filipinos as well as Americans. I consulted Filipinos and Americans who had lived many years in close association and mutual appreciation, and I hope I have been fair to both cultures. One of the difficulties in trying to do this is in depicting accents. It is possible to print English as the Americans hear Filipinos speak it, but not possible to print phonetically the way American accents sound to Filipinos. After one becomes accustomed to another accent it no longer affects one's feeling for that person but putting it in cold print does. Therefore, to print Filipino speech in dialect gives a false impression of that person's intelligence and sophistication. (See Note, p. 91.)

I wish to express my appreciation for assistance given me by my daughter Eunice Poethig and her family who lived in Manila and provided occasional blessed relief from Peace Corps life and were a trusted and valuable source of information and explanation of Filipinos. I was also encouraged by Dr. David Baradas, Filipino anthropologist, and several friends who read portions of the manuscript. Dr. William Taeusch, former dean of the College of Wooster, gave professional advice on syntax and style—"too many adjectives!" Bill and Betty Taeusch read the manuscript as I wrote it and led me to believe it was worth finishing. Thanks to Harriet Schroeder for help in proofreading.

Kathy Brown (now Wingert) was my roommate in training and helped bridge the gap to the other young volunteers. She adopted the nickname "Lola" for me, Tagalog for "grandmother." And when her boyfriends called me "Lola-babe" I knew I had "made it."

Marie Rapp (now Laing) and I lived in a house on the campus of the University of the Philippines, Quezon City, like the one in the story. We established a harmonious household while retaining our independence. Elena Aspi was our Filipino helper and is not the prototype for Mona. By her dawn shopping in local markets and her personal care she kept us well fed and clean and in addition gave us valuable insights into Filipino family mores.

Would I do it again? Mercy no, but I am glad I did. I don't know how much practical value Peace Corps was—is—to the host countries, but I know that the effect on volunteers was invaluable. We not only learned something about the non-Western world but more about our own country and ourselves. We knew the excitement of crossing, if not eliminating traditional boundaries of race, sex, age, nationality, religion, economic status, and social structure. We experienced the frustration and disappointment in the deep differences that separate societies but also the satisfaction of intercultural exchange and the joy of sometimes achieving understanding.

ANTS HAVE NO TASTE

1

To Dance or Not to Dance

The music whanged, slithered, and jerked. The dancers flung and twisted their bodies to match motion to sound. Feet slid and stomped; knees bent and snapped, opened and crossed; hips oozed, circled, and thrust at angles opposite to bouncing breasts; arms swung or flapped as the bodies dictated or struck out on their own. The animals of the jungle had come forth; the writhing snake, the bounding kangaroo, the stalk-legged stork, and the mischievous monkey. It was the beginning of Peace Corps training.

Along the wall and clustered in the corners of the room the non-dancers sat on straight classroom chairs and looked on. All Peace Corps trainees were supposed to participate in everything; it was the touchstone of the program. But it was impossible to talk or even to think, as the sound and rhythm dragged everything into its vortex. One group was set up for bridge but eyes were not on the cards, and there was a frequent nudge as lips formed the words, "Your bid." Most of the sitters made no attempt to follow their own pursuits. The weaving feet, knees, and hips were too fascinating. The pimpled eyeglass fringe saw it all as though through an opaque glass, while a few faces, the older ones, were set in disapproval, reading invitation to lust in the posturing.

One young woman stood alone by an open window at the edge of the dance floor, watching, yearning, loathing. To her young muscles and pounding blood, the dance was irresistible. Her toes curled tensely within her patent pumps, each short breath stretched the bosom of her yellow cotton frock. Yet her mind rejected its coarseness, its aggressiveness.

The music stopped. Laughter and gasps of exhaustion and the sounds of relaxation filled the room. Laura remained standing, miserably rigid as the dancers left the floor and slumped in chairs or pressed toward the windows. The breeze sent the sting of perspiration to her nostrils. She scarcely noticed that she was out of the chattering groups, absorbed as she was in one consuming thought, *Laura Mathews, you will learn to dance like that. You have to.*

Music again. Now the record had been changed to the moaning sigh of muted sax, smothered strings, and the soft thump of the bass. This she could dance to, but there was no one who knew it, no one who cared to find out. A girl does not walk out to the center of the room and say, "Look—here I am—I'm young—I'm alone—I want to *dance.*" She slipped behind a pillar, casually looked into her purse as if she had just thought of that place where girls go alone with their purses, and took a quick turn through the outer door.

The night was dark and starless. Beyond the campus, lights shone from houses on the hill. People were in those houses, people who belonged to other people. A cold loneliness struck her as of a physical pain, and tears stung her eyelids. She walked faster. She would learn that dance. She was free, white, and twenty-one. Quickly she crossed out the "white"; not even in the darkest corners of one's thought was that distinction allowed in the Peace Corps. She didn't really think that way, it was just a carry-over from childhood. Now she had almost rid herself of all manner of carry-overs.

Passing a two-story frame house, she saw a lamp on a table in the exact center of the picture window, drapes hanging limp on either side, almost a duplicate of the front window at home which she had faced night after night. "No neighbor watching me go in and wondering, 'Now where has Laura Mathews been this time of night?' " Her step became lighter, she rolled her hips sideways, then a forward rock, a side slip. Amazed at herself, she whispered to the people behind the safe picture window, "I've almost got it. It's not hard. Stay in there, if you want to, I'm out—out—*out!*" she finished aloud.

"Look out, lady!" boomed a man's voice behind her. She turned swiftly at the voice which came from a large figure which filled the sidewalk. He set down a suitcase and a duffel bag with a weary grunt.

"Excuse me, but you weren't looking where you were going." Seeing that she was not a "lady" but a girl, her slight form silhouetted against the picture window, he changed his tone. "Hi! Say, can you tell me where the men's dorm is? I've hoofed it all around this damned campus and there's nobody to ask." It must be a trick of the light that made her eyes so shiny. "You see, I'm getting in late. The men's dorm?" Why didn't she say something?

Laura suddenly felt as if she were standing in a pool of lovely warm water in the middle of nowhere. She consciously dragged herself out onto firm land.

"Men's dorm? Oh, you must be Dick Blumberg. Everyone has been asking where you were . . . yes, of course." Now she was climbing out fast onto the safe dry land. He was just a late volunteer.

"The men's dorm is two blocks back down the street. Everyone is dancing, back there. *Do you dance?*" The words tore themselves out of her heart.

"Do . . . do I dance?" The man-boy laughed, all over. "Madam, you are looking at the original gigolo, pride of Chi Epsilon." Picking up his duffel bag, hugging it to him, he started to shuffle and sway. Just as quickly he dropped it, caught up Laura in his arms, whirled a few steps and put her back on her feet.

"That's it," she said in a controlled voice. "Now go do it like the others." In a swift movement she side-stepped the suitcase and disappeared into the shadows.

It had begun wrong, she would tell herself many times in the years ahead. Startled out of her natural rut, she had given a wrong impression. But that first encounter was a precious one which she wrapped up carefully and hid in her heart. Sometimes she would take it out and relive it and be glad that her first meeting with Dick had been just that way.

Now she ran lightly up the steps of Rockford Hall. Her feeling of being on the outside looking in had vanished and she did not mind the echo of her steps in the long hollow hall on the second floor. The door to room 230 was not locked, and she was glad she could have it to herself even briefly. She stepped over a tennis racket in the doorway, picked up a black sweater, and tossed it across the room to the other bed. Then stretching out on her back in the dark, she gave herself to arranging her thoughts.

"This is a strange place for me to be. How did I get here?" she began wondering for about the hundredth time since Monday. It was not the dorm life which was strange; she had known that for four years at Midland College. It was partly being in California, 2,000 miles from Paddington, Kentucky. But this was only exciting, not worrisome. This she courted, being far away from home. Six months ago she had calmly, thoughtfully and—yes, prayerfully—made up her mind to apply to the Peace Corps. This was no longer considered far out; it was just one of the ordinary post-college choices. There were several kinds of overseas jobs open, or the more permanent, better-paying ones in the U.S. As much as anything she had been influenced by the Peace Corps recruiter who had come to the campus. He made it all sound so exciting, so fresh, so good in a world that seemed to hold little but work and war and woe.

She looked back at the day she had told her family of her decision to go into training for the Philippines. Dad was disappointed, he had counted on her going into church work. There was no son to follow his footsteps into the pulpit. "But why the Peace Corps?" he kept asking. "There are many other ways of getting overseas missions," he finished hopefully.

"Now, dad," Laura had said, "you know those days are about over. Americans don't go overseas to win souls anymore or tell people how to behave. Peace Corps works *with* people at *their* own level for what *they* want." She had read her recruiting literature well, but somehow it didn't sound as impressive when repeated in the living room at home.

"Yes, yes," agreed dad a bit sadly. This new reality conflicted with his own ideals now so widely ignored by the world.

Mothers are supposed to object to daughters going far afield, but Mrs. Mathews was a strong believer in the get-it-out-of-your-system theology. Let her use nail polish, she'll get tired of it. Let her take art lessons, father, she has no great talent. So now as Mrs. Mathews turned up the hem of a dress, she used the same logic. Laura looked at her mother, gray hair, comfortable figure, little fortyish lines appearing at eyes and mouth. She seemed satisfied with a long life of turning things up or down. Now she snipped a thread and put her needle into a red strawberry pin cushion.

"How short do they wear skirts in the Philippines?" They all knew Laura had won.

No, she wasn't running away, defying parents, or spurning a lover, like so many of the volunteers. Then why the inner discomfort? She had never set foot outside her own country. But Kentucky is not necessarily an inland island. The table by the sofa at home was piled with more magazines than they could read. The repetitive world news broadcasts could scarcely be avoided. There were friends who traveled, professors who went on Fulbright exchanges and came back to blast or praise or entertain their students with tales of "those people." Besides, she was going to the Philippines, an English-speaking, American oriented, modern-at-least-in-cities country. She was not afraid of differences, either race, nationality, religion, or culture—or was she? From long experience in rational analysis of her own attitudes she felt the suspicion that she was getting close to the sensitive core of her trouble. Why was she lying in bed when every other PCV was wriggling to dissonance? In every psychological test, one learned not to blacken the square that said you disliked noisy parties, just as you did not indicate that you feared to be alone, or hated your father. Extremes were frowned upon, even the extreme of never choosing an extreme. Now things were coming clear. There were no black squares to fill in, no grades to be given, no one to question her. She could admit it: she didn't like extremes. She was comfortable in the great middle-class American majority. She liked being a midwestern, average-income, educated, Protestant, solid citizen. WASP—White, Anglo-Saxon, Protestant. But she was a minority within the majority. She fit neatly into small town life, into a small coeducational, church-related college, vacations as camp counsellor, parties without drinking. She was lonely in the stadium at Ohio State, the one time her father had splurged and taken her to a Big Ten football game. Maybe her kind of people weren't numerically the majority but they were her majority and she liked the feeling of belonging. Being different was OK, if it was getting on the dean's list, being homecoming queen, and the daughter of the minister of the biggest church in town. But those differences had carried prestige with them.

Now the truth made her open her eyes to the dark. Here she was a minority, here she was different, and there was no prestige to go with it. Nobody even noticed. This first week all the volunteers seemed alike to her because she felt strange but so many students from so many places just couldn't be all that alike, could they? Maybe each one felt different, a thought that gave her hope. Surely they would sort themselves out in the days ahead, and she would find she wasn't alone. In the meantime . . .

She would dance. That shuffle was easy. She sat up and swung her feet to the floor. One foot forward, knee straight, weight on the back foot, shift and thrust out the hips. Hands shoulder high, palms out . . . Noise and laughter at the end of the hall warned that the party was over. She quickly stepped out of her shoes, put them in the closet, unzipped her dress, taking time to hang it up. She slid under the covers with face to the wall just as the door flung open with a bang.

A muffled, "Gosh, I'm sorry," did not arouse her.

2

From Dao Street to U.P.

Turn off almost any paved street in Manila and you are in a barrio, a village within the city inhabited by people transplanted from the provinces. Dao Street looked like hundreds of others. Beside the dirt road the stench of the ditches of stagnant water and floating garbage testified that they were often used for personal purposes. 'A film of oil was evidence of the half-hearted attempts of the city to discourage the breeding of insects. Rows of houses, their boards weathered dull gray by rain and sun, leaned on each other for support. In some places strips of tin from oil cans had replaced rotten wood. Windows of small panes made of shells looked out over the strip of carefully swept dirt to the row of cans from which bougainvillea blossomed in unruly splashes of crimson, pink, and magenta. Halfway up the street the shacks had been pushed aside by an aggressive, self-important new building of blue and peach concrete disdainfully proclaiming the expanding city.

A bare brown child played quietly in the ditch with a piece of broken glass. Piles of trash burned on the broken sidewalk, the acrid smoke waving in the heat of the afternoon sun.

Emerging from one of the houses, stepping out as daintily as Venus from her shell, came a vision in a pink cotton dress that swirled about her slender body. Unrelated to the sordidness of her surroundings, her beauty was a surprise seeming to glow in the torpid heat. Her skin was clear as iced tea, dark hair puffed around a face serene as polished wood, except for dark eyes, which eagerly looked up the street. She idled beside a bougainvillea and picked a pink sprig, taking no notice of the child who now sat on the edge of the ditch licking the piece of glass. He reached up and tried to pull at her skirt but she swished it away. In her high-heeled, pointed-toed black pumps she carefully picked her way over the broken boards spanning the ditch and arrived at the edge of the road at the exact moment a slim young man stepped in front of her. In his crisp white shirt, with his narrow hips in tight dark trousers, he might have stepped out of a travel bureau to guide a Federated Club Tour.

There were no greetings, no change of expression, only a furtive glance back at the house. Without a sign of recognition, the girl and boy passed a group of children poking at a dead frog. One boy whistled as they watched the pair proceed without haste to the end of the road where it met the paved street.

At the corner by the *sari-sari* store they stopped; both looked intently up the street, not at each other. Jeepneys threatened each other for space and customers, the drivers holding up fingers for the number of seats available. Luz started to step toward one marked Quiapo, but José stood still, and she put her toe back on the curb. He let several of the small extended jeeps that had survived service in World War II rattle by. When a newer jeepney came along, bright with red and yellow paint, polished metal and fringe along the top, José did not raise a hand, but the driver swerved to the curb. Before it was quite stopped, José had stepped up on the back steps. Then he remembered Luz and hesitated. He swung himself up, stooping to miss the top, and climbing over the feet of passengers he squeezed into half enough space. Luz followed him. Arranging her pink skirt carefully, she sat down opposite on a pie-shaped red plastic seat. The man beside her shifted his hips to give her an inch more room.

Maybe they won't know we're together, hoped Luz. Then she saw the woman in black in the first seat look from her to José and back to her. *It's none of her business*, protested Luz to herself. But she knew better. Any deviation from custom was everybody's business. The news would travel from pursed lips to shaking heads. *A girl and a boy got on the jeepney together at Dao Street.* The woman at the *sari-sari* store knew her, of course. *What was her mother thinking of to let her out? Ought to shut her in the house. This is Manila,* Luz defended herself to herself, *not the province. I am a teacher, twenty years old and earn my living. José is a university student and a good man. From your barrio? No, but . . . From your province, then? No, it doesn't matter . . .*

Luz was still arguing it out with herself when the jeepney pulled to the curb. They crossed to the main sidewalk and for the first time smiled at each other. Here they were free, unnoticed in the busy shopping center. They strolled along pretending to be looking at the small shops which lined the covered walkway. From a bakery came the tempting odor of fresh-baked crusty *pan de sal.* In a glass case birthday cakes bravely supported elaborate decorations. Luz pointed to a fly cozily nestled in a rose. They paused at one of the many shoe shops only a few feet wide and Luz looked intently at the display of gay colored plastic slippers outside the door. When an energetic clerk approached, they moved on.

About halfway up the block, Luz and José paused.

"Bus stops here," explained José in English, avoiding Tagalog, the national language, because Luz's family came from a Viscayan region and José's native language was Ilocano from Mountain Province. So English, learned in school, was their common coin. Red, green, brown, and blue buses pulled past, three abreast. José stretched on tiptoe to see over them and abruptly darted out into the street to swing Luz on to one marked UP BALARA.

This time they sat together. The conductress in starched brown cotton uniform banged on the side of the bus with her hand, and they were off. She collected twenty *centavos* from José and gave him ticket stubs torn from her packet. Luz felt more at ease every block they traveled out of the city.

"It's Swan Lake," said José.

"Oh . . . yes," agreed Luz, as if she didn't know. He had already told her three times that was the performance they were going to see at the Music Hall at the University of the Philippines. She had looked it up in the ragged set of *Encyclopedia Americana* in the library at the Normal School. But part of the page had been torn off or eaten by rats, so she didn't know the ending.

It was a lovely ride to the campus. The wind through the open windows cooled her moist skin and ruffled the thin scarf tied over her hair. The city shops, markets, and rooming houses gave way to cement-washed houses and apartments behind walls. After they crossed Highway 54 that circled the city there were open fields. The unfinished memorial to President Quezon loomed straight ahead. As they circled it José pointed out the new government buildings, which would one day line the boulevard. The field around the monument, now occupied by grazing carabaos, would be a park.

"Look," he pointed, "that's our atomic reactor!"

Across the fields a white box and dome rose starkly. Luz thrilled to it without understanding. "Atomic" meant the modern world, science, power. And José did understand it, or would when he finished his engineering course. She was proud but afraid, and stole an appraising look at him as he faced the window. *He doesn't eat enough*, she thought. *The line of his jaw is too sharp; his shirt hangs too loose on his shoulders.* Then she gave in to the excitement of the drive up the avenue to the entrance of the campus with its flowers and little struggling trees and the statue of man with wide-flung arms in front of the enormous administration building, welcoming all who would come to learn. She had come today to learn, to live. The house on Dao Street, the baby playing in the ditch, her brothers in the street, her mother inside worrying, seemed very far away.

Through a crack between the boards of the front of her *sala*, Maria Aspi had watched her daughter go. Once she started to call her back, but quickly pressed her palm against her mouth. This was what Manila was doing to her family, tearing it apart just as she had known it would. There was Luz, twenty and not yet married. A teacher, that was all right, but not married! Back in the province in the barrio, life had been so safe. Hard, but safe. Her eyes filled with tears now as she thought of her house, the snug walls made of double layers of woven bamboo splits, the nipa-thatched roof that let in the air but kept out the rain—most of it—the split bamboo floor high above the ground that let the dirt fall through, yet sheltered the pigs and chickens below. Always at sundown the family was inside. It wasn't crowded, even with the eight of them, just comfortable—and safe.

But papa complained of the low price he got for his rice and of the rats that ate a third of it. Luz wanted to go to Manila to normal school. The boys wanted excitement. Then their carabao died and papa said that was the end of it. Oh, it was a beautiful picture he sketched of the opportunities in Manila. Other neighbors had done it before, so they naturally went where they had friends. They weren't squatters; they paid rent for this house, but the opportunities seemed to dry up, with hungry times in between. She didn't know what they would do without the two hundred pesos Luz brought in each month.

The tears came again as she thought that back in the province Juan was waiting for Luz, working his three hectares of rice. It was about harvest time now. She could see as plain as anything the hot fields of yellow grain. But here were bare, packed dirt in front of her door and a row of pots of bougainvillea she had brought from home, the plants drooping from lack of water.

And Luz, her eldest, her prettiest with the lightest skin, out alone with a boy—a man. She didn't know his parents and had never seen the barrio from which he came. But it was in the north, and she couldn't have talked to him if he ever did come to call in the proper fashion. Anger overwhelmed her sadness and she called sharply in Tagalog to the three children who were still playing with the dead frog. She went outside and picked up the baby from the ditch, wiped his bottom and feet with her full skirt and hugged him close, rubbing her cheek against the soft skin of his shoulder. If children would only stay little!

On the stage in the Music Hall the lovely swan queen and her maidens glided through their airy dances. The gossamer layers of their stiff ballet skirts gleamed softly in the blue light against the illusion of moonlight on the lake. Luz sat rigid in her cushioned seat, her muscles aching to respond in time with the graceful points and whirls. She had never imagined that anything could be so beautiful. In the last act her tension mounted with the seductive threat of the black swan. She suffered with Odette as she tried to warn her prince.

As tragedy neared she gave herself up to the relief of tears. Without turning his head, José knew and he put his hand over hers lightly. She did not draw it away while she was part of the brief happy reunion of queen and prince.

At this moment the paper disk moon hanging in the sky by a string jerked and dropped. A titter bubbled up from the audience and the spell was broken. The swan and the prince plunged into the lake. Abruptly, Luz was aware of José by her side, the approaching trip home in the dark, the problem of entering the house, facing her parents. Even the sight of a crowned swan pulling the lovers along in a voyage to the world of eternal bliss couldn't lift her spirits again.

She withdrew her hand, blew her nose, and put her handkerchief back in her straw purse. She looked José straight in the eyes for the first time. In her teacher's tone that settled all questions she said, "Now we go home."

3

Utang Na Loob

"This may not hold true for all barrios—I can only report on the *palacion* where I lived for eighteen months—but from my observations and the research of other eminent anthropologists, it seems safe to generalize that a system called *Utang*—" there was a wave of movement in the classroom at San Francisco State College, "—*na Loob*," the seats creaked and pens stopped writing. Smiles ran around the room. The visiting lecturer sensed a change and looked up from his notes.

"It may be you have heard that term before?"

Had they heard it! Two whole lectures, three required readings for Philippine Studies. This was only the third week and "*utang*" had already become a byword, and any outsider who used it from now on would be greeted with ridicule. This anthropologist, however, was a comfortably egocentric intellectual who thought his slightest observation was an original discovery, so he proceeded to give details. Laura continued to take notes, partly from habit, partly because she was embarrassed by the rudeness of the class who had given up all pretense of listening, some sleeping, some writing letters or reading for another class.

"*Utang*," she wrote, "a system of reciprocal obligation, built up act by act between: 1) relatives; 2) landlord and tenant; 3) employer and employee . . .

"Carries over into gov.
   into marriage arrangements,
   into international affairs—US friend of Phil.
  so give aid, etc.
You vote for me—I get contract for you."

There was a tap on her shoulder, "Can I *utang* you for a piece of paper?" came in a male whisper from behind her. She turned back with a quick smile. It couldn't be that Jimmy was taking notes. No, the flyleaf of the book on the arm of his chair was covered with cartoons of the speaker.

"I can't get his ears," he complained.

That's not the only thing you can't get, thought Laura. Why was Jimmy even in the Peace Corps? she wondered. With his up-standing hair, quick darting eyes and broad nose he should be a high school coach. Boys would love him. Here he seemed bored.

Jimmy sketched in large ears, but his mind had veered off in another direction. Why he was in PC was nobody's business. Back on the south side of Chicago there was a girl crying her eyes out for him. He couldn't take it, not at twenty-two, with the army closing in on him. Military, marriage, or the PC—he had chosen the one he knew least about, although he knew it was only a temporary reprieve from the other two.

"The kinship pattern extends to distant cousins . . . young men become marriageable. The family will look for a girl . . . friends of the family . . . good Catholic . . . family with a carabao." The speaker's mouth was not in the middle of his face. People's faces were like that. From the back, Laura, with a long neck, should have had a long nose. But she didn't. It was kind of a pug, he could see from the side. Piquant was the word for her face—rangy, rural Kentucky. "Kayntucky," she said it.

"Professor, may I interrupt?" The question was laid down across the wordstream, a temporary dam. The professor was confused, the flow hunting for a new channel. His little eyes darted from row to row of young faces. Dick didn't wait to be recognized.

"Isn't it rather inconsistent to describe Filipinos as bound into a pattern of reciprocal behavior and then claim that in marriage they try to break out of this pattern into a new level? How can everyone marry higher?" There was an appreciative murmur, punctuated by a snort.

"That's a good question," came the teacher's traditional time-gainer. "As I tried to make clear in my earlier remarks, *Utang na loob* operates only between certain individuals."

"But you called it a system of obligation."

Laura held her pen poised. Dick did this frequently, moved

in politely and cautiously on a teacher until he cornered him with his own words.

"Sir, you said—"

"Of course, we cannot make every detail absolutely clear in an hour."

One hour and forty-nine minutes, corrected Jimmy silently.

"But, sir, in *Noli*, Rizal himself depicts the Filipino marriage customs in detail but never once mentions *Utang na loob*. So I wonder if it can be that important."

"I'm sorry, I will not be able to finish the lecture this period. Those of you who are interested may come to the lounge at four, I believe. At that time I would be glad to document my observations . . ." Now that escape was near, he regained his confidence, "of this very complicated aspect of Filipino culture." The note of finality in his voice was a cue for the volunteers to rise. Seats banged up. There was release from boredom in the cheerful clatter. Laura capped her pen, gathered up books, and arrived at the end of her row just as Dick came by.

"You are angry, aren't you?" she thrust at him.

Dick lost his mask of sincere, inquiring student. "That two-penny expert on humanity! What does he know about people, chopping them to bits to show to us, sticking them in notebooks."

"He lived there eighteen months," truth forced Laura to point out.

"What's that? He's a trained observer, that's all. He knows what they eat, where they urinate, who names who, and when a baby starts to show . . ."

"Hi, IQ. Balled him up, didn't you, fella?" Jimmy gave Dick a dig in the ribs and went on by.

Dick took no notice. " . . . but he never tried to feel as they feel. It would bug me to have a white American—one of that breed that stood on my neck for forty-seven years—come and live next door to me and pretend he was interested in little ole me and put it all in a notebook to blab to the whole world. It's disgusting, just disgusting."

"Ye—ah, maybe," Laura wanted to agree with him, but, "but how would we get to understand another culture if some anthro hadn't observed it and could tell us about it in detail?"

They had reached the end of the cafeteria line. "What's for lunch, Tom?" Dick shouted up the line.

"Hamburger."

"Oh, great, great!"

At the change in his voice, Laura looked at him sharply as she put her books on the shelf. So fast, so completely, he changed from standard-bearer to all-American boy. Absorbed by food or a cause, he didn't seem to be aware of her. She slipped her red zipper jacket off one shoulder, thinking he might help her with it. But he didn't, so she hung it on a hook herself philosophically. Three weeks ago she might have slipped back a few paces in line, hoping he would wait for her, but with her new aggressive spirit in command she stood her ground beside him. Shy maneuvering was out. So, chattering about mail—had it come? Who got it?—with the top of her mind, she picked up a plastic tray, fork, knife, spoon, napkin, pear-and-cottage cheese salad, large bun cut open, thick circle of ground beef matching it in size, bottle of milk, and two cookies. Keeping close but not tagging, she followed Dick to the table by the middle window.

"I'm surprised at you," she stated flatly as she tucked in her blue striped pleats and curled her feet around the chair legs.

"Ah, so?"

"Yes, always sitting in the same place. It doesn't seem up to your brand of individuality."

"So, you noticed. Why?"

"I noticed. I have brown hair, a square chin, I notice. I notice Jimmy eats with his left hand but draws with his right." She smiled lightly across the table at him.

"I notice," mimicked Dick, "that her eyes are the same color as the freckles."

She could feel the heat rising to her temples.

Next to her, Isobel joined the game. "I noticed that professor what's-his-name rubbed one shoe on the other when Dick started chopping him."

"His mouth isn't in the middle of his face," complained Jimmy.

"I notice yours isn't either," from Dick.

"Oh, lay off."

"What's for American Studies?" The conversation lapsed into impersonal student griping.

Dick finished his lunch first and took his tray to the carry-out line. Laura took her time and was surprised to see him standing beside her jacket. She reached for it and he actually gave it an awkward tug over her shoulder.

"I notice," he mumbled in her ear, "that you are going to

have the second dance with me at the Glowing Coals tonight?"

"The second?"

"Sure, we had the first in the street, remember? Bring your ID card."

4

The Glowing Coals

The room was dark. It took a few minutes for Laura's eyes to adjust. The outlines of objects began to form in the light of smoking kerosene lamps that cast a weak circle of light on the square wooden tables. In the corner a huge iron stove with the firedoor open showed fake coals glowing. Laura and Dick chose a table with other volunteers. There was Isobel, her honey hair draped across one blue eye. She was good at Tagalog and always had a man beside her. Tonight it was Gabe Levi, who always had an answer. Kathy and George Chaplin—married eight months, fourteen days, they explained—ardent civil rights workers, were sharing a highball, taking turns with sips. Over near the stove a group sat on the floor. Mary Jo, with her guitar, her un-made-up face and long braid flung over one shoulder, seemed to be with Chris, whom nobody knew.

This wasn't a haven for twosomes or steady couples. The crowd was mostly volunteers fumbling to find each other. At the bar a few townsmen occasionally turned curiously to watch this strange collection of young people. The volunteers themselves were aware of a common characteristic; they felt that life began *now*. They never volunteered information about their families or their past or welcomed questions. The Foreign Legion must have been like this, Laura mused. "What was your university?" was about the only opener to personal conversation. Some she knew by now: Gabe, NYU; Isobel, Bennington (it would have to be); Kathy and George, Pitt; Mary Jo, University of Utah; Chris, "various ones" he admitted vaguely with some allusion to a dad in the diplomatic corps and a casual dropping of the Sorbonne. Eighty-four volunteers from as many institutions of higher learning, according to a note on the information sheet. Laura wasn't sure Midland College qualified as "higher" learning, but she could line up with Jimmy from a southern school no one had heard of.

"Laura, where are you, gal?" Dick pretended a whine. "You are supposed to be entertaining me."

"Am I? I thought you were entertaining me."

"I brought you, and bought you . . ."

"No, you didn't."

"Oh, well, if you must be accurate." He put his arm companionably around her shoulders. "We're all equal here, aren't you glad? No sex superiority. We each get the same dollar fifty walk-around money each week, so we spend it drinking around. In service to our country. But you aren't doing it very well, drinking beer—after all the trouble of going back for your card."

He couldn't see Laura's embarrassed flush and her tight lips. She would not tell him she didn't go to places where she had to prove her age. When they had met in the dorm lobby he had asked if she had her ID.

"Hell, you're twenty-one, aren't you?"

"Yes, but—well, I . . ."

"Well, gosh go get it," he had commanded good humoredly.

Obediently she went back to her room, wondering what to do in a situation she had not foreseen. Gloria was in bed with a bad reaction to a yellow fever shot. Laura stood uncertainly in the doorway, then managed to swallow her independence, her pride, or whatever it was that was stiffening her spine while her heart wanted it to bend.

"Gloria," she said, "I'm in a fix."

Gloria rolled toward her, surprised at the tone. "Fix? You?"

"Yea. I'm going to The Glowing Coals with Dick and I need an ID card and . . ."

"Great, that's great. You just cut loose, see, and you'll—"

"But I don't have my ID card," miserably.

"Aren't you twenty-one?"

"Yes, of course, but," —why did they have to drag it out of her?

"Well, we'll fix that." Gloria stood up, reached for her purse on the desk and groaned, "Oh, my arm. Get it, will you? It's in the plastic case, blue."

"But yours—"

"They won't look, dummy. The Coals likes us, see? Peace Corps Washington told them to be nice to us."

Laura clutched the card. A surge of excitement lifted her feet as she ran. Downstairs she waved the card triumphantly at Dick and stuck it in her purse before he could look at it.

"Off again into the wild fog yonder," he sang, tucked her elbow under his arm and pushed open the glass door to the soft gray world.

Now safely in, without question, this crazy dark room with light patches was cozy. The warm closeness of human beings gradually relaxing soon reached her cool inner self. *Nice,* she thought, *just kind of nice,* and moved closer to Dick.

He thoughtfully swiveled his bourbon on ice. "Do you know the difference between kittens and puppies?" he inquired very seriously. When no one answered he went on. "Kittens nestle when they are happy. Puppies wriggle."

"Very profound, Professor Blumberg. At this moment I'm a kitten."

"Right. And you'll never be a puppy."

"Woof, woof," she teased.

"No, you can't be, because puppies keep on being wriggly happy even when you wish they weren't, but you can never tell about kittens. Just when you are getting comfortable with them they may yawn and walk away."

Laura laughed. "Well, wait till I yawn." She turned to look at him curiously. How had he found out that much about her so soon?

Isobel and Gabe were absorbed in each other. Gabe's finger caressed the fall of silky hair down beside her cheek, her throat, and on down to the curve of her breast. She picked up his finger as with a set of tongs and dropped his hand on the table.

"My mama done tol' me," she intoned.

Gabe snorted. "Your mama! She tol' you to be disturbing, that's the way she made you." He pulled her closer.

"Not *my* mama," she protested.

Dick, overhearing, was curious. "And why not your mama? Don't all mamas push, wheedle, stake out their daughters to attract the male?"

Laura sat up straight. "No, they don't. Some protect them, won't let them go."

Kathy and George were drawn into it. "You remember that personality Peace Corps test?" George began writing on the checkered cloth with his finger; "Question four thirty-one. 'At what age did you start dating?' Answer by Kathryn Chapin, 'Fourteen, to George Chapin.'"

"George!" Kathy squealed, "you boob, you've forgotten already. I wasn't your wife then."

George took no notice and continued writing, "Isobel at eleven."

"Nope. Twelve," corrected Isobel, "to the boy next door, birthday party."

"Laura?"

"Oh, I don't know. We kind of went around as a bunch until junior-senior prom." Any day she didn't know. It was the first time she ever deceived her mother. She had met Percy at her friend's house and four of them went to a Saturday afternoon movie. It made her so miserable she finally told her mother, who didn't turn a hair. "Now you know. Being sneaky steals the fun," she had said.

"Sixteen and never been kissed," wrote George.

Dick suddenly grabbed Laura's face between his hands and kissed her full on the lips. "We've made up for that," he declared.

Laura wiped her mouth. She didn't want his first kiss to be like that.

He knew it. So he launched into an analysis of motherhood, as if in a classroom. "Mothers are bad for children. Their possessive instincts hamper growth of personality. Mothers want to mold their children, especially girls, to their own patterns. The instinct to preserve the race leads a mother to place the highest valuation on the sexual atractiveness of her daughter."

"Hear, hear," crooned Gabe. "So mama molds and pokes Isobel into shape but says, 'Hang your clothes on a hickory limb but don't go near the water.' God!"

But George wasn't feeling humorous. "Your assumptions fall down, Dick, when it comes to the pill."

A gasp escaped Kathy, "Oh, I forgot—"

"Hush, hon," said George, matter-of-factly, "you can take it tonight. You see, if mothers only wanted to preserve the race they would not give the pill to their unmarried daughters."

"Oh, now wait." Dick was warming up to the argument. "You are forgetting her first desire to perpetuate her own image. Now her traditional patterns—mores—do not include having illegitimate kids. So with present-day options, daughter can be a siren and still not break the social patterns—so that means the pill."

Laura mentally squirmed. She tried to picture her mother handing her a box of pills and saying, "Go and enjoy yourself, dear." Suddenly she laughed and choked on her drink. Dick pounded her on the back. "Whose mother?" she gasped. "Not mine."

"Mine," said Dick, "though she's schizophrenic about it. Our so-called home is an apartment on West 120th. My mother is business manager for a dance studio. Bodies, just bodies, that's what they deal in. Mostly female and they have to stay in shape. So they quietly dispense the pill but every time she sees the bill, it hurts on account of she's a non-practicing Catholic."

In the next half hour as liquor loosened tongues, they learned more about each other than they had during the three weeks of training. The talk of mothers opened gates which had held back memories of home life. Dick with a Catholic mother and Jewish father, professor of Political Science at New York University. Isobel was almost reduced to tears recounting what she called smashing the family controls to go to "far out" Bennington and now the Peace Corps. Kathy and George, both from divorced parents but sure—so sure—of their own ability to make a go of marriage. And Laura, who thought she came from an average, normal, united, loving family, feeling like a stranger again.

Mary Jo, strumming her guitar in the light of the fake coals, was crooning the party into a state of melancholy. Laura walked over and whispered something to Mary Jo. She stood up and began to roam about the room like a troubadour. "Blowing in the Wind" changed to a rollicking oldtimer, "She'll Be Comin' 'Round the Mountain When She Comes." They began to clap in rhythm, voices rose and blended, and the place came to life. People who had other places to go had left. Peace Corps had the Coals to themselves. Tables were pushed back to make a small floor space, and couples began to move to an inner beat. Laura almost panicked. She wasn't ready for a confrontation on the twist this evening. But as Mary Jo began to pick a rhumba and glasses clicked in accent, Laura ripped off her self-consciousness. Carefully removing the glasses, she took the cloth off a table and while the others watched in astonishment, she draped it around like a rebozo and began a Spanish dance. It was easy; she had done it at the May festival at college. With some extra dips and flirtatious glances she became a Carmen, to the delight of the crowd. Dick pulled her down to the floor and joined her. His grace and skill seemed to loosen her unused muscles. She did a backbend across his arm, but when he tried to whirl her by her hands she lost balance and landed on her knees.

A roar of approval and applause climaxed the performance. They had discovered a new PCV. Dick pulled their chairs up to the bare table. "This calls for another round." And another, and another. The party became very loving and very noisy while Laura continued to nurse her second beer, wondering if she would ever enjoy the bitter taste. The few couples on the open space swayed against each other wearily. Mary Jo had signed off and been replaced by a whanging juke box. The cigarette smoke was a fog that concealed faces.

Laura nudged Dick. "Let's go home." But he just pulled her to him and nuzzled her face. *He's going to lick me like a puppy*, she thought and stood up in annoyance. Clutching her purse she ostentatiously took a turn through the door to the little girl's room—and as she had done at the dance slipped through the outer door. They wouldn't miss her.

The cool damp air filled her lungs like a purge. She pulled her sweater close and walked rapidly. They had come through the shopping center, and so she'd better go back that way. The stores were dark, their outlines weaving in the fog.

She heard them before she saw them, a man pushing someone in a wire grocery cart. A squeal of laughter came with a push which sent the cart into the bushes. Laura paused, then recognized the close-cropped head of Jimmy.

"Laura!" he exclaimed, seeing her appear out of the gray. "What you-all doing here? Alone?"

"What are you doing here—not alone?"

"We just hav'n fun, Gloria and me." Cries from the bushes summoned him and he pulled out the cart. Jimmy lifted Gloria out of the basket, and she smoothed down her skirt and long hair.

"Gloria—you were sick!"

"She got well fast when something interestin' turned up—me. What'er you doin?" he insisted.

"I have fun," she defended herself. "It's just that . . ." Dick came running around the corner of a building.

"Laura, you bastard! What the hell . . ."

"Hello."

"Well, hi."

" . . . did you leave me for?" He took her by the shoulders and shook her, then stopped and looked her over silently. "I

was right, you yawned!" Forgivingly, he tucked her elbow tight
to his side, covering her hand with his.
"Come on, kitten, we'll go home."

5

A Great Divide

In looking back Luz would date events *Before* or *After* that July 20. As on any other morning she arrived ten minutes early at Philippine Normal School, took a cloth out of the cupboard, wiped her chair and desk, and brushed a dead cockroach into the wastebasket. From her bottom drawer she took high-heeled shoes and exchanged them for the sandals in which she had left home. The day wore on from 8:00 to 3:00. Bells rang, orderly lines of students filed into Room 240. Bells rang, they filed out. Luz loved it all; the gentle light through the window pane, murky with dirt, her worn desk where venerated teachers had sat before her, students in close packed rows, their eyes upon her. She took pride in her clean yellow cotton shift and pride in their white starched uniforms, knowing the effort it required to keep them clean what with shortages of water and the expense of soap.

She taught English Literature from a textbook published in the U.S. in 1910. It had been used first by the occupying Americans who had started the school to train Filipino teachers. The hard and fast rules about the use of English only had relaxed, and often now she would explain an obscure passage in Filipino and allowed other dialects to be whispered about. As the national language became more widespread, English usage was deteriorating. She knew she didn't speak or write as well as her teachers, nor they as well as their teachers who had been American. But the literature was the same good writing, and she taught Wordsworth, Longfellow, Poe, and Shakespeare with equal enthusiasm.

She had just finished giving the next day's assignment to the last class when there was a knock at the door. She opened it to find a little student who importantly handed her a note, saying loud enough for everyone to hear, "From the office, ma'am."

Every student expectantly watched her start to open it, then the class rustled in disappointment as she refolded it and announced before the bell rang, "Class dismissed." Holding her head high and smiling with a confidence she did not feel, she saw them out, closed the door and opened the note.

Dear Miss Aspi:
Will you be so kind as to wait in your classroom at the close of school today? Miss Rodriguez, Mr. Lopez, and I would like to speak with you.

Most sincerely,
Mrs. Ramos

All three of them at once! Supervisor, Superintendent, Principal. Fortunately, Luz did not have time to worry as they arrived promptly.

Mrs. Ramos was the shape of a bell jar, Luz observed with the lower level of her mind while all her senses in the watch-tower warned her that something was up. Like the girls, Mrs. Ramos always wore white. Her upper portion descended straight, smooth and round from her shoulders to below her hips. At that level, her body hung out over slim legs and neatly formed feet. As Luz hastily placed a chair for her, she noticed for the hundredth time that Mrs. Ramos had no lap.

Mr. Lopez got his own chair. Being Superintendent of an all-female administration he was accustomed to getting his own things. If he ever succumbed to the instincts of thirty-seven women to wait on him, he would have been less of a man than he was. Luz liked him. She liked his hair, dyed black so that never a hint of gray betrayed his age. He couldn't do anything about his limp chin and wrinkled hands, and everyone knew he had graduated at UP long before the war. Nobody begrudged him his slow inching rise to his present post beyond which he would never go. Even without the dyed hair, and the UP year-book, Mr. Lopez was dated by the fact that he always wore a *barong Tagalog*. This thin, long-sleeved shirt had very little embroidery on it, was neatly mended at the collar but was always clean. Luz noticed the frayed cuffs and thought that this *barong* dated from the period of President Magsaysay when those shirts had a revival as a symbol of independence and Filipinism. Now that Filipinos did not feel the same need to

25

proclaim their non-westernness their use was declining. They were expensive, and Luz knew Mr. Lopez had only two, but he wore them proudly, in or out of style. Luz liked him for it and also for his beautiful English which had survived years of Filipino colloquialism since he had graduated from Columbia University.

Miss Rodriguez was a problem in more ways than one. If you got her a chair, she thought you were currying favor. If she was left to get her own, she felt abused. Miss Rodriguez felt the importance of her position as Supervisor and she wore it like a crown. Actually, Luz observed at that lower thought level, she walked like a country woman carrying a basket of fish on her head. The idea pleased her, so she relaxed, pulled a student chair forward, and quietly nodded the Supervisor into it.

Mr. Lopez solved the next embarrassment which now threatened her composure. He hopped up, took her desk chair, turned it around to face them and said, "Be seated." She was, her back straight, her knees together. Her eyes were wary but unafraid and her breath came in soft puffs from the top of her lungs. But the big moment must be approached obliquely. Miss Rodriguez pulled her mouth into a longer line, but did not manage to make a smile out of it.

"Good afternoon, Miss Aspi. It has been some time since I was in your classroom."

"Yes, ma'am, it has."

Silence.

"The Santos boy was absent again today, was he not?" Mrs. Ramos always knew where every student was.

"Yes, ma'am."

"Is his work satisfactory?"

"No, ma'am, he is gone so much." Luz fiddled with a pencil on her desk. They had not come to talk about the Santos boy. The suspense was agonizing but she responded to more unimportant remarks with the proper, "Yes, ma'am, no, ma'am," until finally, Mr. Lopez zeroed in.

"Miss Aspi," he began, "we have been watching your work." Ah, the time-honored door opener! Some ancient manipulator had invented this well-oiled door handle for the administrator who is about to enter the domain of his employee, it may be to look around, or it may be to invite him to larger and better quarters. It might also be possible the purpose is to move him over to make room for another desk. But this—any of these—

must be the result of ponderous meshing of administrative gears. The raise, the little raise, must be made to seem a great reward for special service. *No,* reasoned Luz, *it can't be that. The government just came through with the automatics.* The big raise, if such it be, must be accompanied by a tightening of the screws. *No, it couldn't be. She had no connections in high places to secure her an unusual raise.*

"We . . . " he had begun, meaning, *Don't blame me for what follows or don't take advantage of your luck.*

"We think you show promise."

"Would you explain the matter, Miss Rodriguez?"

Luz curled her toes inside her shoes. She had given Rosario Lumpo a "3" and his mother was second cousin to Miss Roddriguez's aunt. She had also sent Mario out of the room, and he was . . . She was so engrossed in running down the list of relatives of her discipline problems that she missed the Supervisor's first words.

" . . . we think you can profit by the experience. So this agency of the United States government will be sending a teacher to assist you this year and take your place next year, when you take graduate work at U.P."

Luz sat perfectly still. A breeze rattled the loose window sash.

Mr. Lopez watched her. "I think the American is called a co-teacher, isn't it?"

"Yes," said Miss Rodriguez crisply. "It is the coming educational method. The planning is joint and teaching is shared." She wished Miss Aspi would show some interest. After all, they had passed up several other teachers to select her.

"The Peace Corps Director . . . "

"Mr. Jacobs," supplied Mr. Lopez, who hadn't forgotten a name in fifty years.

"Yes, of course, Mr. Jacobs, as I was saying, was quite insistent that we select a young teacher to work with his volunteer."

"Volunteer?" Luz's eyes lighted up at last.

"That is what they call their workers. I think they receive limited compensation."

So do I, thought Luz, *but nobody calls me a volunteer.* She laid that idea face down for later consideration and directed her attention to Mr. Lopez.

"Is this good, sir?" Hot color warmed her cheeks. She

should not have asked that but it had just come out. *She had to know.*

Mr. Lopez laid his *barong Tagalog* cuffs straight and looked at her straight, "Yes, Miss Aspi, it is good."

"Of course," Miss Rodriguez spoke impressively, "this is an honor to Philippine Normal. We have had Fulbrights, and AID and exchange students and we would not want to be left out of this new project." She was slipping into Ilocano speech cadence and it was not a good sign.

"Yes, ma'am."

Mrs. Ramos had said nothing. She looked over Luz's head at a calendar with a picture of the president. Nobody seemed to notice. She was the one who had to deal with Fulbrights and AID experts and now Peace Corps. It was her school they tried to make over—in their own image. But nobody ever asked her if she wanted them. They just came. She endured it and they left. Now it would be Luz she would lose, just as she was getting her in shape in *her* image, the Filipino image. Her own education had not been marred by any jaunt to the States. She knew her students, their families, and their kinds of barrios.

Mr. Lopez fingered some coins in his pocket. Miss Rodriguez snapped her black purse open and shut. Mrs. Ramos shifted her gaze from the calendar to the door. They all knew the meeting was over but someone had to give the general signal.

Luz precipitated the matter by starting to ask a question, "When . . . ?"

All three rose and moved toward the door.

"Yes, yes, we will let you know," agreed Mr. Lopez heartily.

"Mr. Jacobs will finalize plans at a future date. We must talk again."

Mrs. Ramos said nothing and was first at the door. Nobody, least of all the Superintendent, the Supervisor, and the Principal wanted to discuss details. Nobody really knew such things as when, how, what, and where.

Luz was left alone with it all whirling in her head. Should she be happy? Was it an honor, an opportunity? Certainly she wanted a master's degree sometime and this would mean a start on it. Or had her teaching been so poor, her accent so Filipino, that they were easing her out? Overriding all else she felt invaded. Must she share her cozy room, her precious students with a stranger? An American, a rich, fussy, well-educated American woman?

All the excitement, the bubble of hope burst. She stared at the floor, the dark oil-soaked uneven boards. A rat sat beside the wastebasket, waiting to jump in and scavenge any fragrant bits. He always came at this time, confidently, as coinhabitant of this, her room. She knew him by the ragged tip of one ear. Tears overflowed and ran down the smooth curve of her cheek into her mouth. She put her arms on the desk and held her face in her hands. Probably schools in the States didn't have rats!

6

Mid-Point

Martha Wagner walked up the road from the dorm to the Humanities Building to her afternoon class. She could have waited for Norine and Ruth, after lunch, but out of habit she avoided the other elderly trainees. The youngest of the not-so-young, she had had her troubles, not being willing to flock with the other eight. There were only five now, since mid-training selection. It was a chilling thought and she put it away. So she mingled with the young ones, always choosing to set her cafeteria tray down with a table of them. They were polite, but they didn't seem to know what to do with her. Actually, she was surprised by the difficulty in gaining acceptance with the majority of the twenty-one- to twenty-three-year-old volunteers. In spite of the Peace Corps watchword of equality, the young ones could not bring themselves to call the old ones by their first names—though she was sure they had given them all nicknames. Maybe being a teacher was a barrier to acceptance. Probably they had had enough of teachers and didn't want to live with them day and night.

Or maybe it was the "Miss"—at her age. Surely they must have aunts, if only as occasional visitors or household pests. Of course, they knew some career women but not as fellow students.

Martha had always intended to get married. It was the ordinary thing to do, and it never occurred to her she was anything but emphatically ordinary. She had dated in high school to movies and school dances. Then came Ohio State where she had lived in one of those giant steel-and-concrete honeycombs. She majored in education and went to teaching as naturally as the right hand fits the right glove. Mount Vernon, Ohio, a nice midwest town, became her home. Wide streets, once brick-paved, were lined with elms, before the disease took them. The red brick Methodist church stood on one corner, gray stone Catholic on another, yellow frame Baptist down the street. On the road coming into town was a sign which proudly stated that Mt. Vernon was selected as "typical American town" in 1932. It was complete with town square and Civil War statue.

Suddenly, she was thirty years old. At least it felt sudden that March 28. That morning she stood a long time in front of the mirror over the walnut veneer dresser. How had those eight years since college slipped by? Critically, she looked to see if they had left a mark. Hair still brown and springy. Gray eyes, wide and clear, that could demand truth from sneaky students, skin smooth, nose too long, mouth a bit too thin. But a nice dependable face.

Well, she decided practically, *you'll do, Martha Wagner, but you'll have to get at it. If you are going to get married it will have to be soon.*

So she went to work at it, rationally, purposefully, the way she made lesson plans and wound up her hair every night. Single men were scarce in Mt. Vernon but there were a few young instructors at Kenyon College only five miles away in Gambier. It wasn't difficult to arrange introductions. Several were bored by constant association with soft-bearded, tough-minded male students.

There was one more bored than the rest and handsome, with a New York accent. Of course she wasn't prejudiced, but he was Jewish and she Catholic. Anyway, about that time a nice midwesterner appeared in town selling farm machinery. Then . . .

At thirty-five she gave up. Not disillusioned, not bitter, just sensible. It wasn't worth the effort. She figured she could do very well by herself. She hadn't found any man who was worth giving up her independence for. The Jewish professor had begun saying the same things over and over. The farm boy was more interested in fertilizer than Tolstoy.

Going back to Ohio State for an MA raised her salary to a comfortable $7,000. With the same careful attention she had given to hunting a husband, she made a home for herself in a sedate old white house made into three apartments. School activities, a drama group, Business and Professional Women's Club made up the rhythm of her life, except for one obsession and one fear. The obsession, so small she wouldn't even call it that, was seeing to it that women whom she liked got married before thirty. She herself had molded spinsterhood into a comfortable garment but she was quite sure others could not do as well. The world was made for twos. She didn't need another woman for her companion; she wanted men to have them. The fear accounted for her being here at San Francisco State University.

As suddenly as she had been thirty she found she was fifty, and the fear became bolder. She jerked it out of hiding and looked at it. It was fear of nothing to do. Not yet, of course, but getting nearer. Even before retirement there would be a letting down. Fewer student organizations would request her for advisor. Business and Professional Women would want younger officers. There would be little reason to go to confession.

The specter was postponed by a book she picked up from the New Aquisitions table in the public library, *Rich Nations, Poor Nations* by Barbara Ward. Martha had never been much concerned with economics beyond her own check book and tax returns. She had never felt any personal connection with foreign countries, regarding them only as the stuff of travel folders and the Foreign Affairs section of *Newsweek.* But she checked the book out because it was written by a woman who was also a Catholic. A few sentences swept her into a whole new world. When she got to the last chapter she found the book had affected her deeply. By the time she reached the end of the last chapter certain sentences stuck in her mind:

. . . but I have the impression when we talk so confidently of liberty we are unaware of the awful servitudes that are created by the ancient enemies of mankind: the servitude of poverty . . . of ignorance when there are no perspectives to which the mind can open because there is no education on which the mind can begin to work . . .

Six months later Martha Wagner was in training for the Peace Corps. It had been easier than she thought to get a leave of absence, sublet her apartment, store her breakables, and cut her ties to Mt. Vernon. The best part was the stir she caused. Friends said she was crazy. Fellow faculty members couldn't figure out why. Students began to treat her with a respect and friendliness she thought they were incapable of. She realized she had not even been a person to them before.

Having closed the Mt. Vernon book, it never occurred to

her that she would not stick with the new one cover to cover. She never left a book unfinished, even if she didn't like it. Therefore, she was quite astonished when she discovered that the Peace Corps selection process was just beginning with training, that it was shrouded in mystery and a topic of apprehensive conjecture among the volunteers. At first she thought this was a put-on, the way the brightest students often worried the most loudly about exams. Ten weeks of training at a university with standards to meet held no threat for her. She had expected physical education to present difficulties, after hearing about the survival training in Puerto Rico Peace Corp camps, and indeed the first few days had been a nightmare. On the third day the gymnastic class was lined up on the edge of the tumbling mat shivering in their university-issued white shorts as the cold wind blew in the window.

"Now I want to see your somersaults," commanded the chunky, no-nonsense coach. "Hit the back of your neck first and land on your feet."

Martha could still turn a somersault as part of her morning exercises in the privacy of her bedroom, but she had never tried hitting the back of her neck first. She watched apprehensively as one after another of the young ones tried it. Some did it, others rolled helplessly on their sides, to the amusement of the coach. As it got nearer and nearer to her turn, all she could think of was a headline in the *Mt. Vernon Chronicle*: "Local Teacher Breaks Neck Turning Somersault." Shutting her eyes, concentrating all thought on the back of her neck, she dove, rolled, landed on her feet, and was rewarded by the astonished exclamation of the coach.

"Huh! a pro!" So she was *in* as far as the "phys. ed." department was concerned. If she could not lift the soccer ball with her toe, or make a basket in the embarrassing relay race, the coach would nod her on. But that early experience with somersaults gave her a false self-confidence. That was before Tagalog.

She found out the first day that there had been a drastic change in language study since she took French at OSU. By the new linguistic method of learning a second language you did not talk *about* it, you *talked* it. You did not explain it until you had experienced it. You didn't learn how it looked but how it sounded. There was no orderly vocabulary, no grammar. The process consisted of drills, questions and answers in the language —with no translation. If you found out what was being said it was incidental. The Filipino instructor, Miss Manalong, would confront a student with *"Mabuhay b'ang tetsa?"*

He was supposed to have found out by repetition that the reply was *"Co mabuhay ang tetsa."*

"Ako b'ang hispania?" She might shake her head to help.

"Hindi, hindi ka ang hispania." After a substitute of "Americano," and "Filipina" they figured out they had said, "No I am not Spanish."

Some volunteers like Dick and Isobel picked it up easily. Jimmy managed to muddle along somehow, beaming at the trim little Filipina, making try after try till she passed him by. But to Martha each class was a nightmare of being dragged along a tunnel blindfolded.

At mid-training there had been exams. American Studies was easy for Martha; she had taught American History for a couple of years. Philippine Studies she was knocking herself out on. The Filipino teachers gave long reading lists that no one could cover. The young ones didn't bother. The more conscientious ones dug in before exam and shared their findings cheerfully with the lazy ones. Somehow this generation of college students had a knack of second-guessing the professors on objective tests. The Tagalog exam was a ghastly experience. A recording had been played with pairs of words. Some ended with a glottal stop at the base of the throat, some didn't, and students were to distinguish or guess which. *BatTA* is *baby*, but *baTA'* (stop) is *bathrobe*. You would not get those mixed when used in context but isolated it was next to impossible to distinguish between them.

"Ang" was the real hangup. Sometimes it came before what might be considered a subject, sometimes after, sometimes it was shortened to "ng." It was used as a verb, sometimes as an adjective, or article. Of course these terms were never used, its function never explained. On the exam English sentences were to be put in Tagalog, which they had never seen in print.

The entire class had performed so poorly that Miss Manalong was almost humanly angry and retaliated by writing some sentences on the board. Martha learned more that day than in the four weeks before. Emboldened by finding out she could learn from seeing, Martha stole a workbook. The class was not supposed to see language written, at this stage. However, there was a pile of exercise manuals on the table which they had not been allowed to see. As Martha was passing the desk on her way out of class, on an impulse she took one, slipping it among other books. Laura was the only one she had told about this thievery and together they figured out which of the printed dialogues they were using. Right or wrong, she always attributed her survival of selection into the Peace Corps to that desperate, unethical, and extremely practical act.

After mid-training exams, interviewers had come from PC Washington, these experts who flitted in and out of Peace Corps in the early days, lending their experience and reputations briefly and casually to the experimental government program as yet unhampered by Civil Service, which promised excitement rather than security. Martha was surprised at the trauma among the volunteers caused by the interviewers, as they had already become accustomed to being observed by counsellors and psychologists, to having group sessions in which they were to bare their problems. So this, she reasoned, couldn't be much worse. In fact, she had had a very pleasant half-hour. The man was about her age, a professor in a state university and obviously not the usual government bureaucrat—at least as she imagined one. She had conducted enough interviews herself to know some of the tricks of the interviewee. Keep the conversation general, friendly and open. Steer it away from any sensitive personal areas and above all don't get cornered in a defensive position.

Before he asked, she volunteered her difficulties with Tagalog, but also commented that all university education was conducted in English in the Philippines. She pointed out the age gap here but felt it would be less troublesome in a country where elders were not expected to play basketball or guitars and youth respected the status of years.

But from the conversations in Laura's room that night others had had different experiences. They were piled on the beds and curled on the floor and shouted to be heard.

" . . . so he sez to me, 'How are you?' and I sez, 'Fine, how are you?' and he had to think up another one, see. 'How do you like San Francisco State?' and I sez, 'Fine, how do you?'"

"Oh, Sally, did you really?" They could just see Sal, the unquenchable, who sang gospel songs in the shower, talking back to the PC staffer.

"Didn't he ever chop you?"

"Sure thing, he tried." Her black eyes flashed. "But when you've gone to school with white kids all your life, see, you know how to let it ro-o-l-l-l off." She made motions like water rolling off a duck's back.

Others joined in with their stories.

"He said things to me, yuno, nobody ought to have to take," protested Isobel who was taking up half a bed with her feet in Laura's lap. "He accused me of being like insincere, even a show-off. I told him about all the honors I had won in high school. I'm a drama major and I think I have a lot to give."

"Did you hear they told Mary Jo she had to put her hair up?"

"How dumb! Even in high school they don't tell you how to dress anymore."

" . . . and Gabe, they jumped him because he cut so many classes."

"Well, they have no business requiring class attendance, they don't at OSU."

"Nor Minnesota," . . . "nor Western" . . . nor . . . nor . . .

"Look, we each went to a different college. Did any of them require it?"

"Mine did," confessed Laura uncomfortably.

"Oh—a church school," someone said disparagingly.

"Yea, but did you hear what Dick said in American Studies?" put in Gloria. "He said he thought it was different here. They are really paying us for going to classes."

"Jeez, they gota pay me more than walk-around money to go to classes from eight to four and phys. ed. after that!"

They began to add up those who had finally been selected out.

"Hatchet face, up the hall."

"Oh, she left two weeks ago. Said she couldn't stand eating her meals off a tray. Half of the old ones are out."

"Not me," Martha reminded them cheerily, "you're going to have to put up with me—except that Tagalog will get me if I—don't—watch—out." At that she got up from the floor slowly, with a helpful push, and went to her room.

Martha's steps slowed as she got nearer to her next class, Tagalog. She tried to postpone thinking about it by noticing the flowers, mammoth dahlias, pink and yellow, glads in rainbow colors. The night fog was good for flowers. At home in Mt. Vernon they would be blooming too, but smaller. Were the tenants watering her zinnias and daisies?

"Hi, Mart." Dick came from behind on a lope.

"Maganda umaga po," she flung at him.

"Gosh, you're coming along. Stick with it." He passed her and caught up with Isobel. Martha's matchmaking obsession did not reach out to Isobel, who could take care of herself. But she wasn't right for Dick. Laura was, but Dick didn't seem to know that he needed her stability. She wanted to steer Dick in the right direction; he was one of the few who treated her like one of the gang.

Class had started to gather when Martha reached the room. Isobel had chosen a seat at the middle table, with a man on either side. Martha eased herself into a chair on the right side of the open square formed by the tables. She had figured out that the teacher started her questions on the other side and moved clockwise around the tables, thus giving Martha a little time to catch on to the patterns of the exchange. Sometimes she could surreptitiously scribble down what she thought they were saying. What a sorry picture of herself! She, Martha Wagner, BA, MA, with twenty-eight years' teaching experience, reduced to using tricks to get around a foreign girl half her age. And why? So she could spend two years with kids who didn't want her, in a country she didn't care about, doing something she was not equipped for, driven by . . .

"*Na kanino ang manika?*" (Something about a doll.)

"*Na kay Nene?*" If the question didn't change before it got to her, she could say, "*Na kay Eddie.*"

7

Embarkation—Out or In

Passengers checking in at the airline counters in the San Francisco airport looked curiously at the group of young people standing in the midst of an odd assortment of luggage. Not well enough dressed for a tour group, too mixed in age to be returning to college, obviously self-confident, feeling on the verge of something exciting, they were easily identified as Peace Corps. Every few minutes a new arrival brought shouts and back-slapping welcome.

"Act as if they own the place," muttered one gentleman as he maneuvered his own luggage around their piles.

The selection process had not been finished before the volunteers had left San Francisco and had gone home for several days before leaving for the Philippines. So there were several whose fate was still unknown.

"George, fella you made it!"

" . . . and Kathy. Did they try to separate you two?"

"No, by golly, but Kathy's gonna stay out of those commie bookstores. We had a hell of a time convincing the interviewers she didn't know any better." He and his wife sat down on their suitcases to receive greetings. In a minute George was up.

"Say, don't we check in or something?"

"Oh, sure, over at Pan Am. It'll go when they get the wings tied on."

"Jet?"

"Jeez, no, not for PCV's. Good ole DC-8. It'll probably take us a week, barring accidents."

George and Kathy went to check in, and the conversation resumed about the absent ones.

"Where's Gabe?"

"Selected out."

"Cripes—he's smarter than most of us!"

Dick, in blue-and-white striped blazer, was busy circulating, happily telling each knot of volunteers about his difficulties.

"You know, I hadn't got my security clearance when we went home from training. They just said 'Wait at home, we'll notify you.' I'd get a call from Washington every few days with friendly messages. 'Go ahead and pack. Yes, send your air freight. Let us know where you are at all times'—like that."

"But what took so long?"

"My past," Dick explained darkly. "I changed universities three times. I'd worked for the Progressive Party in New York. I ran a flop house."

"Oh, come off," giggled Gloria.

"Well, you'd think so. They went back to my ancestors. My father's uncle escaped from Germany under Bismarck. I haven't got clearance yet, but they said go ahead." He had everyone enthralled, but, as usual, no one knew how much to believe. He was sprawled in one of the few seats beside Laura when he was paged, "Mr. Blumberg, Richard Blumberg, come to the Pan American information counter, please."

"That's it!" In one motion he gathered his long frame together and was up and off. All eyes followed him. Underneath all the nonsense he had been worried sick.

"Selection doesn't make sense." Martha spoke what they were all thinking.

"I miss Gabe," said Isobel in a mournful voice.

"Remember how they jumped on him at mid-point?"

"Yes, but look how he changed. He really was subdued the last few weeks—he wanted to come."

"And the Cobra, now *she* was a teacher. She really would have been useful."

"Better than a lot of us who never stood up to a class in our lives."

"But the Filipino teachers hated her. She told 'em how to give tests and they never forgave her."

"Well, they could have used a little help," Martha put in, defending her profession.

"Yeah, but we gotta live with 'm. Training was where we found out if we could."

Conversation slackened. Dick didn't come back. Laura turned away from the direction he had gone; she wouldn't look expectant. But her stomach felt empty and her breathing was shallow. It couldn't be, it just couldn't!

Then he came. Striding down the aisle, shouldering his way through the crowd as if running for a touchdown. They could see a yellow paper clutched in his fist before they saw his hard-set, bleached face. Without a word he picked up his duffel bag and suitcase. Not even glancing at Laura, he turned and left. At the edge of the crowd he tossed them the crumpled telegram.

George caught it, smoothed it out, and with the others looking on, he read it silently and then passed it on. Finally, it reached Laura.

Regret to inform you, clearance has been denied stop Do not proceed to Manila. Parson, Peace Corps Personnel Director.

Angry tears stung her eyes. What a way to do it! Plain cruelty, to lead him on, then to humiliate him before his friends. And why . . . ?

Why? Why? It passed from person to person and with it went an unspoken "What if it was me?" Gloom settled darkly over the group in the realization that one's hopes, expectations and the ability to manage one's own life could be arbitrarily cancelled out by fate, by the U.S. government. It was a frightening thought, but it did not make them huddle in mutual sympathy. They were too young, too individualistic, too competitive. Their spirits lifted with the reassuring thought, "So I'm lucky," and it was not long before they drifted apart, leaving a few tired ones to watch the clutter of luggage.

At last they were stowed on board, and the prop revved up. The sturdy old plane roared down the runway and wheeled above the Golden Gate Bridge. Martha had deposited herself beside Laura without a word. She didn't care whether the girl wanted her or not, she just figured she was the best person in the group to cope with the raw nerve ends which were so obviously bruised.

Flight bags, handbags, cosmetic cases, cameras were stowed around their feet. Martha took off the jacket of her permapress durable blue travel dress, then put it on again as they gained altitude. Laura kept her black sweater on over her red cotton, not knowing whether she was hot or cold. Face close to the window, she watched the city slipping away beneath them, a sense of loss, rather than departure, nagging at her spirit. The waves breaking along the shore became thin squiggles of white paint on blue. Soon the world outside the round window was a shining nothingness of blues and grays. The United States had disappeared. Laura felt a ripple of pleasure at the sense of being suspended in time and space, and she turned to give

Martha a weak smile. Martha returned it warmly, relieved that she wouldn't have to sit all the way to Manila in dramatic non-communication. *The sun doesn't set with one man when you are twenty-one,* she was thinking. *Only when you are over thirty.* But such a thought belonged in the closed lower cupboard of her mind.

Laura was the first to speak. "I'm not taking it very well, am I?"

"It's a rotten shame," ejaculated Martha, glad of a chance to say it out loud. "What right has PC Washington got to treat a fine upstanding young . . ."

"Oh, they've got the right, all right! They pick us, they train us, they take us, they reject us. Oh, they've got the right."

"But Dick is bright and, and—eager, and so interested."

"But argumentative, egotistical, rude. Often." Even as she said it Laura was surprised at her rationalizing his rejection.

"Well, sure, and few teachers can take that." Martha cast a hasty glance back at her own classrooms. Had she ever cut down a grade because a student was uppity? "But I don't think it was the professors who turned him down."

"Who then?"

"You know, Laura, how he was about people. People he thought needed defending."

Yes, she knew, and she loved him for it. The blacks for whom he had marched to get the vote, the Filipinos whom he sympathized with as they were scrutinized by anthropologists.

"Why, I heard him raking Jimmy over the coals one day about how the Negroes are treated and how they should stand up and fight for their rights. He was all burned up but he couldn't light a fire under Jimmy."

"M-mhuh, Jimmy knew his chance out was with the Peace Corps and he wasn't taking any risks." Laura remembered other times. The laundry man who didn't get paid enough— he'd advised him to strike.

"Sometimes, I thought he was playacting," admitted Martha.

"Oh, no, no, *never.* Even about the Formosans."

"The Formosans?"

"Oh, yes, he'd met some Formosan students in New York who got him aroused about injustices of Chiang Kai-shek and the thousands he killed when Nationalist China took over Taiwan, and how they were going to fight for their independence and needed help."

"Taiwan, yes. He did start that once in Philippine Studies.

Got precious little sympathy from our Filipino teachers as I remember."

"Well, he added the Formosans to the list of U.S. government stupidities in foreign policy."

"Now, *that's* what I mean. He never had a good word for the U.S. Now, why would a government send him out to represent his country?"

"Jeepers, Mart, half the PCV's are like that."

"Not so loudly so. Anyway, they can't stop him."

"They did," Laura snapped.

"No, they only blocked him. That kind of will and purpose can't be stopped for long."

"You can't try out for the Peace Corps more than once, you know that."

"Oh, Peace Corps!" Martha dismissed the whole business with a scornful wave of her hand. "What did people do before PC when they wanted to make over the world? He'll think of something. There are lots of roads around the world." Martha eased off her shoes and put her seat back. "And it is round," she added emphatically.

Laura yawned. There was an understanding silence between them. The engines hummed relentlessly on one tone, screwing the propeller blades through the air.

"Mart?"

"Hmm," Martha encouraged without opening her eyes.

"If we get a chance to choose our location and living arrangements, how about us teaming up?"

Martha squeezed her eyelids down, suppressed the smile her lips wanted to make and offered a casual, "Suits me."

"Thanks, Mart."

"Thanks, Laura."

8

Sunset and Sunrise

The plane pointed its nose to the southwest to follow the sun, which was sinking slowly into the Pacific. At the same time, 7,000 islands off the coast of Asia were awaking to its light. The volunteers had learned not to call these the "Philippine *Islands*." They had learned to spell the "Philippines" with one 'l' and two 'p's," but they could not yet be as familiar as "R.P." for the Republic of the Philippines, and they were a long way from "Pilipinas" which appeared on the nation's stamps.

The Filipinos (whether spelled "F," "Ph," or "P,") were not waiting expectantly for the arrival of the latest load of young Americans with their goodwill, friendship, and eagerness to share. One batch of Americans more or less was really of no great concern to the 23,000,000 inhabitants whose islands had been washed by waves of migrations since prehistoric times and invaded by successions of conquering armies. The lovely islands with their tall forests, rich valleys, volcanic mountains, gold and pearls had lured the wanderers, the traders, adventurers, and empire builders. They came, plundered, moved over or succumbed to the next wave. As each wave receded it left a pool of people and a thin layer of cultural sediment. But Filipinos had developed a pragmatic talent for accommodation and adaptation to whomever they had to live with or under. They kept and used what they liked, letting the alien tints wash over the surface without changing the strong primary colors. By devious methods and circumlocution, smooth relations were maintained between peon and *datu,* tenant and landlord, student and teacher, worker and employer, subjects and imperialist. It was indeed a pleasant quality, and Filipino teachers in Peace Corps training laid great stress on the importance and understanding of "Smooth Interpersonal Relations." "SIR" had entered the Peace Corps vocabulary. Yet SIR was not the strongest quality of the volunteers, nor the Peace Corps directors—nor Martha's own, for that matter. Maybe she would absorb it from living with Filipinos.

As the Pacific Ocean slipped eastward underneath the plane, Laura slept and Martha floated in that beautiful state of the traveler suspended between what was and what will be. She stretched her feet as far as they would go, put her head back, and gave herself up to trying to piece together what she had learned in the last ten weeks about the country she was going to and the people she would work with. From lectures, books, and government documents, she had crammed into her memory quite a mass of information. But she wondered now how accurate her overall impressions were and what holes there were in her information. She mused away several hours trying to assemble her store of knowledge into an orderly classroom form, pretending she was to give a course on the subject. Her mind worked comfortably in textbook style.

I. ORIGINS OF THE PEOPLE OF THE PHILIPPINES

The origins of the small, wiry, brown-skinned people defy classification with their diversity-within-similarities. In the foggy prehistoric past the Java man-like men came by land and sea; then came the Australoid type, the pygmies, Indonesians, people from Indochina. Various migrations of Malays settled on the central islands. There were traders from Borneo, China, Cambodia, Java, while various local empires rose and fell. At one period tribute was paid to China and there was some limited Chinese colonization. The Muslim influence began with missionaries and was consolidated by conquest.

II. THE SPANISH PERIOD

The barriers of water and mountains kept the different migrations apart and distinctive, and it was not until the sixteenth century that the Spanish imperialist pulled the diverse peoples together into an over-arching structure, and they began the long road to nationhood.

It took Magellan's insatiable ambition and his ruthless soldiers to conquer these tribal peoples and name them "Philippinas" after his ruler King Philip. The parish priests from Spain welded the cross to the sword of the conquistador. [That was a nice phrase she had coined—or had she read it somewhere?] The priest was a total authority figure which was familiar to the people, merely topping the power of the chief or *datu.* Catholic saints were merged with pagan deities, pagan rites became Christian sacraments, and a fiesta for whatever excuse was always welcome.

Martha's mind wandered from her "lecture" to the special meeting that had been held during training for Catholic volunteers. They had been warned that the Catholicism they would find in the Philippines was 16th-century Spanish type. No one questioned the right of the parish priest to the biggest house and the prettiest girl. In fact, to be a blue-eyed Filipino was a mark of distinction. It was said (she would have to check this if she ever really used it) that the pope and the Islamic emir divided the islands between them, respecting each other's religious hegemony: the Muslims in the southern islands and the Catholics in all that lay north of the island of Mindanao. The Jewish volunteers said that at their special meeting they were told the Filipinos would ask them if they believed in God. All the volunteers were told that if asked that they should say yes. It was only for two years. They would have to get along with the local priest; unless he was for them they could make no progress. The volunteers also learned that the Spaniards all but destroyed the emerging literature written in a local alphabet, that the Spanish language had been reserved for the privileged class, but Spanish names were mandatory for all.

Martha wasn't much interested in the intricacies and intrigues of the Spanish period except for Rizal. Oh my, yes, she couldn't leave out Rizal, the revolutionary hero, prophet, martyr, and author all rolled into one. One of the few requirements in Philippine Studies had been the reading of a slightly expurgated translation of his *Nole Me Tangere, Touch Me Not.* That novel, with its not-too-well-concealed revolutionary undertones, seemed to be the one book that every Filipino student read over and over. The visual evidence of Rizal's status as national hero was his statue in every village square, the Filipino teachers informed the volunteers. That brought Martha to —

III. THE AMERICAN PERIOD

Under the powerful Spanish umbrella during the 400-year period of the 16th through the 19th centuries, the people and former kingdoms grew in the consciousness of a Philippine entity. At the end of the

19th century the Americans sailed in from the northeast, demolishing the rule of Spain and claiming the islands for themselves—under the noblest of banners: Christianity and Democracy. [Martha really believed this and silently despised the cynicism of the young volunteers who laughed at it.] It was a shock to the Americans to find that after "rescuing" the Philippines from the Spanish they had a vicious war with Filipinos on their hands. [This had surprised Martha as much as the other volunteers and she resolved that there would be some changes in the teaching of American History when she got back to Mount Vernon High School.] Those gay, amiable people whom the missionaries called "little brown brothers" had kept the American army at bay for three years as Aguinaldo and his band of ragged guerillas fought for their independence. But when the Filipinos found out the Americans intended to stay, they calmed down and began to adjust to the new rulers. In some ways the Americans couldn't be accommodated as easily as the Spanish. They insisted on change that struck at the very roots of the island way of life. But the Filipinos worked things out and SIR won. They accepted required schooling and learned English in order to survive. Some became Protestants as the way to power and thus accepted, on the surface, American systems of orderliness, regular work, land titles, and dozens of other innovations which disrupted their traditional ways of living.

At this point in their studies the Peace Corps volunteers had become indignant. They railed at "imposing American culture" and vowed that they would demonstrate a different kind of American to Filipinos. As respect for their own government decreased, respect for the people they were to work among increased by leaps and bounds. Armed with headfuls of facts, ethnic details, and political theories, they were coming to do battle for humanity—they, who had never battled for anything more important than a basketball game, a boy scout badge or open dorms. And Martha kept silent.

The window circle of the plane had turned black long ago. Martha yawned, eased out of her seat and took a lurching trip to the rear of the plane. As she passed the young people now lolling in awkward positions of cramped sleep, or playing cards by dim light, an unfamiliar motherly feeling came over her. They were so young, so confident, with something of a crusader in each of them. Oddly, and touchingly, they were even prepared for failure and disillusionment, sure they could be patient with the anti-Americanism they were certain they would find. They didn't expect to change people, only to befriend them and help them reach their goals, then move on where they were not quite certain. What the PCV really wanted was experience, strange, exotic, new. Most really preferred that it be hard, demanding, or at least look that way, as the PC recruiters had promised. They thought they were ready for anything. It might be they were more ready than she was, Martha admitted to herself.

When she returned to her seat a dark thought sneaked across her mind. Maybe the Peace Corps was intended only for the young. Pushing it away she closed her eyes and yawned again. She seemed to be surrounded by gray fog filled with half-formed images of green islands—bamboo huts—carabao—rice fields—small brown people hungry for food and knowledge—eagerly looking for a plane bringing help—.

Martha suddenly brought her seat up straight, roused from her half-sleep by a problem she was struggling with subconsciously.

Unkindly she nudged Laura. "Say, Laura, what do the Filipinos want?"

Laura was startled into an uneasy wakefulness. "Want? Who wants?"

"What do *they* want? The Filipinos. Suppose we were wrong about what they want."

Laura was awake now. "Well, you know, they want us to help raise the level of English and new Math and new Biology and —"

"That's what their government wants, or what our government says they want. What do the people want—the ones we are going to live with, the farmers, the ordinary rural little people—you know, nipa huts and carabao."

"Oh, goshalmighty, Mart, I don't know and probably they don't, except for what everybody wants, food, clothes, jobs, education. It's too early or late to argue. My foot's asleep." She twisted it and rubbed it, but Martha was not to be put off. She felt she was on the edge of an awful truth.

"Well, do you know what I think? I think ninety percent of the volunteers on this plane aren't even sure what they are going for or what they have to offer or who wants it!"

"Could be."

"They don't even know who they are. Who are you?" was Martha's next challenge.

"Me?"

"Yes, you know; 'Who am I?' you kids are always asking. I

never asked that. I don't remember my generation searching for identity."

"Well, who are *you*?"

"I'm a middle-aged, middle-class, college-educated American made up of a mixture of races, ethnic stock, religions, and—a lot of other things. Do you know who you are?"

"Yes, I know. Sometimes I wish I didn't."

"Why, for goodness sake?"

"Because if I didn't know maybe I'd find out I was more exciting than I think I am."

"Why should you be exciting?"

"Because exciting people have exciting things happen to them."

"Well, isn't it exciting enough to be on a plane over the Pacific going to a strange country we really know very little about? That's what woke me up."

"Mart, I was half-awake worrying, too, if you've got to know. Not about who I am, but about who *she* is."

"She?"

"The 'she' I am going to co-teach with. Suppose she is old and—set—I'd be scared to death. You don't suppose it could be a 'he,' do you?"

"Put your tray down for breakfast, please," a cheery hostess voice commanded.

About the time the passengers on Pan Am flight 438 were having their first breakfast, Don Jacobs, Peace Corps Director in the Philippines, propped up his feet on his office desk and longingly measured two hours till he could escape to his air-conditioned apartment. His phone rang and the Filipina operator informed him that a Miss Aspi was calling. Could he please inform Miss Aspi as to the time of arrival of Peace Corps Group Eight? He checked the bulletin board on the wall behind him, then told her cordially that they were due tomorrow about four P.M. on Pan Am 438. The woman, obviously young and timid, murmured something about being interested because she was to have one of them in her class. That was enough to brighten his day. It gave him a nice human interest note to spark up his monthly report to PC Washington. He'd polish up something about local Filipina teachers so eager to have PC help they kept calling the headquarters to inquire about new arrivals so they could welcome them at the airport. The timing couldn't be better, with Congress debating appropriations.

Lucky she called, too. He had forgotten that a new group was to arrive tomorrow. Waiting at the airport was deadly; he'd send his deputy.

Luz replaced the phone hastily as the janitor came in with broom and rag. It had taken ingenuity and courage to make that call. She had not wanted to ask anyone at the school about the time of arrival, and she would not for the world have anyone know she thought of calling Peace Corps headquarters direct. There was only one phone in the building, and that was in Mrs. Ramos's office. So she had stayed in the library long after all the others had left. She was elated at the information about the plane; the next day was Saturday so she could go to the airport. Somehow she just had to do this, though she would have been ashamed to admit it to her family or anyone at school.

Luz had had plenty to worry about since the momentous announcement that she was to have a Peace Corps Volunteer in her class. The Peace Corps was like a stone thrown into the peaceful flow of her life. For weeks her thoughts had been eddying around it curiously. Now, tomorrow, she would know its size, shape, texture. No previous experience provided her with any clues as to the kind of relationship which would develop. Would it be teacher-pupil, teacher-supervisor, competitive, antagonistic, friendly? Could they possibly become real friends? Friends with an American who had come to help you? Whoever heard of that? Co-teacher meant nothing to her. She had never known a co-anything except on paper. Someone had to be on top.

So she had made the call to Peace Corps headquarters to learn the time at which the awful mystery would begin to show its face.

Another person in Manila also was interested in arriving PCV's. Sam Lee Wong's store was fifth on the left on Pin-a-pin Street, with its broken pavement and one-lane sidewalks that stroll between two thoroughfares. Sam sat on a stool with his head against a roll of matting in the back room taking his afternoon nap. Around him were stacked in dust-covered confusion rattan chairs, long poles of bamboo, aluminum kettles, bamboo and wood tables, lamps with woven shades, and the other kinds of Filipino-made furniture typical of Pin-a-pin. A fly crawled cozily over his left ear but he didn't brush it away. In his half sleep he fondly stroked the three hairs curling from the mole on his left cheek. A small carbon copy of Wong padded in with bare feet and whispered in his ear, "Americanos." Wong's eyes popped open and instantly he was totally awake. Americans meant money and amusement. He never allowed anyone but himself to wait on them.

There were two of them in the front part of the store. They were not from the Embassy, of course, nor USOM as they had the PX in which to shop and didn't patronize Chinese merchants. Not tourists, either, curious to see a "native" market. Certainly not missionaries; they were too young and they had not brought a Filipino with them. They were the new breed, Peace Corps. His day brightened. These were real shoppers who wanted things but knew that they should bargain for them. They were not very good at this game, and Wong made it his business to give them valuable practice.

"*Maganda happon po*," the redhead began with a smile intended to put Wong at his ease.

"Good afternoon," he replied. These *were* newcomers; what did they take him for? He who had learned his English from his father who had learned it in a mission school in Shanghai, "Something for you?"

"Why, yes," Redhead had the grace to blush at her mistake. "We'd like to see a chair, one of those sort of round ones," making motions with her hands.

"Yes, yes, this way, please." Wong led them around a pile of mats to point out a highbacked intricately woven fan chair he knew they would not buy. The girls bubbled over it, especially the one with the long hair.

"How much?"

"One hundred and twenty pesos, please," Wong put the price sky high.

"Oh, I'm sorry," said Redhead, who seemed to be the spokesman, "we're Peace Corps and we have only a small allowance, you know." Of course he knew, that was his business. That allowance was about twice as much as that of most of Wong's customers. But he bowed in recognition of their poverty and showed them a sturdy bamboo and rattan chair. "Ninety pesos, please." He could see them dividing it in their minds by four to relate it to dollars. Both of them shook their heads.

"No, it's nice but we just want one of those kind of two half circles—there, that's it," pointing. "How much is that?"

"Vely nice chair, make it to you vely cheap," cooed Wong, lapsing into the accent he knew they expected. Fourth uncle from Los Angeles talked that way. "Forty pesos, made in our own shop. Second daughter does the weaving." For some reason this always pleased them, so why tell them the chairs were shipped in by the hundred from Leyte?

Long Hair almost said they would take it but the redhead poked her none too subtly. "I'm afraid that is still too high," she stated with regret. "What is your best price?"

Some Filipino had taught them that phrase! "Thirty-five," said Wong firmly.

"Twenty-five is all we have," lied Long Hair unconvincingly.

"Thirty," compromised Wong, "just for you, because you are Peace Corps." That always clinched it. They were happy at his generosity, and he was happy with double his usual price. Then the problem arose as to how to get it to their apartment on Tennessee Street. They had no car, one of the facts that distinguished them from other Americans. They abandoned the idea of trying to get it on a jeepney. Wong suggested that if they needed some other item he could have both delivered, a settee perhaps, or a cooking pot? But it seemed all they needed was some cloth for bedspreads. Well, that was easy. His cousin had the best selection in Manila and would give them a good price, just over on Risal Avenue and it could all be sent together. Which store was it? Very close, third son would take them (and incidentally pass the word along that they were easy prey).

The girls were pleased, such a friendly system of being passed on to relatives. Brotherly love in action. They would tell the next PCV's about him.

"Next?" He made the question sound casual but his antenna was up.

Yes, Group Eight was coming soon, they didn't know just when. Some of them would be out at UP, Diliman, and some in high school. They would need to furnish houses and apartments, too.

Wong tucked that valuable bit of information into his secret mental file. Some day, one of these nice young Americans would be useful to him. He could be patient till the right one came along.

"Joe," he called sharply to his image lurking among the tables, and explained to the inquiring looks, "He Filipino." Smiling and bowing, he ushered his customers out as though they had done him the highest favor by choosing to come in. As indeed they had.

9

West to the East

As their plane approached from the northeast, a typhoon from the southeast headed for Samar, the most easterly of the islands. It would travel inland following the usual track northwest across Luzon toward Manila. The pilot of the DC-8 had no desire to race the storm to the airport. These PC kids would get their feet wet soon enough in the stinking rice paddies. So he dawdled at Guam and Midway until word came that the storm had veered to the south and its main force would bypass Manila to spend itself over Hong Kong.

Hours and hours of water and sky had floated by since the last stop at Guam. The suppressed anxiety of the volunteers which had erupted first in singing, razzing, and roughhousing had gradually been dampened by delays and boredom. Arguments about the time had started humorously, become acrimonious, and finally quarrelsome. "So we keep losing time and gotta make it up, cross the dateline, skip a whole day," she heard someone mumble from across the aisle.

"Lose a whole day's meals? The hell I do, I'll sue 'em!" threatened Jimmy loudly.

Laura flopped from a left side curl to a right, "Shut up, you idiots."

Martha grumbled, "You should have learned time change in fifth grade."

"So you're so smart, when do we get to Manila?"

"Saturday afternoon."

"Saturday! We left Thursday. It can't take us two days."

"Twenty-two hours minus twelve, plus twenty-four," Martha snapped.

"My stomach never took geography," whimpered Jimmy.

General laughter ended it for that time, to the relief of the regular passengers who had good-naturedly resigned themselves to being an ignored minority.

Now islands below began to break up the endless blue surface like scattered scraps of green velvet ringed with white lace.

"Land-ho!" came a shout from the left side of the plane.

"Land to starboard, mate." That was Jimmy.

In a rush all those on the right rose and pushed over to the left, leaning over to see out the little round windows.

The Philippines? Really? At last! Beautiful! From this height the land resembled crumpled green crepe paper laid over peaks and hollows.

At a lower altitude they could distinguish dark forested mountains, green valleys, white coastline. Then it all disappeared as if they had gone through gray curtains hung from sky to sea.

The hostess came down the aisle urging, "Please be seated. The seat belt sign has been turned on."

The pilot's cheery voice came over the loudspeaker. "We will encounter some delay due to weather conditions over Manila. Get your boots out, folks, it will be wet."

The first response was silence underscored by shock, disappointment, irritation, resignation, fear, as each personality dictated. Then restraint and boy scout good sportsmanship broke.

"To hell with it."

"Back to L.A."

"Come on, gang, let's mutiny."

"Like I told you guys, they don't want us."

Mary Jo exhaled a deep sigh, unsheathed her guitar—she knew her role—and began to strum, "What shall we do with the drunken sailor."

Her throaty crooning voice was joined by others from seat to seat until it swelled to a rocking chorus. "Put him in the longboat 'til he's sober."

Original verses were added until they were out of breath.

Half-an-hour later the plane made a dive that brought cries of pain from those with sensitive ears. It slid through a slit in the angry clouds down a shaft of sunlight and swung toward a strip of concrete. Slightly shaken but joyous, the passengers began to collect belongings, put on shoes, comb hair.

"Please remain seated until the plane is parked at the ramp—"

"Not this time, sweeties!" shouted someone.

Before the plane had slowed to the end of the runway, the aisles were choked with bags, coats, packages—and they were ready to go.

Leaning toward the window, Laura caught a glimpse of the Philippine flag hanging limp over the airport building in the sudden calm, and she felt the first pang of foreignness.

Someone still seated called, "Look, oxen. Right at the airport!"

"Not oxen. They must be caribou."

"*Carabao*, you dumb cluck."

As many of them as could, leaned to look out at the animals they had come to identify with this new land. It seemed to take an unnecessarily long time to roll out the steps to the exit door. Heat seeped in and excitement oozed again.

At last the door opened. Out they poured into the sudden brilliant late afternoon sun. They picked their way around the pools of water steaming in the heat and looked around curiously as they followed the airline official to the entrance. The air was so heavy it seemed to press the breath down their throats.

By the time they reached the door what had begun as a brisk double line disintegrated into a tired straggle with only one thought among them—get out of the sun into shelter.

The heat hit Laura like a slap. She couldn't breathe. Her eyes didn't focus on the building in front of her. As she swayed, Jimmy caught her arm.

"Buck up," he ordered. "We're being watched."

"I'm an idiot," she scolded herself. "A little heat and over I go." By great effort she pulled herself together and walked in under her own power. The airport was a concrete building, new, unadorned but adequate.

"Peace Corps, Peace Corps," called a clipped American voice. "Welcome to the Philippines. This way, please." They followed like a flock of sheep glad to sight the shepherd's staff. They endured the formalities of entering a foreign country, a first experience for most of them: lines to immigration desk, lines to health, lines to customs. Even with the help of American Embassy officials and smiling soft-voiced Filipinos they felt the process to be harassing.

From the observation deck, Luz had watched the silver fish with wings skim out of the clouds and glide toward the runway, glazed by the sun after the rain. The crowd pressed forward. A fat *mestiza* with an umbrella pushed her way through the

packed watchers. Luz felt her but did not look. She clutched
the rail, maintaining her vantage point. Now as the plane rolled
past them heads could be seen at the small round windows. Luz
had a momentary flash of pride that the passengers were seeing
the new modern airport building. The *mestiza* tried to elbow her
aside. Luz did not turn her head but her peripheral vision took
in the heaving bosom, the stiff piled black hair, but she tried to
screen out the voice.

"My son's arriving—four years in the States, yes, yes, doctor
of laws—no, he won't stay—more money there."

"Mom, I can't see," complained a boy's voice as a small
body wriggled in below Luz's knees, his sandals stepping on her
perfectly white pumps. Gently she removed him with one hand
while she maintained her staked claim with the other.

"What's she look like?"

"She'll be different."

"Suppose she doesn't come, already?"

The worried questions voiced by others echoed in her
heart. She knew it was silly of her to have taken this long trip
out from Dao Street just to see the arrival of the Peace Corps,
when she wouldn't know which one of them she was going to
have in her class room. But she wanted to see them before they
saw her.

When the plane rolled to a stop below them there was a
moment of silence, of suspended emotion. The steps were
rolled out. The door opened and the first passenger stepped
out.

"Rafael, it is not. Is! Oh, my god!" a woman's thankful cry.
No one took any notice of her as each pair of eyes pulled at
that door, willing the one waited for to appear. Luz waited
quietly, knowing the one she waited for was there. But she
would have no visual confrontation, no welcome for her, and
no rejection.

There they came, tumbling out of the rear door of tourist
section down the steps. Young Americans, they would be recognized anywhere.

"Peace Corps, *mabuhay!*" shouted a large man waving his
cigar. "They'll make Americans out of us," he muttered loudly
to his companions.

No they won't, Luz wanted to tell him. *They're different.* She
was surprised at the protective feeling that swelled within her.
One of those tousled, hurrying Americans was hers. So big.
Even the girls. That blond girl peeling her red sweater as she

stopped with her huge purse between her feet, her skirt so short you could see the back of her knees when she stooped to pick it up. It was a mixed-up crowd: red hair, brown, gray, black as any Filipino. There were all shades of skin, too, from milk to ink. A sudden horrible thought struck Luz. "Oh, mother of god, don't let her be black," she prayed and quickly crossed herself. They weren't very neat with rumpled skirts, moist shirts, dirty canvas shoes. Then she chided herself. *They must be exhausted. Why didn't somebody welcome them? The day had passed when incoming Peace Corps groups lined up and sang the Philippine national anthem, but somebody should greet them.* If she could just find hers she'd help her, get her a drink of water.

They were all in the gate now, and Luz turned to leave. The bank of clouds had reformed, and the edge of the typhoon would probably hit before she got home.

10

Discovering the Philippines

Deputy Peace Corps Director Charles Lawrence herded the volunteers into two buses that headquarters had hired. He tried not to show impatience, but he did want to get them settled for the night before the storm hit. These groups of newcomers always brought out the fatherly in him. So tired, so bewildered, yet trying to cover it up with boisterousness and nonchalance. But they'd make out OK, given a few weeks. He never got over being amazed at how they adjusted. Most of them. This group was a little older than the last one, three with gray hair, even. That might mean they'd be more stable and less trouble, or maybe not fit in as well. Who could tell?

Now the buses were loaded. He hoped to God they had all their luggage. Being a baggage man was not his idea of an educator's job, and that was what he was supposed to be, back in Fayetteville, Arkansas, as assistant principal of Lincoln High. He got on last, stepped over suitcases in the aisle and squeezed in beside one of the men. It was an hour's ride to U. P., where they would be quartered for the night. How to begin conversation with this young man. Strange, he always felt ill at ease and —well, it was silly, but kind of inferior. He couldn't quite be sure of the Peace Corps type. They were so confident, so sure of their ability to cope.

"Long trip!" he offered, a safe opener.

"Yes, sir."

Easterner, from one of those private prep schools, Lawrence surmised. He felt more at ease. At least this guy wouldn't blast him at the first meeting.

"First time out of the States?"

"Yes —no. Just to Europe, not like this."

So, at least the guy knew that. Good. The bus turned onto the highway.

"This is Highway 54," explained Lawrence. "Goes around Manila. New sections out here, industry, lots of building." He wanted these superior westerners to know Manila was a city.

"Jeez, suburbia!" came loudly from across the aisle.

"But walls. Every house has a wall around it; wonder why?"

No use telling them now, they'd think he was prejudiced. Wait till they had a few things stolen. Both sides of the highway were lined with small new factories or offices, many with familiar names.

"Colgate!"

"Coca-Cola."

"Oh, that's all over. Every little store."

This was business closing time, and the two-lane road was choked with vehicles. The bus lurched to the side as they swerved to miss an open truck packed with workers standing up. There were squeals and laughter as they replaced parcels and found something solid to hang onto as they wove in and out of traffic for several miles. Cars thinned out as they turned off Highway 54 onto Quezon Boulevard.

"Now we go straight to the University of the Philippines," Mr. Lawrence announced loudly, "about ten minutes." While he still had their attention, "Pretty soon we go around a circle with a statue in the middle, and this is where they are beginning to build new government buildings."

To the newcomers the new capital didn't look very impressive. A few poured concrete box-like buildings streaked with dirt around a big circle where carabao grazed. They couldn't see the top of the statue but at the base were some half-finished concrete or stone structures. Nobody commented because at that moment the clouds that had parted to let their plane land came together. Without a warning of thunder or lightning, the wind slashed rain across the road with a force that seemed about to tip the bus. There was a rush to close windows but most of them wouldn't budge. Martha manged to pull down a blind beside her, but others pushed to the center of the bus trying to get out of range of the pelting rain.

So they did not notice the flowers and shrubs on the road into the campus. They did not see the imposing Administration Building nor the beautiful statue welcoming them to seek freedom in knowledge.

The buses pulled up in front of a building so new there were no walks in from the street. The volunteers looked at the stretch of mud across which a few planks had been laid and made no move to get out.

Charles Lawrence stood up, and, packing good cheer into his voice, called out, "Better go barefoot, folks."

Good-natured guffaws and profanity responded to this and the "folks" began to comply. Martha couldn't do it; she had on a girdle and hose. She rummaged in her flight bag for a plastic raincoat. Out they piled, carrying their shoes and anything else they could manage. Many slipped off the boards as they ran and splashed ankle deep in the mud. The sexual equality standard of Peace Corps completely broke down. At this point the girls made straight for the door and shoved through first into dry safety. Grumbling, the men gallantly went back and carried in the luggage.

"What an ungodly mess!" exploded Isobel. "I just know my clothes are soaked right through that canvas suitcase."

"Well, so is everyone's."

"Who cares? We're *here!*"

"We're here, we're here!" It became a shout as they stood around, between and on top of duffle bags, boxes, suitcases, victors whose war had not even begun.

Jimmy jumped on a chair and waving his arms sang, "Let every good fellow now join in a song."

"*Vive la compagnie,*" a few joined in. There were shouts of "No, no," and someone started, "*Paro, Parong bukid.*"

"Oh, cut it, fellas."

"For chrisake, where do we go?"

"Just a minute, folks," Mr. Lawrence waved his arms for attention. "This is a new dorm —"

"Oh, yeah?" They were beginning to act natural, he noticed.

"The men will go to the rooms on my right, the girls to my left. I think you will find what you need for tonight. Tomorrow the buses will pick you up at eight A.M. to go to Los Banas, where you will begin orientation."

"*Begin* orientation? We've had it!"

"When do we start work?"

"Soon, soon, but there are some things that can only be learned in the host country. To eat you can go a couple of blocks up the street to the student cafeteria. Goodnight. See you in the morning." And he was out the door before they could ask another question. George peered out after him into the deepening gloom.

"Now it's stopped. Wouldn't you know."

There was a momentary silence as the strangeness, the aloneness began to penetrate. Then they rummaged around until each had found at least one bag and they dispersed. Two long halls opened off the entrance with rooms on either side, all alike. Gloria walked the full length of the hall hoping for something better than she saw through the open doorways, found a stairs at the end and went up. Others followed till there was no one left in the hall.

The men found the same arrangements and settled in, except for the married couples. At San Francisco State they had stayed in the men's dorm with separate bathrooms. But here each room had four cots. After complete inspection, George and Kathryn and the Allens conferred.

"Guess we'll have to double up," Ken Allen suggested.

Kathy looked at George. Suddenly, George had had enough. He went into the nearest unclaimed room, picked up a bamboo bed, and tossed it out into the hall. Another followed.

"Kick someone else out or sleep in the hall, this is ours." He dragged in his embarrassed wife and slammed the door.

In the female wing, the first discovery was—no lights in the bedrooms. There were ceiling lights in the hall and bathrooms but the bedrooms were dark.

"Here's a fixture," Mary Jo called out. "but no bulbs."

"Go ask the fellas," Isobel called back from across the hall.

Mary Jo walked to the center hall and called, "Hey, guys, you got any lights?"

"Nope," came the response.

George, still in a do-something-about-it state, came out of their room. "There must be a janitor or something. Where's the phone?"

Discovery number two—no phone, anywhere. No outlet for one.

How can you have a dorm without a phone? The question made the rounds. It was a staggering thought.

Doors were left open to the light in the hall, and some light came in from the street. In the semi-darkness they groped around and made more discoveries. "No springs."

"Well, at least there's a mattress."

"Pad, you mean."

On each cot was a folded sheet and towel.

"I've got only one sheet."

"That's all there is."

"No blanket."

"Blanket! Who wants a blanket? That rain didn't cool off anything."

The urge for a bath seemed to hit them all at the same moment, overwhelming every other need. The first ones in the showers were delighted to find that they worked. At the same time they made another major discovery—no hot water. They shouted to each other, in urgent need for talk.

"This place certainly wasn't ready for us."

"Cold feels good, I'm so hot."

"I don't feel clean, though."

"Hey, girls, hurry up! We want in."

Martha waited her turn, then dug around in the dark for some pajamas. She spread her sheet over the pad and stretched out with a sweater for a pillow.

"You going to bed?" asked Laura in the doorway. "It's only eight o'clock."

"Eight o'clock what?" asked someone down the hall.

"Eight o'clock when? Morning or night?"

"Or tomorrow morning?"

"Well, isn't anyone hungry?"

"No! We ate all the way across the Pacific."

"I'm not hungry and I don't care what time it is. I'm bushed," sighed Martha. "Let them make something out of it."

With that the female end of the dorm collapsed. The hours of sitting, of ears continuously assaulted by droning motors, the excitement and apprehension of arrival, and then the rain— more than clothing had dampened. Fatigue descended like a blanket, muffling movement and voices.

In the end room Mary Jo braided her hair. "What's that noise?" she whispered. "Sounds like something outside." Warily she looked out the window, "Can't see anything except some things crawling around the eaves."

"*Things?*" Isobel sat up.

"Well, frogs or something. Maybe they do it."

Isobel swung her feet to the floor and let out a piercing scream. "I stepped on it!"

"On what?" Mary Jo jumped on her bed and they huddled together.

"I don't know. I can't see."

Heads popped out of doors and retreated hurriedly to get their own feet off the floor.

"I won't sleep here," wailed Isobel, all control gone.

"Where will you go?" asked Martha practically as she appeared with a pocket flash she always kept in her purse. She shone the light by Isobel's bed, and they all leaned down to look. Isobel screamed again, "It's a tarantula! I'll die!"

Mary Jo looked again. "No, it's only a spider. You half killed him." Mary Jo was a biology major.

"You don't know Philippine spiders," accused Isobel defensively.

Laura had followed Martha and looked over her shoulder at the biggest, blackest spider she had ever seen, hairy legs curled up. She shuddered and ran back to bed. Any spider could make a coward out of her.

"It's got a mate," Isobel wept. "It'll come to look for it."

"That's snakes," scorned Mary Jo. "Here, I'll take it out." She took her towel, threw it over the offender, gathered it up and shook it out the window.

For the first time Martha noticed there were no window screens. Back in her room she prudently shone her flash around and under her own bed.

"Mine, too, please," Laura pleaded.

Over in the men's ward they had made the same discoveries as the girls but they accepted matters more easily. Some of them simply dropped their shoes, sprawled on the cots and slept. Others took to the showers and found to their disgust that this dorm was built for girls only.

Hunger drove Jimmy and Joe to hunt for the cafeteria, hoping for at least a sandwich at this hour. They walked up the street in the direction Mr. Lawrence had pointed, and odors led them to a large low shack. To their surprise, although it was after eight, lines of men students were loading their plates from big kettles on long counters. They joined the line at the end but immediately a plump man with a wide smile came from behind a counter, shook their hands, and ushered them past the waiting students up to the serving tables, explaining loudly, "Piss Corp, Piss Corp."

"Oh, no," protested Jimmy, "we'll just wait, thank you."

But it did no good. "We just want a sandwich," he suggested weakly.

Pairs of curious eyes stared. No one smiled, but the looks were friendly somehow. The women behind the kettles heaped enameled plates high with rice, a soupy meat mixture, and another strange conglomerate. The plump man led them to a table from which he brushed bits of food onto the floor and brought them bottles of Coke. At that moment they realized they had passed the cashier.

"Wait," Joe called to the man, "we haven't paid." He pulled some coins from his pocket—quarters. Of course, they had no Filipino money yet. Embarrassed, he started to apologize.

"No, no," grandly gestured their host. "I'll be the one."

So they sat down and ate.

"What did that PC guy expect us to do, without money?"

"Just what we did, probably."

"Gosh," ejaculated Jimmy. "Would we do that in the U. S.?" Then as he looked at the formidable pile of unfamiliar food on his plate, "And I don't even like rice."

"Shut up and eat it," ordered Joe.

11

Three Letters Home

On the west side of U. P. Diliman campus between the co-op grocery and the infirmary is a street which in early Peace Corps days was dirt without a name. The first houses were temporary wooden huts thrown together during World War II as barracks for troops. Past these an uneven row of small cement block cottages squatted among weeds and gravel. Behind them a ditch bordered by banana plants straggled toward one tall proud mango tree.

In the late afternoon heat, nothing was moving on the street. One would have passed the last house thinking it was empty. Inside, three Americans were writing letters. Laura wrote on her lap with her paper on a book. Martha had pulled up a small table to her bamboo chair. Isobel had things spread out on the dining table at one end of the kitchen. This was the first time all of them had sat down at once since moving in. But they were not together now. Each was trying to shrink the miles of space between her and someone back home. This was the first time they were trying to express just how things were, just how it felt to be a PCV in the Philippines. As the replies came back they would know that they had failed.

Dear Alice:

About this time of day the sixth period is over and you are clearing your desk for the night. I can see Room 201 at Central High so plainly. Actually, you are not doing that because you are twelve hours different in time. (You should hear all these college graduates trying to figure out time changes. Something must be wrong with social studies textbooks!) Anyway, it is 4:00 P.M. here and I want to tell you what has happened to your erstwhile fellow teacher since I arrived in the Philippines. You can tell Social Studies IV for me that there is a lot more to the Pacific Ocean than appears on a map. It took thirty hours to fly over it, with two stops. Also, typhoons are not to be put in the same class as a summer thunder storm in Ohio. One of them blew us into Manila.

We thought we were through training when we left the U. S. but there was two weeks more of it here. It became apparent that we were not going to be in the kind of programs that had been envisioned in Peace Corps Headquarters in Washington. [It took Martha a long time to phrase that sentence. She couldn't tell the teachers at home, and certainly not the students, about the consternation that came as the volunteers gradually realized that those "felt needs" they had come to fill seem to have been felt only in Washington.]

We were given a great deal of freedom in the choice of our individual locations. Certain schools were "open" and we would work with counterpart teachers as kind of assistants. There are only four of us at the University of the Philippines, where we thought most of us were to teach in a remedial English program. I am one of these. The campus is about ten miles out of Manila and was built by the United States after the downtown campus was partially destroyed in World War II. It has thousands of acres and a central quadrangle so big we ride in jeepneys to get around. A jeepney is a World War II jeep with an extended body, painted up like a circus car.

There are about 5,000 students on this campus and the university has other campuses and two high schools. I am located at the Graduate College of Education, with a variety of responsibilities. [Maybe it wasn't quite honest to sound as if she had walked into a university position with accompanying status. Actually, she had felt like an inexperienced twenty-one-year-old, clutching her diploma and applying for her first job. No, it was worse, with Mr. Lawrence along, going from department to department peddling her services, which embarrassed deans politely indicated they didn't need, even though free.] Tomorrow I will find out more about my specific duties.

The students look very young and actually are, as there are only six grades here before high school. It is a big step from high school to U. P. where all the textbooks are published in the States, and they try to maintain a level with U. S. universities. I have visited classes and you would be amazed as I am at the passivity of the students. They seldom ask questions even when the professor gives them an opportunity, and never argue. It should make teaching easy, but possibly boring, too.

I must admit I am glad to be here instead of out in the provinces.

Manila is an odd mixture of modern city and rural slum, but people look so clean and neat in western clothes and the latest hair-dos. They look so American, but they are *different*. I hope I will understand it better after I have been here longer. I am glad I came though I do miss the routine and the friends in Mt. Vernon. Give my regards to anyone who is interested.

Sincerely,

Very dull letter, Martha thought as she sealed the envelope and sighed. *Just the kind a teacher would write back to her school.*

FROM LAURA

UP Diliman, Quezon City, Philippines

Dear Mumsey: [Funny she had written that old pet name. She had not used it for years.]

The above will be my address from now on. We pick up our mail, so you don't need a street address. I don't have thatch in my hair or rice between my toes, because I am located on a very civilized modern university campus. Isn't that a surprise? I know it has been several weeks since that first quick note I wrote after our arrival. I kept planning to write but impressions came so fast it didn't seem to be any use describing them till they began to coagulate. I'm not sure that's a good metaphor. But I guess I expect too much too fast.

The PC director is Dr. Jacobs, who was dean at Rutgers. So he must be good, and I will say he makes the whole PC program sound just great But it seems kind of vague, so far. There weren't any definite assignments for us, just some openings like. "They would like to have two volunteers in Dumaguete," and, "What part of the country do you want to go to?" I don't know anything about the country. How could I pick a place to go? [That was the best she could do to describe the sensation of complete letdown at the realization that no one was eagerly waiting for her talents and goodwill.]

Martha Wagner helped decide it for me. She is the older woman I told you about. She wanted to stay in Manila and we decided to stick together, if we could. So when they said there was a "cordial" request for an English teacher at Philippine Normal School I piped up and said I'd like it. There are about eight others of our group around Manila and the rest are scattered from Loaog way up north to Davao in the southeast. We may never get together again. Dick, the boy I went around with some at San Francisco, was selected out at the last minute. Several others were, too. [That sounded casual enough.]

Well, I suppose you would like to know how we live. We are lucky there. Three of us, Martha, Isobel Swartz, and I, have a little cement-block house on the university campus built by a Rockefeller grant. It is new and clean and painted wild colors. Blue, green, and brown all in the same room, and cement floors painted red and still sticky. I'll draw a plan for you. We drew lots on bedrooms and, wonder of wonders, I got one alone—only the company, if we have any, will sleep with me. The third bedroom is occupied by a maid. Now don't faint, *everyone* here has them. And *you* helped get her for us, because you wrote to Rev. Williams that I was coming. He and Mrs. W. found out through PC office where I was and came to call the day we moved in. Oh, was she a help! She showed us where to do washing—on the back stoop in a low pan called a *batya*. Told us what kind of an iron to buy—Japanese without a thermostat, so we burned everything the first week, and where to buy mats for the floors—from the Chinese stores on Pin-a-pin Street. One big problem is shopping for food. There are no near groceries except the co-op store, which doesn't have much. She said the local markets are much better and cheaper and have fresh things but they are down in Manila. She asked did we want a helper. Well, we said no, PC can't afford that and we are supposed to live like our counterparts. She laughed and said every Filipino teacher had several. You pay about fifty or sixty pesos (that's $15.00) a month—that's right, a *month*. She knew of a good girl from the same province her helpers were from and who wanted to go to school, too. We fell for it. None of us want to wash in a pan on the floor or go to market at 6 A.M.

Mrs. Williams looked around and said our house was built for Filipinos not Americans, and when I asked her how she knew she said, "Because there is no room for a helper."

"But you said they all have them."

"They do, but they sleep on the kitchen floor."

Can you imagine that! So ours has a whole room and a bed to herself. I'll bet she feels like a queen. He name is Mona and we can hardly understand a word she says, although it is supposed to be English. None of us ever had a servant before and we don't know how to behave and we must call her "helper." We are so afraid of hurting her feelings. Well, I guess I'll have to write a whole letter about her and the food, sometime.

Our stove is electric—but don't get visions of one like yours. This is Philippine made, three burner and the oven won't bake. We also have a refrigerator that almost keeps things kind of cool. I repainted it. If we just had screens in the windows we'd feel like American suburbanites. They have been promised by the Department of Buildings at U. P. We make Martha go up and ask about them every few days. But now we cohabit with flies and mosquitoes and cockroaches. I thought those came with garbage and dirt, but we had them in the dorm we stayed in which was new and here, too, huge ones. I hate them and I won't let Mona step on them they crunch so.

We have a bathroom with a tile shower and only cold water. But that feels good, the air is so hot. The best thing about Manila—the very best—is that we don't have to boil our water. We can drink what comes from the faucet.

We *worked* for our furniture. We found it in the university store room, *"Bodega"* is the word. It was filthy, worm-eaten rattan but we scrubbed it and painted it and covered cushions and it's just great.

We are learning how to use local fruits and vegetables. Everything has to be peeled or cooked. We pooled our settling-in money and got plain white dishes and steel forks and stuff in the market. Oh, I could take a book to describe those markets. Am I ever glad you made me take sheets. They only make them short here and even they are expensive. Each shop has a different item and there are hundreds of stalls close together for cloth, hardware, baskets, mats, etc., etc. Lots of clerks—not like self-service in the states.

Well, to go back to my job. Mr. Lawrence, deputy PC Director, took me to the Normal School. It's on Taft Avenue right downtown and a long way from here. I have to take a bus and then a jeepney. But there's no nice place to live down there and we get to live in this house because Mart and Isobel work at UP. Anyway, so he took me and introduced me to the Supervisor, Miss Rodriguez; the Superintendent, a sweet elderly man, Mr. Lopez; and the Principal, a sourpuss if there ever was one, Mrs. Ramos. We sat in a row of straight chairs and they told me the history of the school, started by Americans during commonwealth days. It was all very formal but I didn't meet the teacher I am to "assist." They called her Miss Aspi. I hope she is not too old. I still don't know what I am supposed to *do*. Mr. L. just said, "Work it out." [Work it out? Laura stopped writing and took some long breaths to keep those knots from tying up her insides. She had never taught a class in her life. In training, English had been taught the same way as Tagalog, as a second language. But these people already spoke English.]

Tomorrow I will go again and meet the teacher I am to work with and I hope she wants me.

Now I must stop. The others are through with their letters and I offered to walk them to the P. O. I have been getting your letters that you sent to PC Headquarters. Keep them coming. Pet Matilda for me and give her some milk. She wouldn't get any here, or liver either.

Lots of love,

68

Hi, Sharon, Darling:

Here I am at last in this beautiful, fabulous country. Oh, I just wish I could show it to you. I am living in a darling little house with two other PCV's on the edge of a huge gorgeous campus of the best university in the Philippines. We are near the mountains here so it is much cooler than in Manila. I am so lucky to have been chosen as one of the few stationed here at the University of the Philippines. I will teach in the Dept. of Speech and coach plays in the high school, just my bag. I haven't really got started yet but I have visited classes and the kids are dear. All have black, black hair, big brown, almost black eyes that just tear at your heart and they are so polite. They all speak English, of course, with a cute accent and they are eager to improve their pronunciation, that's why we are here. I will be using tapes in a lab with the latest recording equipment.

Just imagine being able to step right into a university job my first year out of college! A lot of the students here take six or seven years to get through because their preparation is so poor, so they are my age. The fellows look keen in short-sleeved white shirts and slim dark slacks. And they say they do all the latest dances. The only teeny weeny trouble is they are kind of short. We were warned in training about their dating patterns, sounds wild, but if you stay out with them past 10 o'clock they will brag they slept with you even if they didn't. But I expect that's exaggerated. Leave it to me to find out. Anyway, I think all that PC training junk we went through as to Philippine culture and customs and how to act is for the birds. They look just like us and I have never yet seen a two-legged animal I couldn't handle. So I'll just do my thing—as usual—like crazy.

Tell the girls at the house that this is the best way to get free travel and new experience, and I know we can be a lot of help to these darling people. The girls here are slim and straight up and down and look neat in the starched print shifts they wear. All the high school kids are in uniform, no less, blue jumpers and white blouses. Well, it saves the agony I used to go through if I had to wear the same dress twice in a week. But I'm sure it must stifle their individuality.

PCV's are scattered all over the Philippines and we're not supposed to fraternize with the Americans in the military or at the embassy, so I'll have to do my own hunting. If anyone at the Delt House is still interested (!) tell them (him) I am staking out a claim for the son of a former Philippine president I'm going to have in speech lab. They pointed him out to me yesterday.

So long, angel, this is the life for me.

"Damn!" Isobel exclaimed. "All these envelopes are stuck together. How am I supposed to get a letter in? And I am stuck to the chair!" She got up, pulling her skirt off with a ripping sound.

12

The Day

September the twenty-eighth began with the playing of
"U. P. Beloved" by the carillon in the auditorium tower, a
pleasant way to start the day. Laura opened her eyes to the
6:30 sunlight, stretched, and for a few minutes breathed deeply
of the coolish early morning air. This was the best time of the
day. Best for sleeping and best for doing things; and a choice
had to be made quickly, before the all-persuasive sun took over.
There was no choice open this morning, however. This was *The
Day*. The day she started her Peace Corps work, at last. She
could hear Mona rattling pans in the kitchen and hoped mildly
that she had washed her hands. She undoubtedly had worms,
and one of their girls must remember to tell her to get a
check-up at the infirmary. Isobel was already in the shower so
there was no use hurrying.

She was fully aroused by Martha's loud voice, "Go away, go
away! I tell you, off! Out! Stop looking at —*Mona!*"

Mona and Laura arrived at her door at the same time to
see Martha clutching a robe to her front with her back against
the wall, wildly making motions to a man at the window seated
on a carabao, which was just the right height for him to see in.

"Mona, make him go!" Martha commanded.

Mona spoke a few words indignantly in Tagalog and the
man turned slowly by digging his heels in the carabao's stomach
and ambled off.

Laura plunked down on Martha's bed rocking with laughter. "It is worth the price of admission to see you scared!"

Martha was not amused; she was visibly shaken and angry.
"What does that man mean by staring into my bedroom? What's
he doing on a carabao in our yard, anyway?"

"He tek heem to water, eber morning, mum."

"Every morning!"

"Yes, I saw him go by the house yesterday," agreed Laura. "I guess he just discovered you today."

"Well, *well*, we'll see about that! You see about that, Mona —please?"

"OK, mum," agreed Mona happily. She liked taking care of these Americans. Being last in a family of nine, she had never known this pleasant sense of superiority.

The three of them sat down at the table. It was set for four, but Mona would never sit with them without a special invitation. This had been one of the first cultural problems. Mrs. Williams had said Filipina helpers never sat with the family, but since their dining table was at one end of the kitchen they could not endure having Mona stand by the sink and watch them eat. So for breakfast and dinner she was persuaded to sit with them. For lunch, it was every girl for herself.

The bright wedges of papaya were firm but juicy with just the right tang from the juice of half a calamancy, a small green lime-like fruit they had come to appreciate. Maxwell House coffee was a staple Philippine import, so that was fine, although Isobel kept reminding them that they should use Filipino-grown products. It required Mona's full attention to toast baker's bread on an old electric toaster with drop-down sides lent them by Mrs. Williams. They would learn from exclamations of envy by other PCV's that toast was a luxury in the Philippines.

"No eggs?" queried Isobel.

"We had eggs yesterday," Martha reminded her.

"Bacon?" hopefully.

"Don't be silly," reproved Laura.

"Well, y'know when it's my turn —"

"All right," Martha cut in, "when it's your week to cook and plan you can spend our kitty on eggs and even canned butter, if you want to. If we all starve at the end of the month we'll see how you like it."

"Well, I don't mind that coconut oil stuff they use for butter," said Isobel. "I think they do awfully well with all their substitutes."

"They aren't substitutes —except to Americans," observed Laura. "Mona, what do you eat for breakfast at home?"

Mona thought. Actually, she couldn't think of a meal that resembled what they called breakfast. "Rice," she hazarded.

"Rice? What else?"

"Ricup, mum."

"Ricup, what's that?"

"Soup, I betcha," surmised Isobel. "Like this, Mona?" She made motions of a spoon and a bowl and loud slurping.

Mona giggled delightedly, "Yes, mum. Ricup."

"Oh, dear," Laura rose hastily. "I have to catch a bus at seven-thirty. I hate to walk up that road in good shoes, but I guess I'd better, the first day."

"Wipe them off on the bus," advised Martha.

"Well, I'm not going to walk around this campus in heels, I can tell you," announced Isobel. "My flats are good enough for this dust."

"What do you think I should take?" Laura called from her room, "a notebook? Or would that look like I was going to report something?"

"Just your sweet self, dear," said Isobel.

"A pencil," advised Martha practically.

Laura settled for a pencil and a few sheets of paper tucked in her handbag as she ran out the door.

"Slow down!" Martha called after her. "Well, she's off. Now I start today too, and I don't know any more than she does about what's expected." She lingered over the last swallow of coffee. "What about you?"

Isobel yawned and brushed some crumbs off her pink duster. "I don't know. Nobody said when I should come, y'know. I guess I'll wash my hair."

It was Martha's week to get dinners. The girls had reasoned that they were not paying Mona cook's wages so they should at least do dinners. But Mona, to whom this job was pure luxury, considered the kitchen her domain. She hovered about, recognizing this as an opportunity to learn American ways so that she could advance in status to the level of helper who had cooked for Americans. Jobs with Americans were always better than with Filipinos.

Miss Wagner let her cook the rice.

"How long does it take?" Martha asked, figuring out when to start the other preparations.

Mona was stumped. How did anyone know how long it took to cook rice? You just put it in a regular kettle, with water two finger joints above the rice, and boiled it till it was done.

"I don't know, mum."

It was Martha's turn to be stumped. How did you get the

food all done at the same time if you didn't know how long to allow for cooking? But she knew that time was not important to Filipinos. *Introduce change slowly,* she reminded herself.

"Well, you cook it and we'll watch the clock this time. I expect half an hour will do it. I'll fry the fish. Are you sure it is ocean fish, not river?"

"Yes, mum." Mona hadn't the slightest idea. She saw it in the market this morning, it didn't smell bad, so she bought it. But if Miss Wagner wanted it from the ocean, it was.

"Did you get bananas?"

"Yes, mum."

"I'll make a salad —Oh, no lettuce. They're green!'

"Yes, mum, dey *saba* por cookeen, mum.""

"Oh, the kind you slice and fry and roll in sugar? You do it for us. But we have only one skillet. Well, when the fish is done we'll put it in that oven that doesn't get hot, and then you do the bananas —the *saba*. OK?"

"OK, mum."

"That'll do for a vegetable, even if it is a starch, and for dessert, too."

The call to dinner brought Laura and Isobel from their rooms. The table of wood and rattan which they had painted white (the better to see cockroaches crawling up the legs) looked inviting. Inexpensive reed-and-yellow abaca placemats set off their plain white china. Laura sighed as she sat down with a weariness that a nap after her return from school had not dispelled. Isobel was bouncy after her day of rest. "Fish and it's not Friday, and you a Catholic," she teased Martha.

"Fish on Friday doesn't matter in the Philippines, I found out," Martha explained seriously, "because they eat it almost every day."

"And they eat rice like it was going out of style. I was in the cafeteria line today and do they heap it up!"

Martha felt defensive. "Potatoes are expensive, if you want to have them when —"

"I know, when it's my turn to cook. It's OK, Mart, I'm just kidding you. Food looks great."

Martha felt hostess responsibility. "How was your day, Laura?"

Laura felt a sudden dash of hominess that unsettled her. That was almost exactly what her mother asked her father every night of the world.

"Well, I'll have to start at the beginning. The bus stopped

almost every corner all down Quezon Boulevard. Then I got off at Quiapo, as Mr. Lawrence told me to get a jeepney to Taft Avenue. There are thousands of them and they all looked full. Two slowed down for me but I couldn't see any place to sit. It was getting late so I climbed on the back steps of the next one and the others squeezed over so I had a few inches. It costs only ten centavos. I couldn't think of how to say I want to get off."

"Stop!" offered Isobel.

"No, I listened to the others and they said, '*Parah*.' That's what it sounded like, so when I saw the school, I said it too and the driver stopped —at least almost stopped and I about fell off. It was almost eight thirty and I ran across the street and got in as the kids streamed in. My gosh, they all look exactly alike in white uniforms. I was out of breath when I got to the office and asked for Miss Aspi's room. But I needn't have hurried. Girl at the desk said 'Have a seat.' So I sat and waited and waited, I didn't know for what."

"Me too," put in Martha. "I thought I had an appointment with Dean Gonzalez, but he wasn't in his office and his secretary didn't know where he was and didn't make any move to find out. Every time I stood up to get her attention she'd smile and say, 'Pliss bi sitted.'"

"I'm glad I didn't go," said Isobel with self-satisfaction. "Let them come for me if they want me."

Laura was not to be sidetracked. "So, finally after about an hour, the Principal, Mrs. Ramos, came in. She's the fat one and kind of huffy, but somehow I think I can talk to her better than the Supervisor, Miss Rodriguez, who came after we had waited some more. I don't know where Mr. Lopez was. He's cute. So the official dignitaries escorted me to the second floor to Room 240. The classrooms are built around an open square with an open passageway on the inside. The door of the room was open and we marched in. At last I was face-to-face with my teacher."

"Your counterpart, you mean."

"Your co-teacher."

"Anyway, whatever you call her, she is young, pretty as a picture, and I judge as scared as I was. But I think Ramos and Rodriguez enjoyed it. They introduced me and Miss Aspi told two students to give up their chairs, the kind of student ones with an arm desk. They stood against the wall while we all sat down. The room was deathly still. I'll swear no one breathed. Maybe they understood the ceremony, but I didn't. It seemed like a play where the actors hadn't been given the script. After some murmurings and nodding and more silence, the others went away and Miss Aspi and I and the students were left to figure it all out.

"Miss Aspi introduced me to the class as 'Piss Corps from the States' and then what do you suppose she said? 'Miss Madoos will spik to us.'

"I was horrified. I hadn't the slightest idea what to say, but there I was!"

"You could have recited the Declaration of Independence," suggested Isobel.

"Well, I told them how glad I was to meet them and be in their lovely country, and I tried to think of something to say that would make them smile, but not a glimmer did I get. I told them a little about where I had come from and why I joined the Peace Corps."

"Why?"

"Oh shut up, Isobel. Wait till you have to do it. All those black eyes staring at me, out of those deadpan faces, judging me. It was devastating. So I stopped and they dutifully clapped and I sat down, and there I sat for the rest of the morning."

"Eat your dinner," commanded Martha. "You probably did all right. I hope nobody does that to me."

"Oh, Mart, for you it would be OK. You're a teacher and you're used to facing classes. I'm going to get some stories all thought up—and probably never get a chance to tell them, because I'll be in a speech lab with only a few at a time."

After a few bites she went on. "Miss Aspi took me to the cafeteria for lunch."

"Rice?"

"Yes, rice and some kind of mixture, mostly onions and some chunks of yellow things in it. But, my dears—the toilet. I didn't need to ask where it was. You can smell it a block away."

"No towels, I'll bet," said Isobel.

"No towels—if that was all! No soap, no toilet paper, yet."

"Do you know what they do at U. P.?" interposed Martha. "I saw them today. The professors, the women anyway, keep toilet paper in their desks and when they go to the ladies' room they carry a tray or box with a roll of paper and soap and towels in it right in plain sight down the hall."

Suddenly they were conscious of Mona.

"Well, paper is expensive and I doubt that most people have it in their home," reasoned Martha out loud, conciliatorily.

"I remember how at my grandmother's house in the country they used Sears Roebuck catalogues in the outhouse."

"We're terribly spoiled with pink rolls. So soft," Isobel said dreamily.

"Scented, even. It's silly."

"We are lucky there are bathrooms, so who's complaining?"

The attempt to cover up their criticism left something to be desired, they all knew, but it was the best they could do.

Laura wasn't finished. "I got through the day without any more boners, but I did something wrong after classes were out and I don't know what it was. Nobody had told me my teacher's first name, but I saw it on one of her books. 'L-u-z'. I didn't know whether that was a nickname or for real, but since it was in a book I decided that was her name. It seemed to me we must get on a friendly basis if we were to be in the same room every day. She's about my age and I felt silly having her call me Miss Mathews even when we were alone. So I said so and told her my name was Laura and I'd be happy to have her call me that if I could call her Luz. Well, she froze. I mean I could see it. Froze isn't right because her face got red and she said something so low I could hardly hear it about being teachers and what would the students think and then she said goodbye quickly and left. Did I insult her some way? Isn't that her name?"

Mona spoke up from the stove where she was frying more bananas. "Loose."

"Loose? What's loose?"

"Iss her name, mum. Loose."

"Loose? Luz? L-u-z is Loose?" Laura gasped in dismay. "Oh, my gosh, how stupid!"

"Loose, of course, that's the Spanish of it!" ejaculated Martha.

"They didn't teach us any useful things like that in training. Only Tagalog, but not how they pronounce English."

"But her name. Names are very important, she may never forgive me."

"Don't take it so hard. We came here to teach English and 'z' is a voiced consonant, as every dictionary will tell you, so that's where you start —telling her how to pronounce her name."

"Oh, Mart, that would be awful, to try and change the way you have said your own name all your life," protested Laura.

"Well, if we aren't here to change things then we better have stayed at home."

"That's cultural imperialism and not . . . "

A loud knocking at the door startled them. They looked at one another with anticipation mingled with apprehension. Mona went to the door, opened it a crack, and quickly shut it.

"Iss a man, mum, Americano."

"Open it, for heaven's sake"—"Joy be"—"Now who?" They all spoke at once.

The knock was repeated and a familiar voice asked, "Is Laura Mathews in there?"

Laura jumped up and gasped in disbelief, "Dick!" All three went to the door and flung it open in happy excitement.

"Dick Blumberg! How did you get here?"

"How did you find us?"

Dick walked in, plunked two suitcases down in the middle of the floor and announced with histrionic extravagance, "Behold, behold, damsels, I am here in the flesh. The stone which the builders rejected got up and walked!"

Laura laughed. Suddenly everything was funny. "Where did you heathen pick up that mixed quote?"

"Oh, I was brang up right—by half my parents, anyway."

"Well tell us quickly, no funny business, what are you doing here?" Martha demanded.

"I, Mr. Richard L. Blumberg, am head salesman in southeast Asia for Great Drugs, Inc."

"Oh for heaven's sake!" from Martha. She had predicted he would come, but this was crazy.

"How did you ever get to be that?" asked Isobel.

"You, a drug salesman? That doesn't fit."

"Yes, it does, and I'll tell you all about it. Why don't you introduce me?" he asked, looking over at Mona who stood stiffly in the doorway to the kitchen.

"Oh, sure, Mona, this is Dick Blumberg, a friend of ours. Dick, this is Mona, our helper."

Dick walked over easily and offered Mona his hand. She hesitated, put forward a limp one of her own, and then ran to her room.

"Now what's that for?" asked Dick in surprise.

"She's shy," explained Isobel.

"And probably no American man ever offered to shake hands with her before," whispered Laura. "Oh, you've got a lot to learn, Mr. Americano," she added, feeling slightly superior.

"U-huh," Dick looked around. "Well, you gals got a nice little pad here. What strings did you pull?"

"We didn't!" protested Laura. "Now what strings did you pull?"

"I didn't. I just made it happen."

"Tell us!"

"You haven't even asked me to sit down yet. A—you having dinner?"

"Oh, haven't you eaten?" Martha asked guiltily.

"Somewhere over the Pacific, I guess."

"Did you *just* get here?"

"Just. I took a taxi to the Peace Corps office. The driver even knew where it was; I sure didn't. Got there just before it closed and asked were there any PCVs in Manila. The Filipina girl at the desk was very nice. Just gave me a list—and there you were. So I took another taxi and we've been driving around this damn campus in the dark, not knowing what to look for. Finally I had him stop at that clinic or hospital and they said there were some Peace Corps down the street."

"Well, we'll find you something to eat. Unfortunately, there's no fish or rice left—we run a close budget—but there's a can of cheese and bread and, oh, bananas—Mona," Martha called, "will you please come and fry some more bananas?"

"Just milk will do," Dick said as he folded his long frame into a bamboo chair.

"Milk!" they all laughed.

"Do you like it dry or mixed with water?" Laura asked.

"I, well—jeez, I forgot. No milk, huh?"

"It's not so bad without," Isobel reassured him. "We make cocoa with powdered and there's Coke and beer. Even it's kind of cool in our so-called refrigerator."

"We can even drink the water," Laura boasted.

Soon he was seated with a cheese sandwich, fried bananas, and a Coke. The girls sat with him around the table, having coffee; his was the last Coke. Between bites he told his story.

"I went home from the airport and for the first three days I was mad. My mother felt sorry for me but was glad, and my father wanted to complain to his congressman, but I wouldn't let him. Then for a week I wandered around New York looking for a job. *Gawd* what stupid ones I was offered!"

"Worse than a drug salesman?" Isobel quipped.

"Now wait, you'll hear about that. I knew New York was not for me. Not after planning on Asia and big deals. So I looked up my Formosan friends at International House. They were all for having me stow away on a freighter and go to

Taiwan and start a revolution. But I don't know any Chinese and I do know Tagalog."

"Some!"

"Enough! So we thought it would be better if I went to the Philippines and got in touch with some of their Huk friends."

"Huks!" exclaimed Martha. "You mean those communists who caused trouble after the war? I thought they had all been lured to the farmland."

"Not all. There are more in the mountains than the Philippine government likes to admit."

"Sounds like TV intrigue," shivered Isobel.

"Sounds like a comic opera. Big American sneaks in and overthrows president—and his sisters and his cousins and his aunts," said Laura scornfully.

"It was kind of far out," Dick admitted, "but those Formosans keep up their spirits by talking wild schemes, and I was just in the mood for anything. Anyway, it started me thinking of how I might get here, and I had a brilliant idea."

"Always a modest guy," murmured Isobel.

"You remember how in training they said Filipinos were wedded to Colgate toothpaste and Camay soap because they got here first? Well, I got to thinking about the poor Filipinos without any choice, just the same old toothpaste every day, and it seemed like some enterprising U.S. firm ought to give those old American firms some competition. So I did some research on drug and soap companies and I talked to a guy in the National Chamber of Commerce and we came up with three companies that might want to expand their export business. I went to see the Jewish one first and, believe it or not, Great Drugs swallowed my bait. I told them I'd come out and investigate the market. See how their products sold. They wouldn't have anything much to lose; it's a bargain for them. All I get is my expenses and a commission. I figured out I couldn't make less than PC makes! And it would leave me time for any little interesting projects of my own."

"Well, I must say—," began Laura lamely, but she didn't say it.

"Of course it wasn't quite as easy as it sounds," went on Dick. "There was the little matter of a passport and something called pre-arranged employment and you just don't walk into a country and start selling things. It could have taken six months to get me in."

"Then how —?"

"That's where tricky Dick came in. I had my passport that PC had made a mistake of giving me before I was cleared, all visaed and everything. So I just came in smoothly as a late PCV. No questions asked. I'll worry about what to do next when I have to."

Martha looked smug. She wanted to say, "I told you he'd get here." Instead she asked practically, "Where are you staying?"

"A —hm-m —a —"

"Our guest bed is in Laura's room," Isobel offered sweetly.

Laura could not control the blood that rose to her cheeks but she managed to toss off lightly, "We Filipinas provide mats on the *sala* floor for our guests, they tell me."

"Good enough for me," Dick accepted.

"For one night," Martha settled the matter. "Any more bananas, Mona? Where's Mona?"

"Marched to her room," said Isobel. "She doesn't approve of our loose ways."

"Loose," moaned Laura. "Oh, I made the most awful mistake today . . ."

13

The Other Side of the Day

Luz awakened to the early light pushing open the cracks between the boards in the wall by her bed. She reached across her young brother and ran her finger along the edge of a board etched by light. The air outside was still cool. Wide awake now, she still hesitated to get up and start this *Special Day*. She could hear her mother blowing on the charcoals to coax them to life under the rice kettle and knew she must get moving if she were to have any privacy before the children awoke. Gently disengaging the old skirt she had slept in from the other sleeping child, she eased her bare feet to the floor and tiptoed over the weathered boards, past her mother to the roofless enclosure that leaned against the back of the house. After looking around to make sure she had no audience, she stepped out of her skirt and blouse. She never felt really safe since they had built the apartment house next door. Anyone could look out a high window over the side walls. So usually she bathed at night, but today she must be last-minute fresh. From a bucket she dipped water into a white enameled basin and bathed herself, rubbing her smooth pecan-tinted skin with her hands. She dried herself with one of her precious private possessions, a terrycloth towel recently bought in the market.

Last night she had washed and ironed her best dress, the pink one she had worn the afternoon she went to U. P. with José. It was laid out on the table in the sala. By the time she was dressed, the children were up and clamoring for food, and her father had left. This was one of their fortunate periods; he had a job at San Maguil Brewery. If he kept it a few months more Luz would be able to spend some of her salary on herself.

"Pinapay," called the bread man, was coming up the street with

a tray of fresh bread on his head. Luz took thirty-five centavos from her purse and without asking her mother went out to greet him and to buy seven *pan de sal*, the large crusty rolls, soft white inside, that the Spaniards had introduced. This was a treat in recognition of the importance of this day. Sometimes only mama and papa and Luz got the rolls, but today it would be for all except Ben, the baby. Each of them would pinch off a bit for him.

By 7:30 Luz was walking toward Buendia Street in her high heels, carrying an armload of books. She arrived at the corner just as a jeepney pulled to the curb. Arranging her skirts to produce the fewest wrinkles, she sat tight into a corner. The jeepney would be full by the time they got to Taft Avenue. All the way Luz repeated to herself opening words to her Peace Corps assistant, or "co-teacher" as Mr. Lopez had called her. He had such nice ways of saying things. But beyond those few memorized words a great wasteland seemed to stretch to the far corners of the day ahead. Nobody had even hinted at what she was supposed to do with this American lady. But certainly the lady herself, Miss Mathews, would know. Americans always seemed so sure of what to do. Would she teach the class or watch? Or—a shiver shook Luz's small shoulders—would she correct mistakes? Luz knew she made errors in English, and so did her pupils. They were studying the paragraph and she would stick to the book, an American book, so that should be safe. They were passing a cathedral, and she crossed herself offering a little silent Ave Maria prayer for mercy and a little Luz prayer for courage. In her eagerness, she arrived at the school before the janitor.

That same evening a small quiet drama was enacted on Dao Street. Luz sat in a straight wooden chair on one side of a straight wooden table. Opposite her José sat in a similar chair. A jam jar holding a spray of pink bougainvillea sat in the center of a crocheted doily in the center of the table. This was an official courting call. It had taken place hundreds of thousands of times in hundreds of thousands of Filipino homes, but this one was missing some of the actors. Those present didn't know their lines, and the stage setting was wrong. Mama Aspi was in the kitchen alcove standing over a kettle of guinatan, salting it with her tears. In the barrio she would have known exactly how to behave. But here it was all wrong. She should be sitting with them, Lola, too, and the uncles. They would talk, about the crops and the neighbors, about his family and hers.

But she couldn't even talk to this young man, and Luz had told her she could not sit with them all the time; it was old-fashioned. Of course it was better he had come than this sneaking out Luz had been doing. And he did look nice, she had to admit. But what was he *saying*? Luz would never tell her. They talked in English. How would he put in the work he owed the family if he were to marry her. And if he didn't why was he here? Luz had told her he was from Mountain Province. His father was a constabulary, his grandfather had been a barrio chief. But *land*. How much land did they have? Jobs didn't count. That she had found out in Manila. They took you in, then they shut you out. You had to buy rice with pesos, and then there were no pesos. But land is always there. That a wife could count on as the babies came. But Luz said he was a university student, as if that was the greatest thing, and she didn't even know how much *land*.

Luz was uncomfortable but uncompromising. This had to be done, at least this much of a bow to tradition. She couldn't keep on pretending to her mother that José just wasn't there.

José accepted the fact that it was proper to call on a girl's family. But he had experimented enough in American-style dating to prefer the freedom it gave him compared to the Filipino courting customs in which the whole family took part or had even prearranged. Well, they hadn't prearranged this. There had been no go-between and no marriage broker, and it wasn't settled, by a long shot. He knew he had pulled Luz out of her provincialism as far as she would go, and if he wanted any more of her he would have to make a nod to the family. So here he was. He ran his finger down the crease in his dark slacks and tried to listen to Luz. She was really chattering, must be upset about something.

"—so I didn't know what to do with her and she didn't know either. Miss Rodriguez and Mrs. Ramos introduced her and then just left and there we were. I asked her to speak to the class and that seemed to surprise her. Don't Americans who come to U. P. always make speeches? The students were very attentive, thank goodness, but I'm sure they couldn't understand her. She comes from Kentucky, isn't that in the South?"

"Yes, and a southern American accent makes it worse. They leave off their 'r's' and do something queer with their 'a's.' A Fulbright professor at U. P. came from Georgia and we never did catch onto the way he talked."

"Well, hers wasn't so bad if I listened very hard, but—"

Luz hesitated and worked at a fold in her skirt.

"But what?" José had never seen Luz so fluttery.

"Well, I suppose it isn't too important, but—well, she called me 'Luz'!"

José slapped his knee and rocked back on the legs of his chair, laughing. "Luz! Well, of course, that's the way it looks to them. 'U's' are the worst. They say 'alumni' instead of 'aloom-nee' and a 'z' they say hard instead of 'sss'. You just have to watch some of the letters they always say wrong and figure out what they mean, kind of translate."

"But José, they came to improve our English. Probably she thinks I'm wrong. Mr. Lopez does talk more like her than I do. Shouldn't I let her teach my children good English?"

"Oh, what's good English or bad?" José was serious now and on the defensive. "You don't want to pick up an American accent, it would sound like you were putting on airs."

"I don't know what I want to do or what she expects me to do." Her eyes filled with tears, and it was a good thing mama bustled in with *merienda.* She put down bowls of *guinatan,* a plate of *macupuno* cakes and bottles of Coke.

"Mama, come and eat with us," invited Luz. But she would not. She should have been there all the time, and if that wasn't allowed by these ignorant young people she wouldn't sit now when she was serving her guests. With a toss of her head she went back to the stove.

With the big spoon José scooped up the food. When he had emptied the bowl and drained the Coke he rose.

"I have to get to U. P. at eight. We have a meeting of the KM."

"The Kabataan Makabayan; do you belong to that? Isn't it communist?" The last word was whispered.

"No, no, not really. But we want some things to happen around here. And if you try to start anything on that campus you're called communists."

"What do you want to happen?" asked Luz, hoping he wouldn't tell her.

"We don't know exactly. We just want room to breathe in. We want to be Asians."

"Asian! What for?"

"Well, not Asian, Filipino. First we make ourselves Spanish, all our names are Spanish, then American, all our streets are states of the U. S. Now we should be ourselves."

"And talk Filipino," Luz said scornfully. "You talk Ilacano

and I talk Tagalog, and to each other we talk English. Does that make me an American?"

"You will be if you live with that Peace Corps teacher very long!"

"No I won't!" Luz shut her lips in a tight line and walked with José to the door. She watched him jump the drainage ditch and saunter toward Buendia. Now she would do up the dishes and explain it all —or some of it to mama. She sighed. It was a strange first visit. Five heads appeared around the corner of the house from the alley. "Can we come in now?"

14

The Meaning of Conceiving

English Composition 2, Room 240, was very quiet. Luz, in starched yellow cotton, black hair piled high, looked very perky seated at the teacher's desk. Laura sat at a side table, her no-iron, good, blue shift showed dark circles at back and underarms. Her attention was on the pile of papers before her. "Consultation Period" this was called, and it was her idea. Compositions were usually turned in and were turned back with no marks. On the other hand, Miss Malano, the other English teacher, used a red pencil so viciously that the writers were left in tears.

"There must be a middle ground," Laura had insisted to Luz. "Can't we explain their mistakes to them?"

"Yes, Mu—Miss Mathews, but —"

"But what? Now try to tell me, please."

"But eet will hut der fillin's."

"How else will they learn?"

"Yes, mum, I know." How well she knew. She thought of that school in the barrio, the dirt floor, the sun slanting through the *nipa* thatch onto the scarred double desks. "This is a mango. It is yellow." All the time her mind had been saying it in Tagalog and when she said it out loud it was, "Dees eess mohn*go*. Eet eess yallow."

"Dey tink in dialect, alreaddy," she explained.

"Still?" asked Laura, gently, hoping Luz would grasp the correction without her pointing it out. "But they have been taught in English since third grade."

"Only in school."

Laura tried to imagine this. American immigrants had similar problems with language. German, Swedish, Spanish were spoken at home, English in school. It separated generations cruelly, but the children soon learned to negotiate the new language and made it their own. Evidently to Filipinos English was still a foreign language even though it had been the medium of instruction for sixty years. "We'll just have to try harder. Let's start by explaining their mistakes to them. Is 'consultation' a good word?"

"Yes, very good." Luz was looking intently in her top drawer fingering the pencils.

So that was it. The teachers corrected what had been handed in and called each student up to talk it over while the others were writing an assignment.

"Emanuel," Laura called.

The big boy in dark slacks and white shirt ambled to the desk and sat down. He scratched a remote spot on his back. Someone snickered. The room settled back not to silence but to the usual rustle.

Laura smiled at him and began encouragingly, "This is quite good, Emanuel. You like basketball, don't you."

"Yes, mum."

Now, gently, a few corrections. "You say, 'We play Cavite last January fifteen. Now since that was this year and there couldn't be any other January fifteenth you don't need to say 'last.'"

"Yes, mum." There was no expression in his face or voice.

"When was Easter this year?"

"Last April four, mum."

"No, just April fourth. I know it was 'last.'"

"Yes, mum."

"So how would you rewrite this?"

"We played Cavite —January fifteen —last?"

It began to seem unimportant. So they add "last." Who cares? She reached around to the back of her dress and pulled it away from her damp skin.

"Let's go on. Here you say, 'We are tossing for a basket already when Ben is jumping —.' Now that is all in the past, isn't it?"

"Yes, ma'am, last January fifteen."

"So, just put it in the past tense, instead of the present participle, that's 'ing' you know. 'We tossed for a basket when Ben jumped —'" No light in those brown eyes, just worry now.

"Ma'am, but Ben is jumping when —"

"Jumped, jumped, past tense. Now correct it."

"We tossed for a basket already when Ben already jumped."

"No, not 'already,' just 'jumped.'"

"Yes, mum."

"Please write it out correctly." Laughter.

Laura picked up another paper. "Angeles." She probably should have pronounced it with a hard "g" like they did that town near the Clark. She should have asked Luz. Angeles would have been called a "flapper" in 1920 USA, or a "dame." Although her white starched uniform was like all the others, she filled it out more. As she walked to the desk she slouched so that the back of the skirt was longer than the front, and her hips gave it a swish. When she sat down Laura could see the gentle divided curve where the top button of her blouse was not closed. She wondered again about the composition before her. "A New Day." She had read it three times, surprised by a teenager who had written a composition like a detective story in which she discovered that there was to be another baby in the family. What did it indicate about this girl or her culture? Earthy, frank, or trying to be sophisticated? Begin with tenses, that's always safe.

"Angeles, you have created interest in your readers who want to find out, as you do, why your mother doesn't eat breakfast. Your spelling is excellent but you must watch your verb tense. Now you say your mother 'is conceiving.' That should be past tense, 'conceived' or 'had conceived.'" Somehow the room had become warmer. Laura was quite conscious of Luz at the other desk covering a smile. Why had she picked on that verb? But she was into it now and was not about to be routed by a little biology.

"Conceived," she said firmly and too loudly, "an event in the past which just happens once, when life begins. After that we say a woman is pregnant, or going to have a baby or — or —in the family way. Which would you rather say?"

Angeles was flushed to the roots of her hair. Laura was instantly sorry for her.

"I'll say 'In the family way,'" she whispered.

That consultation was over and Laura was annoyed with herself. She had shamed a student, which she had vowed never to do. It was done often by Filipino teachers, she knew, who used shame as a weapon, to punish inattention or wrong answers. But she had done it without intention. It really would be easier just to grade the compositions and return them.

The class was getting more restless. A boy stood up for no apparent reason and someone giggled. He sat down. Luz rapped on her desk.

"Quiet, please."

Suddenly Oren slipped from his chair to the floor. Forgetting she was not in charge, and seeing the class control about to dissolve, Laura spoke up firmly, "Oren, get up on your chair."

"I'm better here, mum."

"Better? That's silly. Students don't sit on the floor."

"It huits, ma'am."

"What hurts?" She stood up. Luz stood up. The class stood up.

"Tell her, mum, please," pleaded Oren boldly to his teacher, now scratching his bottom without self-consciousness.

Luz hesitated, because she didn't want Laura to know the cause of the distress of her class. But she couldn't let her students down, and she blurted it out.

"Fliss!"

Laura was stunned. Fleas! They were serious. She looked around at the faces, impassive but tense, she could sense in the depths of dark eyes, "How would the American take it, fussy, ignorant Americano?"

"Oh-h?" She managed and sat down. Luz sat down. The class hesitated, then gingerly balanced on the edge of their chairs. She knew about lice in hair, bedbugs in beds, but fleas in these clean starched children? "Where?"

"In de chairs, mum." It came in a chorus. "Dey bite —it huits, too."

Luz sat very still, her hands clasped tightly beneath the desk, embarrassed for her entire schoolroom. Something had to be done, quickly.

"Line up for a spell-down," directed Laura briskly. "Debby, George, choose sides."

Mercifully, the bell rang just then and students filed out, orderly as usual. Laura sank into her chair, then jumped up in a reflex of fright.

"They're not in that one," said Luz dully. "I exchanged yours with one from the office."

"Fleas, fleas —of all things. Why don't they spray?" wondered the citizen of the birthplace of DDT.

"They do, ordinarily, during vacation, but our apportionment was cut so they diluted it, the janitor told me, and it didn't work very well. This building was built fifty years ago, you know. By Americans."

"And the chairs came with it," added Laura, "and in this climate —. I'll bring DDT in the morning." But what lasting good would that do? Peace Corps wasn't supposed to give things away. It wasn't supposed to raise the economic standards which people couldn't later support on their own. While she wrestled with governmental policy —and fleas —she became aware that Luz was giggling with her hands over her face.

"Fleas?" she suggested. No, fleas were serious.

"No-no —con-con-ception," Luz gasped out.

Laura's throaty laugh joined the giggle. "I sure was caught! Did you think I got out neatly with 'when life begins'?"

"Yes —a, a but —"

"But what?"

"But that's what we always say, A woman 'is conceiving' for the first three months."*

* After this no attempt will be made to spell the Filipino English the way the Americans heard it, except for Mona. It is not fair to continue it because it is not possible to indicate how an American accent sounds to Filipinos unaccustomed to it. Gradually, Laura became used to the accent and could understand it automatically except for occasional words or very rapid speech from a stranger. However, it never quite ceased to be a barrier to understanding and an occasional irritation for both Filipinos and Americans. (The Author)

15

The Culture Curtain

Laura turned back the top sheet of her bed and inspected it from top to bottom. She brushed out a few dead ants and stretched out with a deep sigh. Stretching her arms above her head she let her back relax inch by inch onto the pad. At shoulder, hips, calves, and feet she could feel the bamboo slats but it was still better than sleeping on the reed mat that some Peace Corps volunteers affected in their determination to identify with Filipinos. She settled her head snugly into her pillow, then impatiently jerked it up and tossed the pillow on the floor. Now the space between the back of her neck and the mattress made possible a slight movement of air.

Holding her transistor radio close to her ear, she listened to snatches of programs offered by the nine Manila stations. There was a choice of American jazz, classical, western music from a church station, a drama in Tagalog dripping with emotion, or news. At last they had all signed off with the playing of the National Anthem.

"Bayang magilaw, Perlas ng silanganan"

She remembered that much from training but beyond that the Tagalog got too fast for her.

Now all was quiet except for regular breathing of her housemates coming slowly and evenly across the partition, and the chatter of the lizards along the eaves. The street light shone fitfully through the leaves of the mango tree, weaving patterns on the closet door. As she watched, they faded and she floated in that lovely space between waking and sleeping.

A cry —or was it a laugh? She tried to decide afterwards — stiffened her muscles. Without moving or breathing she listened. Again a low cry or laugh. Mona's room. She jumped to her feet and called, "Mona!"

"What's up?" from Martha's room.

"I'm OK, mum," called Mona.

Laura and Martha met at Mona's door. With her hand on the knob, Laura hesitated. She had been brought up not to enter another person's room without permission.

Martha, majestic in red pajamas and hair rollers, slapped her hand away as noises increased behind the door. She pushed it open, and they both entered in time to see a man struggling to get out the window. With a lunge Martha grabbed his feet.

"Help me, you idiot!" she yelled.

Laura's instincts were to let him go, but she was impelled to action by Martha's string of abuse.

"You rat, you, you—intruder! You're a blasted—get him! Hold his head." They had him down.

"Sit on his chest," commanded Martha as she tried to hold onto his legs. He seemed to be very strong.

"Throw us your sheet. Don't just stand there." This to Mona, who seemed quite helpless.

"I don't have any, mum."

"Then you hold his legs and I'll get one." Martha was in her managerial glory. She relinquished the writhing legs in cotton pants and ran to her room.

Laura obediently though distastefully sat on his bare brown chest. She was frightened by the look in the flashing black eyes above a crooked nose, but she should not have looked away. With a heave, the man tossed her on her back, shot out the door, down the hall, jerked open the front door and was gone.

The two women screamed after him at the door, then suddenly became conscious of their night clothes and the noise they were making. Panting, Martha shut the door and flopped into a chair. Laura threw herself on the sofa as Isobel made an entrance. The street light gilded her pale hair which was gathered smoothly into a ponytail. She was a prim little girl in her wrinkle-free, pink ruffled nightgown.

"My God, what a racket!" the "little girl" spoke.

"Racket! It was a *man*."

" —in Mona's room."

"Where were you?"

"He tried to climb out the window."

"Don't tell me you slept through it!"

"We caught him, Laura sat on him, and Mona held his legs while I—where's Mona?"

Laura hugged a sofa pillow and pressed her face into it, laughing hysterically.

"What a fright—over one man among us four girls. We should have stopped him from escaping."

"Stop it!" Martha commanded. "We chased him, Laura and I—where's Mona?"

"Put on the light."

Nearest to the door, Isobel snapped on the switch. How ordinary everything looked in the bright light. Laura stopped laughing.

"Mona," called Martha, "where are you?"

"Here, mum, in my room."

"Are you hurt?" Martha stood up. But Mona came around the corner from the hall; she flounced, fully dressed. Laura stifled her exclamation of surprise. She knew now that Mona slept in her clothes, on a mat on top of the mattress, with no sheets. Three pairs of eyes were upon her. She looked so daytimish standing there in her bare feet, full blue skirt and rumpled blouse, her black hair scarcely mussed, as if nothing had happened.

"What happened!" It was a command not a question. Mona's eyes went to the floor.

"Sit down, Mona," said Laura gently. "Now tell us."

"Nothing, mum."

"Nothing!" snapped Martha. "A man in your room in the middle of the night is *nothing*?"

"Mona," began Laura conversationally. She wished Martha would not attack her; they'd learn exactly nothing that way.

"Mona, now I was just going to sleep—"

"Yes, mum."

"And I heard you cry out."

"No, mum."

"Well, I heard something."

"Yes, mum."

"Mona, don't just sit there saying, 'Yes, mum, no, mum.' This is upsetting. It's an emergency."

"Now do calm down, Martha. Mona, did the man come in through the window?"

"Ah—yes, mum."

"Did he attack you?"

"Oh, no, mum."

"Was he trying to steal something?"

"No, mum."

"Then what —?" Laura's mind reasoned, *How did he get in the window when he couldn't get out?*

"He not know about de scrin, Mum."

The screen—this didn't make sense. Mona must know that, too. She intently regarded her big toe, slowly crossed it over her next toe and said nothing.

Martha, calm now, was working over the sequence in her own mind. "He went out that door, and I locked it myself last night. He didn't unlock it, because I saw him just jerk it open."

Isobel ran her fingers gently down a satin ribbon on her gown and spoke casually, "That was a nice-looking young man who stopped here yesterday in the jeepney."

"Yes, mum," very softly.

"Mona, you didn't hold his legs, did you?" Martha accused.

"No, mum." It was scarcely audible.

A breeze moved the edge of the curtain, the lizards chattered. Laura could feel the cultural curtain coming down between the three of them and the one of her. "Mona," she pleaded, "please tell us —who is he?"

Mona raised her eyes and with perfect composure said, "My hussbohnd, mum."

A gasp escaped Laura.

"Your *what?*" blurted Martha.

Isobel said, *"Siya mag-asawa!* married," in her aren't-they-darling inflection.

Mona sat primly in her straight chair, her palms up, resting one inside the other, her feet neatly crossed at the ankles.

"My hussbohnd," she repeated plainly. Her eyes brightened and she sucked in her breath sharply. Having decided to tell her story she began to enjoy the center of the stage.

"My parrents arrange it already wid hees parrents whin I wass seextin. Dey leeb in nixt barrio. Heess oncle eess my fader's cosseen by hees firs wife."

"That makes him your —"

"Never mind, Martha, let her tell it." Isobel tucked her feet under her in anticipation of enjoying a romance.

"I not like heem." No emotion, just a statement.

"Why?"

"He hass beeg hahnds, crooked nosse."

"That's not a good reason —"

"I not like heem." Her mouth closed in a firm line and

Laura was afraid that was the end of it. She prodded with a straw drawn from the Philippine Studies class.

"Did he do any work for your father?"

"He mus work for my fadder one yearrrr."

"What for?"

"You know, Isobel; they told us in training. The man does it for dowry."

"Oh, yeah. Go on."

"I not spik to heem."

"For a year?"

"Did he eat at your house?"

"No, not it, work. Rice."

"I remember, now. If you have a daughter, that's how you get the crop in, if you're lucky."

"Hi eess lookin at me. I am not lookin at heem."

"For a year?"

"Why didn't you go away?"

"Where I go?" No one had any suggestion.

"My modder cry. But she say I marry. Hees famly haf one carabao, two hectars rice."

"Two acres?"

"Two hectars, that's five acres," corrected Martha impatiently.

"Would he get any of it?" questioned practical Laura.

"No, but hi ees sharring crop from landlord. My modder get ready for wedding. One night —"

"What did she do to get ready?"

"Oh, Isobel, just let her tell it. We aren't having a lecture in anthropology."

"Yes, we are," Martha stated grimly.

"One night I am slipping. Hi raped me."

"How awful!" from Martha.

"How did he get in?" asked Isobel eager for details. No answer. "What did you do?" No answer.

Laura held back the falling curtain again. "We don't understand, Mona. Why did he do that when he already had your parents' consent to marry you."

"To shame me, mum."

That word again. That dark, painful word. The word Americans shrank from and wouldn't use.

"What good did that do him?" Isobel asked.

Mona looked from one to another in mild surprise. These Americans, so educated, but so stupid. She explained slowly.

"So I had to marry heem, mum."

"Oh!"

"Well, I never! That's outrageous."

"The brute."

"No, mum."

"What do you mean, 'No, mum'? He took advantage of you illegally."

"He hass the right. We were betrothed."

"Oh."

"Huh!"

"So you married him."

"Yes, mum."

"You lived with him."

"No, mum."

"Why not? He's your husband."

"I do not like heem." The hands were now clenched together, the feet wound around the legs of the chair. "I am goin' to schull. So I am runnin' away." The words rushed on. "I am comin' to Maneela, already. I am working. I am sabing money. Sometime I am goin' to schull."

"And what is your husband doing?"

"Hi eess drivin' jipney, mum."

"You should divorce him," Martha told her seething with indignation.

"Martha, you know there's no such thing as divorce in the Philippines."

"You can't marry anyone else, ever."

"Yes, mum."

"But he can have other woman?"

Pause. "Many men haff outside loffs, mum."

Isobel looked at Mona under half-closed, speculative eyes. "So when he wants to sleep with you, you let him in." Laura noted, the sound that woke her had been a laugh, not a cry.

"Hi hass the right."

"Well, not in *my* book!" Martha rose stiffly. She looked at the sheet in her hand rather foolishly, rolled it up and walked uncertainly to her room.

Mona looked at these smart, white, rich American women and a spring of pride lifted her head. None of them had a man who wanted her, except maybe Miss Mathews. Only she, Mona, had a man of her own who couldn't get away.

Laura snapped off the light. She tried to stuff this new knowledge into her mental file of Things Learned, but it was still too live, too human to be fitted anywhere in her real world.

"Well, good night," she offered warily and went to her room. She stretched out again on the bed and resolutely closed her eyes. She drew the comforting folds of her Americanism around her, but she could not shut out those angry black eyes glaring at her as she sat on the man's chest, virtuously keeping a husband from his wife. And she could still hear the clicking of the lizards as they scurried along the eaves.

16

Poison Frogs
and Tasteless Ants

October was a finding-your-groove month, a try-to-stop-overreacting period for the Peace Corps groups. The weather took one last slap at Manila, dumping all the water left in its angry clouds in one crashing deluge. Laura was next door paying a welcoming call on the new Fulbright professor. As she started out the door to go home, a weird yellow light enveloped her. No air was moving except in the top branches of the mango trees which were whipping against an orange sky. Over the roof of their cottage a black mass of cloud billowed upwards as though blasted out of smokestacks.

"I'd better get home before it strikes," she called back to the newcomers. But before she reached the porch the wind and rain struck. At her touch the door flew open, but she couldn't push it shut against the force of wind that blew through the house from the west windows.

"Mona, help me shut the door!" she called.

There was no answer and she turned to see Mona struggling to close the kitchen windows. The rain drove in horizontally, hitting the ceiling and washing across the floor at the same time. Laura abandoned the door and ran to her bedroom. Screens recently installed were on the inside and had to be swung open to reach the slatted windows. As she jerked the screen open a fat frog leaped in and clung for a moment to her wet dress.

"Scat!" she yelled foolishly. With all her strength she pulled the windows shut, jammed down the catch, and swung the screen toward them. Just as she slammed it, she saw another frog on the sill. The frame banged to with a sickening squash.

"Oh, my gosh, I smashed it," she wailed. Breathless and

soaked to the skin, she backed away from the window to the bed. The first frog, frantically seeking shelter, jumped wildly and landed on her shoulder. She screamed and struck at it.

"Mona-a-a, help!" Mona heard her above the drumming of the rain on the tin roof. Having secured the doors and windows, she now competently came to the rescue of "mum."

"A huge frog, big as a plate, yellow," babbled Laura.

"It's poison, mum," comforted Mona as she began looking under the bed and moving out furniture. Laura had regained her control and looked, too, cautiously. There was a streak through the air, a plunk on the floor by the dresser, and Mona popped the wastebasket down on him.

Laura took a long breath and tried to sound casual, more than a little embarrassed by her performance. "But you eat frog legs. How come, they can be poison?"

"Grin fr-r-og wi it, no yahlow. Yahlow, Hapniss bring dem in war. Poison," she pronounced, settling the matter.

Laura was in no position to argue. Mona went to the kitchen and brought back a newspaper. Carefully she eased it under the wastebasket. The frog obligingly jumped up against the inside of the bottom of the wastebasket. Holding the paper tight to the open end, she carried the basket to the door. Laura passed her and opened it and Mr. Japanese Frog was out. Free to bother them again, Laura regretted but there was no way to kill the fat thing neatly.

"Uh, Mona, I think I smashed one behind the screen."

"Yes, mum." She went back to the bedroom while Laura prudently attended to urgent business in the living room. Mona reappeared with a crumple of paper which she carried to the back door.

"You're an angel, Mona, an absolute white-winged angel!" Mona giggled. Laura hoped she would wash her hands, but she didn't.

After that, the weather god, or demon, dried his face and smiled. The long dry season had begun. The sun heated the stagnant pools and they grew smaller each day. The water in the ditch back of the house shrank to a trickle. On its surface, minute mosquito egg rafts floated to which millions of larva clung, just below the surface, till they would be full grown, rise to the surface and on an evil day be released to take to the air.

On the concrete slab in front of the Peace Corps door eleven pairs of shoes, scrubbed of mud and mildew, baked in the sun.

Day after day, Mona happily sloshed clothes in clouds of Tide suds in the low pan on the back stoop. With her own traditional method of whiter-than-white, she spread the slightly soapy slips, pants, bras, and dresses on the stubble that passed for the lawn, sprinkling them with water occasionally so they wouldn't dry too fast. But brighter-than-bright she hadn't mastered, and the colors didn't last long. The nylons turned yellow, and mysterious spots appeared which bespoke the careless bird kingdom. But each article was ironed to perfection, except for an occasional brown mark the shape of the iron.

The girls by now had become accustomed to a certain gaily bedecked jeepney which parked occasionally by the house. If the front door was found unlocked in the morning no one commented. They even found Diego, whom they learned to call "Deeahgo," useful for small services such as transporting a big box of paper, hand and toilet, from the post office which Isobel's mother had insisted on sending airmail. It was luxury, indeed. Once he had even dug holes for the cuttings of San Francisco plants which Mona had "procured" (they called it) from a former employer and with which she made straight borders and round beds for other strange bits of greenery she stuck in the gound.

Since U. P. didn't seem to care whether she worked or not and the PC hierarchy ignored her, Isobel finally became bored enough to go regularly to the Speech Department. So far, charming her fourteen students in two classes in the speech lab three times a week, keeping her hair in shape, cutting the sleeves out of all her dresses, had kept her amused. But she was beginning to make frequent excursions to Manila PC office in search of visiting male volunteers from other towns.

Martha had fumed for a week about nothing to do. "The graduate College of Education of the most prestigious university in the Philippines simply has no use for an American teacher on the loose with only a master's degree to her name. All the regular profs got their own doctorates in the U.S."

"Don't they need any assistants?" asked Laura.

"I guess not. There are lots of those, all hoping to get their chance at the U. S."

"Well, there's always paper work at a university, isn't there? You know, profs using grad students to grade papers or something," Isobel suggested.

"I asked. I said I'd do anything. They're all so polite, and so vague. I get the idea they think they can't ask me to do the menial jobs and they don't want me to do the good ones."

"Threatened," said Isobel.

"Who threatened them?"

"Not 'who threatened,' you didn't. *Who's* threatened? They feel they are. I had a fabulous psych prof who showed us why most people hate newcomers—they're threatened."

"Well, that's nonsense. I don't want their jobs. I merely want to help temporarily." But as the days went by she wondered if it was nonsense after all. Had she ever liked those practice teachers she had to put up with, even though she knew they would be moving on?

It occurred to her that Barbara Ward's phrase, "the poverty of ignorance," which had inspired her to join the Peace Corps was patently inapplicable here. Then her chance came. The editor of the *College Educator* was leaving for a special journalism course at New York University, and the dean of the College of Education could find no one willing to take her place. It had to be someone the editor trusted to give the magazine back to her when she returned, but it could not be a friend who would fear losing a friend by making changes in the magazine. There was that nice Peace Corps woman hanging around who had not made friends and would not be staying long, so why not? So to Martha's great relief she was asssigned an empty desk in a third floor office, handed a stack of past issues and a box of manuscripts waiting to be published.

"You're the editor," beamed the dean, glad to be rid of the sticky problem.

But Martha gently refused the title. It looked too important for a PC volunter. They were supposed to help, not to run things. The dean was mildly amused.

"Assistant editor," insisted Martha. The dean looked more carefully at this American. She looked ordinary enough, tall with straight American features, nose too long, face too pale and firm. But refusing to take a top title, this was something new in Americans. Not wanting to run things? Since when? No Filipino would have refused the title—only the work that went with it. This woman seemed to want the work but not the title. Nuances of human relations were not the dean's field.

"Assistant editor, then," he agreed. "But we can't put out a magazine without an editor."

"Couldn't we have a guest editor, a different one for each issue?" she came up with on the spur of the moment and indulged herself in a moment of self-approval.

The dean beamed. Now this was smart, real smart. He would take the first issue himself. There would be a place for that long article he had already written on "Tests and Measurements in Education."

"It's settled then. Thank you, Miss Wagner, we are very glad to have you aboard."

Laura was the happiest one in the household, except for the fact that Dick had disappeared the morning after his arrival, swallowed up by Manila. It was an odd feeling to know he was here but unreachable. He couldn't phone and was not one to idle time on buses without news or a specific purpose, she kept telling herself. Ever since he had walked away at the San Francisco airport there had been a void deep inside her that she had been stuffing things into, people, impressions, activities. Now it was filled. She refused to define for herself what she wanted from Dick or why she felt at peace knowing he was near. Actually, uncertainty and worry seemed to follow him, rather than peace or fulfillment. She could not lightly dismiss the suspicion that behind that drug-selling front he was working on some crazy scheme wrapped up in his idealistic notions of freedom and justice. When he got the legal mechanisms of the country straightened around he'd come, she told herself.

Laura was feeling more at ease with Luz. Fleas had brought them together, though the two teachers had never discussed the affair since they had laughed about it. Laura was totally ignorant about the life-style of fleas. Maybe the dry weather discouraged them. Anyway, the class had not been totally upset again. She was conscious now and then of furtive scratching and impulsive little jerks of students' bodies, which at first she had thought was nervousness. Now she knew the cause but noticed it less. The semester break would soon be here, and hopefully the spray budget would allow for more permanent relief.

One afternoon, after the close of classes, found her on the way to the Williamses carrying a large white box. She was glad to the change from PC living offered by their invitation to celebrate Tessa's fifth birthday. Tessa was a precious child, always seeming to be on tiptoe. How anything so dainty and elfish had been produced by the serious, practical pair of Brethren missionaries, Laura didn't know. She wondered why there was only one of her. Rev. Williams seemed like the type to have fathered a brood. Laura wanted to take her something special, something her parents wouldn't give her. She had asked if she might bring the cake. Not a homemade one but a Country Bake Shop cake. Laura had seen those cakes when she treated herself just once to chocolate and a sweet roll for lunch in the Bake Shop on United Nations Avenue. Each cake was a work of art, specially decorated under the professional guidance of Doctura Ilano.

Laura had gone in to order the cake the day before, lingering over each intimate decision. Roses, yes, and scallops and her name, T-e-s-s-a, in pink. Her mouth actually watered and she laughed at herself all the way back to school. Whose birthday is this, Laura Mathews? At noon that day she had picked up the cake, gently laid in a white box, and carried it like breakable porcelain all the way back to the Normal School— then tried to figure out what to do with it.

She wished now she had not picked it up till after school because now she faced the problem of getting it the ten blocks up Taft Avenue to Tennessee. She made the extravagant decision to take a taxi. Laura and cake arrived safely at the frame house of the Williamses. The cake was spirited out of Tessa's sight to the kitchen. It was restful to be among her own kind again. No doubt about it, being with Filipinos was a strain, trying to listen, trying to understand, guarding one's words and facial expressions. PC volunteers were easier but different too. Their four-women household was not without its tensions. At the Williamses she could let down. It felt like home, however different it looked. This section of Manila had been bombed flat in the war, and the new buildings and shops hastily put together were interspersed with squatters' shacks, broken sidewalks, and *sari-sari* stores.

Tessa was a butterfly of excitement. In her flounced yellow dress she darted from person to person, resting a moment, sampling the response to her charm, then flitting on. There were presents to look at and exclaim over. She expected one from Laura and although she didn't ask, she kept coming back to her hopefully, glancing curiously around her chair. Finally, Laura couldn't stand the suspense.

"I brought you a surprise, darling," she confided. "You'll see it later."

Tessa hid her face in Laura's skirt, shy at having her thoughts read. Laura touched the soft-honey-colored curls that clung to her fingers.

It was pleasant to be waited on at dinner by two competent Filipina girls. Laura still felt guilty about it. Did missionaries live too well, as some of the volunteers accused? Laura had told Mrs. Williams about their social dilemma of having Mona eat with them, and she had laughed.

"I felt that way at first, too. I had never had anyone work for me, but I found out they didn't want to eat with us. They were miserable watching their manners, eating with our knives and forks, not taking as much food as they wanted. And a wise Filipina woman said, 'Don't force your conscience and what you call equality on us. We have our own way to live, and who's to say your way is more Christian?'"

At last the table was cleared and Laura, excusing herself, went to the kitchen and opened the box. She had not been able to find birthday candles but the cake didn't need them. Making a triumphal entry of it, she returned to the dining room with cake held high, singing, "Happy birthday to you." The others joined in and she placed the cake before Tessa.

"Happy birthday to —" She finished the line with a sharp cry, "Ants! Ants, look at them—in our beautiful cake!" Around the edge of the plate a thin wriggling black line moved in and out of the creamy frosting. A few had crawled onto her hand. She brushed them off angrily and snatched up the cake. "How horrible! That awful school closet!"

Tessa jumped up, too, and held onto the plate, refusing to let the luscious vision go.

"No, no!" she screamed. "I want it!"

Laura looked down at the little flushed face below the cake and said gently, reasonably, "But it has ants in it, dear."

The blue eyes opened wide, pleading. The hands hung on tight, "Aunt Laura," she said sweetly, reproving this ignorant adult, "ants have no taste."

The words stopped Laura dead. They cut straight across her patterns of clean living and made her reasoning unreasonable. The two of them still clutched the plate.

"Probably they only got to the edge," Mrs. Williams saved the birthday. "Aggie, take it to the kitchen and wipe them off."

A minute later Tessa sat, thoroughly content, eating a large piece of cake with a spoon, saving a perfect rose to the end. Laura hated herself but she ate the cake cautiously and didn't touch the frosting. Later she explained to her own household, "I'm sure they wriggle, even if they don't taste." Tessa ran the tip of her tongue slowly around her lips, savoring every trace of rose petal. She looked across at Laura's plate with its ring of untouched frosting. In a very gentle conversational voice she remarked, "I could eat some more frosting, I think."

Laura started and looked at her plate, then at the hopeful cherub face. Momentarily she struggled with herself, then with an exaggerated sweep of her hand, she passed her plate to Tessa and was rewarded with a flashing smile of approval. Aunt Laura was nice.

17

Neon Hallowe'en

A cemetery in the moonlight on Hallowe'en is an eerie place, inhabited by ghosts. But a Philippine cemetery on the eve of All Saints Day comes to life with a bustle of preparation and lights to welcome back the spirits of the dead. At least that is what Laura, Isobel, and Dick had been told and had come to see. Rather reluctantly they left the security of the taxi and walked slowly up the dirt road in the direction the driver had pointed. Dick had an arm around each girl.

"Are you sure this is the way?" whispered Laura. "It's awfully dark."

"He said, the man said," Dick spoke out loudly and it boomed back from the tombstones silhouetted against the light of the rising moon. "We asked him for the Filipino cemetery. Maybe he just didn't want to go any farther."

"Well, where are the lights and the people? I mean a cemetery at night—"

"You are the one that suggested coming," Laura reminded Isobel not too kindly.

And so she had. Dick had appeared at the house about 6:00 P.M., conveniently in time to share a dinner of canned Spam, rice, and green beans that Mona had cooked with bits of onion, tomato, and soy sauce. To their questions he gave short answers. He had a room in Cubao, he had traveled by bus a twenty-five-mile radius of Manila showing samples, not selling. No permit yet. Hours of waiting in lines only to find he had the wrong window, the wrong office, or the wrong man. In fact, it was obvious that Dick the unquenchable had been at least partially subdued by the system he could not cut through.

"When you do get into an office, the first thing they say is,

'Please be seated.'" Sympathetic laughter from all of them who had had the same experience. "So, I don't do it. I pace," grimly.

Laura could see him, all six feet two of him with his crown of red hair, long strides back and forth and all the small Filipinos looking up at him, wondering what was the matter with the Americano.

"After a while it makes them nervous."

"What do you gain by it?" from Martha.

"Not much, actually. Somebody comes and asks me questions and sends me to somebody else."

"Have you tried a bribe?" brightly suggested Isobel.

"I have *not*," proudly.

"Well, you'd better. I know that much about the system already."

"That's not *my* system."

"Have you got a friend who's got a friend who —?"

"No."

"Well good-bye, fella, nice seeing you," Isobel waved in mock farewell.

"Oh, I expect it's no worse than at home," defended Laura rather lamely.

"Yes, it is. You can tell that by reading the papers," said Martha. "But Dick's right. If we came to bow to their system we might just as well have stayed home."

"When in Rome —" began Isobel.

"Shut up. I'm tired of hearing that," Martha cut her off with unusual rudeness.

"Well, let's let Mona get at the dishes," Laura said cheerily. "We can-a-a-what can we do?"

"Bridge?" offered Martha.

"Movie, now that we have a man with us?"

"I looked. All the latest and worst American ones," wet-blanketed Dick.

The gloom descended like a heavy fog in which each one thought, "Now if we were in New York, or L. A. or Midland College —"

"It's Hallowe'en. We could put on masks," began Laura facetiously.

"Hallowe'en! I know, let's go to a cemetery!" was Isobel's idea.

"A cemetery! At night? What for?"

"To see the decorations. My kids were talking about it in speech today. They go to the cemetery and scrub graves and hang lights, and some stay there all night and on All Saints Day families gather and have picnics."

"Oh, for heavens sake!" exclaimed Martha, "that's what she meant. I was invited by one of the assistants in education to come to a picnic tomorrow at the cemetery and I thought I hadn't heard right, so I made some excuse."

Dick stood up. "What are we waiting for? All signals on Go for the graveyard."

"Where is it?"

"Well, it's somewhere west of Quiapo, I gathered. And I don't know how you get there."

"Bus, jeep, there's always a way. Let's go, girls."

"Not me," Martha refused. "A cemetery at night is not my idea of entertainment." So they went off without her, and she knew she must comply with her age bracket sometimes.

They took a bus to Quiapo and finally gave up trying to find a jeepney going the right direction. Dick grandly offered to put a taxi on his expense account. But that didn't solve the problem either. The first two they stopped were sure they wanted to go to the American veterans' cemetery, which was closed. They persuaded the next one that they wanted to go to the Filipino one with *lights*. He had stopped, firmly, where there were no lights.

"Maybe we came in the back way," suggested Laura. "There are no gates. Cemeteries always have gates."

"Filipinos put walls and gates on everything," agreed Isobel. They moved along in silence for a few yards.

"Look, lights! Over there."

Around a bend in the road they stopped in surprise. The moonlight was paled by monuments big and small bedecked with colored lights or outlined in neon.

"Looks like Main Street at Christmas, or a carnival," exclaimed Laura, smiling at the sight, and relieved they had not, after all, made fools of themselves.

"Whoever heard of a gay cemetery?" Dick commented.

"Those Filipinos! Aren't they the greatest!" Isobel exulted. "Look at that tall one."

They walked closer to a monument which dominated the whole area. A round Grecian temple with authentic Ionic columns was topped by a crown with a cross on top, all in blue neon lights. A crucifix stood out in front with floodlights focused on it. The base was circled by lower monuments each with its string of lights.

"Jeez, he must have been a VIP," Dick concluded.

"The president himself, or a cousin, anyway, with lots of relatives," Isobel offered.

"I like this one over here better." Laura had turned away from the extravagant display to a ten-foot stone relief of Mary, Joseph, and the child outlined in white lights with another line arching over it.

They walked on slowly, stopping to comment or wonder at each display. Isobel was amused, Laura amazed, and Dick confused, as he often was, between his mother's piety and his father's Jewish heritage.

"Now that's simplicity itself," said Laura, finding a cross outlined in blue and white, stark against the black sky. Only a name in small blue letters at its base.

"Where are the people? I thought there'd be people." It was too quiet to suit Isobel.

"Finished with their work, I guess. Wait, look there where those lights from a car are shining." The car was turned off the road so that the lights shone on a monument. A man in white trousers and t-shirt, barefoot, squatted on the marble slab, washing the face of the inscription.

"They really do it!" Isobel sounded satisfied.

"I think it's nice," said Laura. "I hope somebody cares enough to wash my tombstone."

"I'll scrub yours if you'll scrub mine," Dick quipped. "That's *utang* for you."

Laura gave his arm a slap and pulled him along. She felt they were intruding on a sacred ceremony. But as they passed, they heard his car radio playing, *"I ain't got anything but love, baby."*

Now the grave markers became less pretentious, and there were fewer lights.

"That one beyond the tree looks like the last," Dick said.

"Cute. Looks like a real little house," observed Isobel.

Two men's figures took shape against the moonlight, one bulky, the other slight. They heard voices as they approached. A Filipino voice said, "What did you take that at?"

"A 25th and 4-F, pure guess," replied an obviously American voice. The three joined the two in front of the lighted "house."

"Pictures!" exclaimed Dick. "I never thought of that!" It was enough of an introduction.

The American looked them over. "Peace Corps." It was a statement not a question.

"Yes," said Laura and Isobel together, so Dick would not have to.

"I'm Isobel Swartz and this is Laura Mathews and Dick Blumberg."

"May I present José Lascon? And I am Phil Thomas. Where are you stationed?"

"At U. P., Dick's in Cubao and Laura—"

"I'm at Philippine Normal School." Laura was quite able to talk for herself.

"Yes, I know," the Filipino spoke up.

"You know?" queried Laura. But José was busy putting his camera in its case.

"José's a student at U. P."

"And you?"

"A—I'm at the Embassy." He said it reluctantly as if, don't judge me by that. He knew what Peace Corps thought of the Embassy.

"This seems to be the end of the show," said Dick to divert any questions. "We thought we could get into the Chinese part from here."

"You must see it. It's spectacular. I was there last year."

"Do we have to go back the way we came?" asked Isobel.

"No, ma'am," said José. "It's right over that way," pointing to an area of unlighted graves.

"You can get in the front way, if you go back out and turn to your right. It might be hard to find from here."

"I'll be the one," José offered. "I will accompany you."

"I'll go along, too. Last year I didn't have my camera. It's a bit rough, though."

They set off on the road to the left that soon dwindled to a path and they stretched out single file. The path disappeared and they wound among monuments that cast long gray shadows in the moonlight. Nobody said anything till they came to the top of a rise and below them lay a miniature city ablaze with light.

"Chinese cemetery, ma'am," José announced importantly.

"How beautiful," breathed Laura.

"They really lay it on, don't they?" from Isobel.

"I'm going to try to get that."

Dick watched the Embassy man enviously as he unhooked

his Leica from the neck strap and found a stone with a flat top to set it on. "Will you get anything from here?" he asked.

"I've got high speed Ektachrome in, but you're right, it'll probably come out like the lights of a city from a plane. I'm always trying that."

He sighted carefully and set his exposure by the light of a penlight. "José, could you rest your hand on the stone and hold the camera steady and I'll use a plunger. How long can you hold your breath?"

"Maybe half a minute, sir."

"We'll try it for that." There was silence while they all held their breath until the click.

In a few minutes they were walking in an Oriental Disneyland. The curving street was paved, bordered on either side by a bewildering assortment of tiny houses, pavilions, grottos in concrete, stone, glass and steel fashioned into architectural creations which vied with each other for attention. Besides the floodlights, strung lights, and neon, there were lighted candles. It all provided an endless opportunity for pictures. José soon used up his film but Phil kept snapping.

"What are you going to do with all those?" asked Dick curiously.

"Part of my job in cultural affairs; I'm taking visual notes now."

They stopped before a fence of iron palings. On a ledge behind it a solid row of fat candles burned, their yellow flames bent by the wind were licking their red sides. On the wall opposite hung a portrait of a man guarded by two enormous candles standing on the polished tile floor.

"That must be the —a —occupant," whispered Isobel.

"We'll be going in," said José.

"Going in! What for?"

"To be seeing," explained José easily.

"Oh, I don't think so," Laura demurred, stepping back.

"It's OK, they expect visitors," Phil agreed.

So they entered. From another room a Chinese family appeared, bowed, shook hands. There were introductions all around, talk and laughter.

"In a tomb. I don't get it," Dick said disapprovingly on the way out.

They went into others which were open, always receiving the same welcome, often followed by invitations to return tomorrow for lunch. After a few tombs Dick caught the spirit and began to enjoy himself. The lights began to go off now, some tombs were barred or chained shut, but the largest still loomed just ahead. It was different from the others, with an imposing dignity and restraint. The polished marble floor of the outer court mirrored magnificent Chinese hangings of red silk embroidered in blue, silver, and gold. Tall vases of fresh flowers, and slender candles on a tiered platform rose toward a portrait of a gentleman in white suit.

"He must be the emperor of the cemetery." Isobel's remark annoyed Laura. Must she always be flip?

"The Wongs," Phil said.

"Wong. That's the name of our rattan furniture man."

"There's thousands of Wongs."

"Do you know them?" Dick asked Phil.

"You can't be in the Philippines long without knowing about the Wongs," Phil replied evasively. "They're in rice and sugar, lumber, and gold—and a few other enterprises not so obvious."

"Wongs are being too powerful, too many, too rich," José spoke with bitterness.

"What do they do that's so bad?" asked Laura. Before she got an answer, the people inside saw the strangers looking through the gate, and a servant was sent to open it.

A tall elderly Chinese gentleman strode toward them. "Welcome, welcome," and they went in. "Ah, Mr. Thomas, I believe, from the American Embassy."

"Good evening, Mr. Valera. I'd like you to meet my friends." There was bowing and handshaking all around.

Isobel nudged Laura, "Isn't that our Sam Wong over by that candle?"

"I can't tell till I see his mole and three hairs."

He recognized them first and came to them, "Miss Peace Corps and Miss Peace Corps!" He was not now the obsequious little merchant they knew. Erect and perfectly groomed, he was confident in the presence of an illustrious ancestor. "My great uncle," he waved toward the portrait. The Peace Corps girls were the real center of attention.

Mr. Valera maneuvered Dick away from the group. "You are not Peace Corps," he began casually.

"No, I was in training but didn't make it." His tone said, make something out of it if you want to.

Mr. Valera chose to make regret out of it. He shook his head. "A pity, government agencies make many mistakes."

Long pause. "But you came anyway."

Dick was tired concealing his problems. A sympathetic listener that was neither Peace Corps nor Filipino nor Embassy, who had no claims on him, broke the protective walls he had so carefully maintained since his arrival.

"Yes, I did. I wanted to come and I *did*."

"And the vehicle?" gently probed the manipulator of men and governments.

"I'm employed by Great Drugs, Inc., of New York."

"Ah, yes." He made it sound as if he already knew the whole scheme of introducing competition into the business. His cordiality and apparent understanding were all Dick needed to relieve himself of his recent history. The whole story came pouring out.

Laura glanced their way from time to time and felt relieved for some reason when the conversation ended with a laugh and a handshake.

The main entrance was not far away. It was obvious to the girls that a change had come over Dick. His depression of the early evening had vanished, and he was his usual buoyant self.

Phil noticed the difference, too, and asked, "Did Mr. Valera offer to do you a favor?"

"What makes you think that? He did invite me back for tomorrow's gathering."

"He likes to be helpful to Americans, and he's in a position to do favors. Can I drop you any place? My car's near the other entrance."

"No thanks," Dick refused quickly. "I know where I am now, and I can get a bus. But you girls—?"

"Don't bother about us." Laura's voice was tinged with sarcasm. "We'll make out."

"I should be delighted to drive you to U. P.," Phil offered formally.

"That would be keen," Isobel accepted promptly and Laura didn't object.

"José?"

"Oh, I'm not far, thank you, Mr. Thomas. See you next week." He crossed the street and disappeared.

Dick made his casual adieus and hailed a bus while the others walked on, the girls feeling a little strange with their unknown escort. He stopped beside a discreet black limousine as a uniformed man appeared and jumped to open the door to the back seat. The girls hesitated; an Embassy car with a chauffeur was not what they had pictured.

Phil spoke rather roughly., "I know you are not supposed to associate with the Embassy. Get in. It isn't bugged."

They obeyed and Laura relaxed in the far corner. A ride in a luxurious American car! She had forgotten they could be so big, so soft, so quiet. You could stretch your legs. "I must admit this beats a jeepney," she murmured and leaned her head back. It had been a long walk.

"Gosh, what a fabulous evening. Simply fabulous!"

"I'll agree with your favorite adjective this time, Isobel. I'll even go so far as to say 'out of this world'."

"That's what that is all about," Phil said from the other corner, "people who are out of this world."

"Into another?"

"Who knows?"

In a moment, Laura sat up straight. "I'm so mixed up. And *it's* all so mixed up, the attempt to pretty-up death, the pretense that they'll come back, trying to make a tragedy light and gay."

"Death isn't always tragedy. For most of the people back there I expect it was a good thing."

"Even the rich ones?" asked Isobel.

"Especially the rich ones."

Laura leaned forward to look across at this man who said strange things so matter-of-factly. "But you go to a cemetery to mourn. Why do they go for picnics?"

"Because they are alive, they think they are lucky."

"Mixed up, all mixed up," she insisted. "Moonlight and neons, worship and sacrilege, superstition and technology."

"Longing to see the dead, yet afraid they will," added Phil.

"Marble and dirt."

"Grief and joy."

"That's life," Isobel summarized brilliantly as they turned into the campus.

18

The Squatters

The houses came down. They were not difficult to demolish, just some old scrap boards, pieces of rusty corregated iron, and flattened oil tins slapped together. So they came apart with a whack of a bolo or a kick. Across the street an old woman squatted on the ground beside a pile of rotten boards. It hadn't been much of a house, but it had been home for eight years ever since the family had come from Samar. She had seen so many homes knocked flat by typhoons she should be used to it. But somehow it seemed less cruel to have a storm do it than to have strange men inside the ring of policemen smashing the walls which had sheltered families. She wasn't thinking, just feeling, that any spot where the family has lived and loved and hated, quarreled and labored in birth, failed and hoped is home.

Around her were stacked their household goods: a table with three legs propped up on a bench, a cooking pot holding a pair of wooden sandals, a cracked mirror, some tattered sleeping mats. A small hammock woven of abaca was flung over a box. It had been nice for the baby, hung between the posts out of the way of the rats. They had brought it from the province. In her hand she held a cup with the bright red enamel cracked off. Manuel had brought it to her on Christmas. She hadn't asked where he got it.

A crash jerked her face towards the broken shacks. A man had stepped through the rotten floor and was hanging on by one hand. People watched but did not reach a hand to help. His foot found a step, and he crawled out of the debris. Farther away fire leaped to devour the last of the shacks and the stinking garbage. Rats ran out ahead of the flames, dogs barked, boys laughed. Her man kept going back into the smoking heaps, ducking under the arm of the police to rescue a bit of tin, a piece of a chair, a few nails. Now he came with an iron bedstead on his head. She looked over at the families sitting in the courtyard of the old church to see if anyone would claim it. She noticed the boy with the scarred face watching the closed door of the church. Maybe he thought the padre would come out like he did after mass on Sunday, speak to his people, put his hand on the boy's head, or maybe the sister who ran the nursery would come. But the door stayed shut.

The woman was so numbed by the shattering of her life that it was some time before she was aware of a pair of slim pale legs standing near her. Slowly she raised her tear-dimmed eyes to the hem of a blue skirt and on up to the face of a young girl. American, she recognized without interest. The girl was saying something softly but the woman knew no English.

Laura had been standing there for several minutes feeling utterly helpless as she watched the hovels being leveled. The open field and the courtyard of the church were almost filled now with clumps of household goods like the one she was near. Over near the newer city yellow flames licked the dry tinder. Joyfully they clawed into the waiting fuel and mounted with a truimphant crackle, then a roar as they swept upwards to the stone walls of the old Spanish buildings which had withstood the bombs and fires of war. Now they would go down at last in a rubbish bonfire. The arches of the vacant window looked down with hollow eyes on the advancing flames. The flames did not dare touch the walls of the big cathedral.

Stopping short, the smoke swirled up as high as the dome, then waved a farewell to the stinking hole it had blackened and thinned to air. St. Augustine was untouchable, indestructible. Laura hated its aloofness to the misery sprawling at its feet. She should have remained aloof, too. But when she read in the morning paper that the mayor of Manila was actually carrying out his threat to demolish the squatter area and move 10,000 people out of the city, she felt driven to see this drastic action to clean out this festering sore of a slum. So without telling anyone where she was going she had put on her oldest and least conspicuous dress, removed everything from her small purse except change, and had found her way by bus and jeepney to Intromuros.

Here within what had been the old Spanish city, partly surrounded by remains of earth-covered crumbling walls, she was seeing human misery such as she had never imagined it could be. People actually lived here, "squatting" from dire necessity on land they neither owned nor rented. An assortment of rickety trucks moved along the alley ahead of the flames, stopping to pick up families and their possessions. The paper had said there were not enough trucks, and some families had waited all night. Crowds gathered around each truck, the aggressive ones elbowing out the others, tossing in the remnants of their huts. People clambered over the side to ride on top, while the oldest and the youngest were pushed or dragged up. Children were everywhere, some enjoying the excitement, others weeping. Most of them looked on blankly, immobilized by fear.

Several children gathered around Laura, staring. They had never been this close to an American. She felt a touch on her leg and looked down to see a tiny brown hand gently stroking her skin. An older girl caught up the child, held him on her hip and asked, "Your name, mum?"

"Laura. What's yours?"

Giggles and nudging produced, "Flora, Ding, Erlinda, and that's Luna," pointing to a little one who was rubbing her cheek on Laura's skirt.

"Where do you go to school?" They must go somewhere, knowing English.

"The sisters," they pointed to a low building near the cathedral. So it wasn't quite oblivious to the people crouching in its shadow.

"Where are you going to live?" she asked and then was sorry she had. There was no answer. Laura tried to think of something to say. She yearned, a physical, out-going desire to do something, to say something reassuring. But she had no words, no help to offer. She wanted to gather these children to her, dirt, sores, smell, and all, and weep with them. Instead, she smiled, putting her heart into it. To her surprise they responded with quick, shy and, she thought, grateful smiles. So an intangible smile could bridge the gap from heart to heart when words could not. She tucked this new knowledge away for future thought. She tried it on the old woman. First only a blank stare, but in a moment there was a flicker in the dull eyes. *I got through to her,* Laura told herself. *Just me, a person and her, a person,* she knows I want to help.

The ring of children had now become a crowd pressing close upon her. The crush of warm bodies and curious fingers was a little frightening, and she slowly worked her way to the edge of the group and walked on aimlessly. In the midst of the noise of crashing roofs, crackling flames, shouting, and crying she felt very much alone. She had not expected to be the only outsider to observe this human upheaval.

She was startled when a white car pulled up beside her and a man's voice called to her, "Pardon me, miss." A man in a white suit leaned out of the window of the car. "I am the Chief of Police of Manila and I don't think it's very safe for you to be walking around here."

"Oh, I'm Peace Corps and I just thought . . . " Well, what had she thought?

The Chief of Police smiled benevolently. "I'm sure your intentions are good, but these people are not very happy about being moved out. So with your permission we will escort you out." A uniformed officer opened the door for her and stood waiting.

Laura did not move. To be delivered home in a police car would certainly crack the Peace Corps image, but she couldn't exactly refuse the gently official "invitation." Before she chose what to do she was surprised by another voice from behind her.

"I'll be responsible for getting her home, officer." She turned to see the Embassy man of the cemetery. He showed his credentials to the chief. who looked, smiled, offered him a cigarette, and drove off leaving her facing Phil Thomas.

"Well! *Well!*" was all she could manage, not knowing whether to be angry or grateful. "What are you doing here?"

"What are you doing here?" he countered with a sort of snort.

"Well, I came to —to —"

"You came to see what was happening to human beings," he finished for her, "and so did I." It was a simple statement and she wanted to believe him. Instead she said, "Taking visual notes —for the government?" She looked for his camera.

"Yes, I am," he said defensively. "I want a record of this." He took his hand out of his pocket and opened it to show a Minox.

They had been walking away from the fire toward the cathedral. She was disappointed, hoping she had been wrong about him. She looked up at the cross on top of the dome, not watching her feet. He steered her around a hole and away from a house wall about to fall.

"Contrast? Power and poverty?"

Laura looked at him sharply. If he knew her thoughts before she spoke them there was no use putting up a front of irritation with him. "Can't they stop it? Doesn't anybody care?"

"Yes, some do, but no one has found a solution. These people come to escape rural poverty and they land in urban poverty, which is worse —no money, no jobs, no housing, no land. So they squat. The church paid a lot of them to get off church land but they came right back. I went to one of their interminable meetings last week. There were social workers who want the garbage collected, lawyers who represent the land owners, congressmen who count on squatters' votes, public health people in despair, police who hunt for petty criminals, priests calling it inhuman, even an American Protestant missionary. Nobody knew what to do. It's a seething cauldron of filth and crime, but who is free from taint? Did you see what the Chief of Police offered me?"

"Why, a cigaret, I guess."

"A *blue seal* cigaret."

"What's that?"

"Haven't you been called 'blue seal' yet?" At her denial he shook his head. "You live in kind of a protected area out there. 'Blue seal' is slang for 'American,' because American cigarettes that have a blue seal were smuggled in and escaped the import tax."

"The police, too?"

"Sure. Smuggling is a national sport. They say it reaches all the way up to Malacanang."

"The president's palace? But squatters —what's the connection?"

"Illegal business thrives on desperation."

"But how can the mayor just clean them out?"

"He's had the advice of United Nations experts. He has created a calculated crisis, and he's spreading his city's abscess over some hills thirty miles out. He has thrown them on the national government by moving them to government land, where they have been promised half an acre."

They had passed through an opening in the old fifteen-foot wall and reached the main street. "In Spanish times no Filipino was allowed to live inside the city. The Americans took the wall down or let it crumble. Would you like to see the next act, where these people are going?"

Laura hesitated.

"I don't have the black monster," Phil said rightly interpreting her reluctance. "I managed to get a jeep and that was a lot harder. The road out there is murder. But I had to take a driver."

A Filipino in army fatigues ran up and opened the door of the drab Army jeep with all the ceremony of a limousine chauffeur.

Laura stood still. It wasn't P. C. rules about fraternizing with the Embassy or the military that bothered her. It was because she wanted so much to go and she didn't know why.

"Pepi, this young lady is a Peace Corps volunteer. Shall we take her to Sapang Palay?"

"Piss Corps? Yesser!" Pepi's face broke up into creases of delight.

"Don't you want to see the other end of the journey?"

He had furnished the rationale. Laura climbed into the high back seat. They rattled over the pavement headed northeast out of the city.

When she had time she must figure out how it was that this man whom she had seen only once before seemed to anticipate her thoughts. But right now she had other questions to ask.

"There's a lot of things about the Philippines I don't understand," she began. "I'm still on the outside of this country looking in. I can't get *in*. I don't know why they do what they do and I feel alien." She sighed and hoped he wouldn't laugh.

He didn't. "You are alien and always will be. You've been here only three months. The longer you stay the more you'll know you don't know."

"That's discouraging! I thought —I think we all thought —it would be easy, if we tried. If we were really friendly. We think nobody else ever has been —but I know that isn't so."

"You have been thousands of years and miles apart, and now a few months together. And you think you can know people in that time?"

"All right, so I'm impatient. So let's get started. How did that Chinese man of the Wong family tomb get the name Valera?"

"Because somewhere along the line a Wong daughter married a Filipino. This is very advantageous because the offspring of such a marriage can become a Filipino citizen and own property, and escape the restrictions on Chinese."

"You mean they can't become citizens otherwise?"

"Nope. Chinese can't automatically become citizens of the Philippines, not even if you are born here, not even if your mother was a Filipina. It must be your father."

"Why, that's crazy! That's worse than U.S. restrictions on immigration."

"Sure."

"Well!" She didn't want to follow up that discovery now. "Why did you ask if he had offered to do a favor for Dick? I mean, why would he? I mean, why would Dick need one?" She got in deeper with every word.

"I wouldn't know. Does he?" Phil asked casually.

Laura had no talent for finesse, and she wasn't going to be maneuvered into double talk. "Yes, he does." She was sure he knew it anyway.

The jeep swerved around a truck packed with squatters' families, all standing.

"So many people do need a favor," said Phil watching them from the window. "It's a good thing, I guess, that there are people who have the power and the money to cut the tangle of red, pink, and blue tape we are all enmeshed in—however they do it. He'll never know how it was done; he'll never get a bill . . ."

"One mystery is cleared up, anyway. I found out how José knew me. He's the boy friend of my co-teacher and she told him my name."

"That figures."

"How come you know so much about this country?" she challenged. "You don't look as if you had been here a thousand years." She twisted around and looked him over carefully. She hadn't paid much attention to him in the cemetery and had been embarrassed by his taking charge of her among the squatters. But now she revised her general impression. He was as solid and squarish as he had looked in the moonlight, but not as stolid as she had thought. His crewcut hair was almost as dark as a Filipino's and crossed his broad brow in a straight line, angling sharply to his large ears. A craggy face, she decided. Shoulders square, too. His square hands she had noticed before.

Phil quietly let her stare. He himself had learned to appraise people quickly and to catalogue faces in his memory file. She had a nice face, unusually high arched brows over eyes he usually filed under "flecked." But they were deep and luminous and escaped easy categorizing. He remembered how they had shone in the candlelight.

Now he looked at her directly and smiled. "Sorry to disappoint you. What good is a diplomat without a streak of white in his hair—and eyeglasses, though Americans gave up monocles with George III. No striped trousers, no cuff links, no . . ."

"Oh, stop it. I'm not as naive as you make out, only . . ."

"OK. My life history in three sentences: My father was in Foreign Service. We moved about between India, Indonesia, Chile, and Washington. We were in the Philippines three times. Now I am starting at the lowest rung of the ladder as Assistant Deputy in Cultural Affairs, but I'm not going to stay there!"

"That was four sentences but thank you. I was beginning to think the State Department indoctrination was better than Peace Corps, but I see experience does it. Now we've finished with the Chinese and you," she teased.

"Oh, no you haven't," he said it a bit grimly. The jeep lurched over broken pavement, potholes, stones, and ruts as they drove into the rolling countryside.

"This area of Sapang Palay we are going to was designated for the resettlement of squatters, several years ago," Phil explained, "but they can't get the people to resettle voluntarily, since there's nothing here for them to do. So now they are just being dumped." They came upon signs of "dumping" as they turned off the road onto a dirt track. A line of trucks ahead of them had stopped. People had clambered out and were standing by the road until they were herded toward a small building.

"Each family will be assigned half an acre somewhere on these hills. Let's walk." They left the jeep and walked past the trucks. At intervals beside the road were piles of junk, pieces of houses, household possessions. Beside each a man or a woman stood guard. One family huddled under a piece of tin propped up by two bamboo sticks. The mother held a baby tight to her breast hanging out of her blouse, but the baby only cried. A woman ran up to them and said softly, politely, "We have no breakfast today. Please tell your government to help us."

"You complain to your own government," said Phil rather sharply. "Our government didn't do this."

"Somebody's got to do something!" Laura began to feel frantic.

"Not the U. S. Everything gets blamed on us."

"So it's *not* our fault. People are hungry so somebody's got to help!" Her face colored with emotion, angry—as she always was —in the presence of real misery.

"Who?"

"I don't know. Churches, agencies, community chest —don't they have some resources?"

"Their government—and it's broke. But it's made some promises and I've heard the Catholic church will build a school. Protestants are sending food. Over on that hill are some houses for people whom they moved out before. A lot of them seeped back into Manila but some have stuck it out. Eventually this will be a community, I guess. What's the crowd?"

Coming toward them in the midst of a cloud of dust, with a group of children following, was a tall figure, his red hair blazing above the dust.

"It's Dick!" exclaimed Laura, her voice reflecting the lift of her heart. "What in the world . . . ?"

"Laura, what the hell are you doing here?" Dick called before he reached them.

"Looking."

"How did you get here?"

"With Phil." His first name came naturally.

"What are *you* doing?" Dick's tone was suspicious.

"Working," replied Phil calmly.

"I'll bet!"

"Dick, don't be mad."

"Mad? Of course, I'm mad. My God, these people have no houses, no food, no stores. One well for forty families. No jobs, no transportation, no nothing. Somebody *better* be mad. You don't see any Filipinos around here doing anything. I came out with a Swede from UNICEF, and I saw your missionary fellow awhile ago. But what can *we* do?"

Laura was looking at the children surrounding Dick. Several had familiar objects clutched in grimy hands.

"Well, I see you've been selling drugs."

"Selling! What do you take me for? But they can't eat toothpaste. It's just all I had with me."

"They don't know they can't eat it." Laura pointed to two little boys with foam on their mouths. There was a wail and the group stepped back from a girl vomiting in the ditch. An older child pounded her on the back. "Soap, mum," she explained to Laura. "Hi et Americano." She pointed at Dick accusingly.

"Jeez! I had to give them something," he said pleadingly.

Laura laughed a tremulous laugh which caught in her throat. *He would; that's just what he would do.* She linked her arm in his and pulled him away from the children.

Phil said, "I don't think we can do any good here. We've seen, now we know. Help, if there is any, is back in Manila where the wheels of government grind slow. Have you a ride?" to Dick.

"UNICEF had to go back but I'll find my way."

"Glad to give you a lift. It may be hours before a bus comes along."

"No, thanks."

"Oh, Dick, don't be so stubborn and rude. Come along," Laura coaxed.

Reluctantly Dick followed them back to the jeep, making sure they saw he was unenthusiastic. When Phil went to find the driver he had a swift change of mood. Drawing Laura close he whispered. "I've got it —visa, permit, everything!"

"Mr. Valera?"

He pushed her away to look at her. "How did you know?"

"Just guessed."

"Well, he's a find. He knows people. Suggested I start in the gold mines. Lots of workers with good pay."

"Start with an empty sample case?" It was unkind of her.

"Oh, well, they'll airmail me some more."

Phil returned with the driver and they piled in. "I'll drop you two where Quezon Boulevard crosses Highway 54 and you can arrive home uncontaminated by the Embassy." Was there irony or amusement in his voice? He was riding with the driver so Laura couldn't see his face.

The road back was just as rough as coming out but it seemed shorter. Conversation soon dwindled and stopped altogether. Laura spoke just once after they reached the city streets. "I wonder what happened to all the people living in downtown Chicago when they moved them out and put the university there?"

No one answered.

19

Maligayang Pasko
at Masaganang Bagong Taon

The day after Christmas was letter-writing day at the PCV house. The volunteers felt an abrupt let-down from what Martha called a "frenzied season in which Catholicism surfaces and spreads over everything." She continued in a letter to Alice, a fellow teacher in Mt. Vernon.

Catholic symbols, ceremonies, saints and celebrations brought by the Spaniards fitted well with Filipino love of fiestas and some pagan folkways.

To these were added the firecrackers and paper fantasies of the Chinese and with the coming of the Americans Christmas customs from the cold climates.

On the nine days before Christmas the churches have mass at 4:00 A.M. In the old days (not so old either) the worshippers carried candles as they came along the dark streets and gathered at the church. Now there are street lights and flashlights of course.

I managed to route myself out and go a few times to the chapel here on the campus. After mass some home in the neighborhood is open for breakfast. There were about fifteen people at the one I went to. And such a lavish spread of food! I think it is a great custom, especially for visitors.

Speaking of food, I tried to make some of my usual Christmas candy.

Martha described the troubles she had with unfamiliar ingredients and damp weather, which affected the consistency. But she learned to adapt:

I cook to a hard ball, not a soft, compensate for coarse sugar that
seems to be less sweet than ours, for chocolate that does not melt,
baking powder that loses its strength, flour with bugs, shortening that
turns hard if it gets as cool as seventy degrees. I can dry my own
coconut, roast my own peanuts and all in all come up with some quite
presentable sweets.

Her letter ended with an attempt to explain Filipino attitude
toward holidays.

Holidays have a way of stretching and multiplying in the Philippines.
Four and five day weekends are frequent. Since this is a new country
they have not yet settled on important events to commemorate so they
just do them all. The birthdays and death days of national leaders pop
up unexpectedly and then there is a Hero's day for any they have
omitted. Not only are we foreigners surprised by holidays but so are
Filipinos. But they don't mind, a holiday is always welcome any time
for any reason.

Christmas, of course, is no surprise and there are dates for beginning and ending the vacation. But these get very blurred. The professors try to keep the students here by giving exams just before vacation and at U.P. there was a tremendous parade the last evening with
floats, bands, torches, and queens. They are so careless with fire, I
thought the whole thing would go up in flames, but it didn't. The
students' ranks had already thinned and they say half of them will not
be back when the university opens after New Year's. It is part of the
disorderliness and casualness that I find very hard to live with. I keep
telling myself that I can't change them in the time I am here so why
fight it.

We have had a stream of volunteers dropping in here which has
wrecked our food budget, I must say. But they are all welcome. This
is more like home than the way they live in the barrios or in dor-
mitories and they seem to like the presence of some of us oldsters—at
least at this season. We are going to have a bunch here tomorrow for
supper. Mona, our helper, has gone to the province so we will cook
up something easy and American, like Italian spaghetti with ground
meat from Australia and Del Monte tomato sauce canned in the
Philippines, served on plates from Japan.

With which international note I shall close, wishing you a traditional Happy New Year.

Martha

Dec. 26

Dear Family:

If you are in a green country dreaming of a white Christmas, the best thing to do is to forget it. Only I'm not dreaming of a white Christmas, I felt very much at home at the Williamses who invited me to spend the day with them.

This is really a gala season in this country. Everybody celebrates. If you have the misfortune to be Jewish or pagan, just shut up and close your eyes and ears till it's over. Customs of the Americans predominate and that calls for Christmas trees. There are many versions: bare sticks of bushes painted white or green; the ubiquitous coconut dried, pressed, shredded, dyed, wound, fluffed, and fashioned into a white pine—more lacy and feathery than the genuine article; frames of wire or wood covered, stuffed, glazed, embroidered to taste in traditional red, green, blue, silver, and gold. For trees there must be lights and Germany and Japan have brought strings of electric bulbs within reach of the purses of the middle class.

We have had Christmas music for weeks, all very western. The Protestant missionaries brought carols and "Jingle Bells." Radio and records have added "Rudolph the Red-Nosed Reindeer," "Santa Claus Is Coming to Town" and "White Christmas." Groups of boys make a seasonal occupation of touring the neighborhood for weeks in advance serenading—for a price. They are so cute we began by giving them too many pesos. Then when they multiplied we got Mona to handle them. I can't get over the incongruity of charming brown kids at our door singing off key to an out-of-tune guitar, "Wee-eespareen hopp owow wahlcam dai voisees." I just barely recognize "Whispering Hope" being sung by Aunt Gertrude when we used to visit grandmother. These kids really murder it.

We haven't known what to do about presents for Filipinos. At one faculty party we didn't take anything because nobody told us to. Then I made a mistake with Luz, my co-teacher. Just naturally I wanted to give her something. So after much thought I decided on a book from our Peace Corps library (we can use these as we see fit). Robert Frost seemed harmless enough. I wrapped it and took it to school on the last day. As soon as I handed it to her, I knew it was wrong, she was so embarrassed. At noon she disappeared and just before we left the room in the afternoon she slipped me a package. Then I was embarrassed. Well, live and learn, I tell myself. It is a lovely scarf of *jusi*, that filmy, silky stuff, in pastels. She has gone to the province (as everyone says) for Christmas. I hoped maybe she would ask me to

128

come with her, some of the other Filipino teachers did. But no, so I will have to wait longer for that.

Tessa was so excited over things yesterday it made it fun. We had fruitcake and kalamanci juice at the end—no ants in the cake this time. Now it is the day after and there is nothing left to do. The carols have been sung hoarse, there's no taste left for parties, the tree is dusty. The noise, the fanfare and the trappings are over and families are alone. Of course for a Filipino family this may mean 30 or 100 people but for us foreigners it is kind of a relief to be just ourselves. We might have time to think about a real star—not a paper one, and a real baby—not a borrowed doll and real people, not wooden figures.

But that time will be short. Peace Corps is in town with a vengeance. A bunch will be out at our house tomorrow night.

Love to all,
Laura

FROM ISOBEL

Dec. 26

Maligayang Pasko at Masaganang Bagong Taon, or just plain Merry Christmas and Happy New Year.

We say it both ways in the Philippines and we say it often and to everyone! I never went much for mangers, carols, and angels but you sure can't avoid them here. And paper, my gosh! You can't get a piece of paper for mimeographing but come Christmas the whole country foams with it. Every door, wall, and ceiling is hung, draped and pasted with tissue, crepe, cutouts, and tassels like crazy.

And parties!! Marymotherofgod (as they rattle it off here) I'm commonly known as a party gal, as you well know. Well, I had my fill, at least of the Filipino brand. At first I thought they were cute but I soon got over that. Parties begin about 5:30, so forget your American six o'clock dinner. Straight chairs are set in rows around the wall. People come and sit down and never move unless on the program or playing a game. Important people sometimes "put in an appearance." There is always a program, folk dances, songs, guitars. After this, group games, musical chairs, spin the bottle kind of thing. There is usually dancing—the most "in" modern ones. But somewhere in the evening comes the climax—impromptu entertainment. Fat old ladies get up and dance, people sing who can't and nobody cares. The catch is they expect us to do something too. And Americans hate to make fools of themselves. Now I don't sing or play the guitar or recite silly

129

poems by myself. So what do I do? I say no, I can't. Then they are sure I want to be coaxed. Well, it's pretty ghastly, I can tell you.

I must tell you about our fabulous Christmas parade. We got the word that there was to be a torchlight parade the last day of classes before the holidays, but we couldn't get any solid information about it, where it would start and when, just that it would go around the quad which is about half a mile long. About dark we hoofed it over to the quad, and squatted on the steps of the Engineering Building. We waited a good hour and then saw some lights moving along the far side and they finally came our way. Floats, my gosh, like houses and boats, out of nothing. Every school, department and campus organization had a queen, but don't say queen—say "muse." Every couple of feet there'd be a band playing like crazy trying to drown out the one on the platform and the loudspeaker, which kept blaring all the time. But those muses! Precious little Filipinas dressed in gorgeous formal gowns, Spanish style, *ternos* (with the butterfly sleeves), Maria Christina (drop shoulders, full skirt), or *patajong* (wraparound skirt), and short kimono. I don't know who paid for them but they were fabulous; silk, satin, *jusi*, beaded, laced. (I'm going to be one next year if it kills me.) The muses were mostly up high on a structure built over a car. They stopped by our steps (we let the judges sit there, too!) and were helped down a ladder so rickety I thought every one of 'em would fall off. Mart was having a fit because of the fire hazards of torches and crepe, sparklers attached to paper-covered wheels and nobody paying any attention. There was one crisis. The Department of Agriculture had a wooden cart piled with straw and pulled by carabao. One of them started to run and the guys tried to pull the muse off. In the excitement someone threw a torch down onto the straw, the skirt of the muse caught fire and everyone screamed and *laughed*. One guy had sense enough to stamp out the flames. That "hero" was a fellow from the Music Department I've been "dating." I put "dating" in quotes because you'd never recognize what passes for that here. He came into the Speech Lab one day with a friend. After several weeks he and a bunch serenaded us one night. We've had these before but these guys really could play and sing so we invited them in and made coffee and ate cookies Mart had made. It was a fun time. But Mona, our helper, told us very plainly afterward that by inviting them in we showed we would accept serious courting and they had stayed too long, 10:30, I think it was!

Anyway, this guy, Ramon Valdez, has come often since, usually at the most inconvenient times, which is when we are about to eat dinner. If we ask him to eat, he says no, but doesn't leave. The others usually go ahead, leaving me to sit with him. How's that for an exciting date? Weird, but better than nothing, I sez. Going *out* in couples at night just isn't done by *nice* people—like *me*. But when the PC fellows come in from the provinces it's different. We spend a week's food money for a steak dinner at Max's or an evening drinking at Korner Klub or even go to a movie in Manila. The PC "leaders" have the use of a jeep and no one pays too much attention to how they use it. Except one story that's going around. The PC director told some of them, "I don't care who you shack down with but for God's sake don't leave a government vehicle parked out in front of the whore house." The director wants to make us all happy so he has frequent parties with plenty of cold San Miguel beer and he doesn't care how many sleep on his living room floor. They say—but don't quote me on this—that he told the PC guys in Davao that they should keep the girls from getting lonely and not to worry, if they got pregnant he would send them to Hong Kong for an abortion. I guess he's having trouble with the PC doctor whose family were missionaries in China and he doesn't go for handing out the *pill.*

We're having a gang here tomorrow night—and no row of chairs around the wall I can promise you.

Say, could you send me some of those nice thin-skinned Band Aids? I've got blisters on my heels that won't heal and the things I can get here look terrible.

Yours, as ever,
Iz

20

Christmas in the Barrio

The bus station in Manila should have been a mad house three days before Christmas, but it wasn't. It was packed with people, of course, standing or squatting among a staggering assortment of bags made of string, paper, or cloth, baskets stuffed to the handles and battered cardboard suitcases. Children. The place was crawling with children. There was a rumble of voices, shouts, and laughter. People pushed their way onto buses, red, yellow, green or blue. Never room for everyone but nobody got angry at being shoved. A few men hung onto the outside as each bus chugged and rattled out of the parking area to the road, rocking slightly with its overload. Those who could not squeeze on, regrouped by another bus going their way. It would leave in an hour—two hours more likely—three—what did it matter? They were going home. Home to the province, to the barrios where they belonged, where there would be a warm welcome. They would reenter the large family circle with its comfort and security.

Luz had not yet become a part of the patient, relaxed crowd. Her mother, father, the boys, and the baby were all there, going to the barrio for the first time since they left, five years before. Her mother was already a different person. She was again head of the house, confident of her ability to cope with a life she knew. She didn't scold the boys when one of them upset the basket stuffed with city delicacies, candy bars, gum, plastic wash basin, fly swatter. She smiled at papa when he bought a plastic toy for the baby that broke in five minutes. They had missed the express bus and now waited for the local. The boys were ready to jump on as soon as it was ready and save space for the family.

But Luz was an observer. She was still a schoolteacher, used to bells for classes to begin and end, accustomed to the deference due her position and order to life which had been difficult to accept when she first came out of the barrio, but which now was difficult to throw off. Besides, she was seeing all this through the eyes of Laura. Laura had wanted to come. She even made hints. Volunteers were coming to Manila for Christmas, but Manila volunteers were going to the provinces to see what Filipino life was really like. Manila was much too Westernized. Luz understood the hint perfectly but ignored it so completely that Laura gave up.

She couldn't bring her, that was all there was to it. Not that she wouldn't be welcome. The relatives would have been honored and would have done everything possible to make her comfortable. That was just it. Luz didn't want them fussing over Laura, making an important person out of her just because she was an American. Luz herself had been fighting this impulse and was just beginning to feel able to be herself, feel on an equal footing and call her "Laura." The relatives would think her naturalness, rudeness to a guest.

That was part of it. Another reason was Laura's reaction to insects and dirt. She was really foolish about it. After the fleas in the chairs there were ants, tiny black ones that didn't do any harm at all. They only swarmed along a crack in the wall from floor to ceiling. Laura kept looking at the crack during class. It seemed to be getting wider. Then one of the students noticed it and raised his hand.

"Ma'am, they is ants, again," he said, pointing. "Should I be wiping them?"

"No, I'll be the one," several students offered. This happened every once in a while in that crack and the students loved to take a cloth and in a long swipe scoop up the thousands of wriggling bodies and shake them out the window. Somebody always wanted to take a handful to biology class. But Laura didn't enjoy this and deliberately turned her back till the last ant had been disposed of. Luz had had to ask the janitor to set a trap for the friendly rat with the notched ear that scavenged in their waste basket every night. It hadn't done a bit of good, just opened the way for several smaller ones and more traps. Evidently grandpa had staked out his own domain and kept off lesser poachers. But Laura saw nothing funny in this. Well, in the barrio there were lots worse things than fleas, ants, rats, spiders, and lizards. Luz didn't know what Laura would do if she met up with a snake. And whatever would she be doing now? Squatting patiently? Her skirts were too tight and too short, and there was no place to sit. She wouldn't complain, but just by standing she would make others uncomfortable.

Then Luz had more intimate problems or problem, singular, José. She felt him moving in on her. Nothing overt, but her instincts told her —which were all she had to guide her since she had neither personal nor cultural experience to draw on —that he would one day make it necessary for her to make a decision regarding him. No traditional Filipina ever had to do this, others did it for her and it was a terrible thing to face, deciding your own life all by yourself. He had shocked her once as they were strolling along Dewey Boulevard near the shore. She was embarrassed because they passed foreigners swimming, girls as well as men in skimpy bathing suits. She kept her eyes on the steamers out at sea. There was no one near them, and José had slipped his arm around her and raised her hand to his lips. The warm soft pressure sent a tingle running up her arm. She had never had such a sensation before, and she was sure it was wicked. She flushed now just remembering it. Not knowing what to do in the unexpected circumstances, she did nothing. He kept her hand against his cheek a moment and then released her. Nothing was said and she did not admit, even to herself, that she hoped he would do it again.

But that moment had become near tragedy. A group of boys ran by them and one snatched her purse. José shouted angrily and then chased them, caught the last one, who dropped the purse and whipped out a knife. Luz saw it flash and screamed. The boy dashed off and José wiped blood off a scratch on his arm.

"You shouldn't do that," Luz had scolded him, angry out of her fright for him. "You know you should never chase or resist a robber, especially a gang. And don't report it, either."

"I see you have been brought up the good old Filipino way," he said unpleasantly. "How do you think we will ever get law in this country if we let them scare us?"

"I don't care, look what they did to you!"

"Not much."

They never mentioned it again, and it almost obliterated the sweet moment before but now as Luz thought about it there was a fluttery feeling inside her, and down under her upper thought she recalled that delightful sensation.

So she welcomed this trip back to the home of her childhood. She would know when she got there whether the city, education, and new experiences had changed her, or whether she could fit back into life in the province. They needed teachers there of course but—well, anyway that was another reason she couldn't bring Laura here. Her presence would have confused Luz's reaction. Also she might have to deal with Rual if he was still hanging around.

A murmur and a lunge in the crowd made her look toward a red and yellow bus. The driver had taken his seat and people were climbing the high step that ran the length of the bus. No standing in line or waiting for turns. So Luz pushed ahead like the rest. The bus was all open, no doors, or windows. Wooden benches ran crossways with no aisle. A board for a seat, two boards for a back. Each bench was supposed to hold seven people; children, packages, chickens didn't count. Five of the family got into one seat but Luz wasn't quick enough, and she was shoved out by an old man and a woman who filled the row. Luz had to push in two rows back where there were already six adults, one child, and two guitars. Between the heads she could see that the choice seat beside the driver had been given to a young American. Of course, she thought resentfully and then chided herself. How could he fit his long legs into the rows of seats? All Americans had long legs. Anyway he must be Peace Corps, only Peace Corps would ride a local bus; in fact, only Peace Corps would ride any bus at all. If she had brought Laura she could have ridden up there.

With a cough and a jerk the bus began to move. Luz dropped her worries and let herself enjoy the fun of a journey, any journey to anywhere! The road south to Cavite was paved and fairly smooth. When they were free of the city, Luz tied a scarf on her head, settled the base of her spine tight against the back board and let the upper part of her body sway with the bus and bounce with the bumps and the holes. This way one could ride for hours. And it was hours to Laguna.

Not far out of Cavite the rice paddies bordered the road. It was planting time for soft rice. Rows of workers, men and women, stood in black mud to their knees. Holding a bunch of bright green rice shoots in one hand, they bent to poke the shoots into the water.

The foreman walking along the strip dividing the paddies, clapped and chanted while the people worked to the rhythm. The row of workers moved back as they planted. Luz didn't know what he was singing so she hummed to herself the tune of a dance her girls had done for the Christmas party. The melody was haunting and the rhythm catching, the words had been translated into English,

Laura should see this. This *was* the Philippines. But if she were here Luz would point out the power lines strung between steel towers that straddled the rice paddies. She must not think rural Philippines was all rice.

The bus turned east, away from the coast and the countryside changed. Passing through coconut groves, they caught glimpses of boys shinnying up the tall slender trunks to get the fruit. The mango groves were even more beautiful. Luz had never noticed before their full cone-shape or how shiny the dark green leaves were. Soon the green mangos would be ready for eating. Her mouth watered at the thought. Vendors did sell green mangos on the streets in Manila, peeling the skin down with a knife, sprinkling on some coarse grayish salt. But it didn't taste like a fresh one just off the tree, so sour it made your eyes water, sweetened with the salt.

They stopped in every little town to let off the city passengers and take on the farmers who had been squatting by the road, waiting. Pigs encased in wicker baskets were hoisted to the top of the bus, sacks of rice were stored under the feet. A woman with a pair of roosters, feet tied together, sat on Luz's bench. They flapped and squawked and Luz wondered how Laura would have enjoyed that.

Now they entered a larger town, Santa Cruz. The bus careened around the corner, scattering naked children and chickens, and jerked to a stop in the main square. The usual statue of Rizal was in the center. Vendors surrounded the bus pressing on the passengers bags of boiled peanuts, shelled *pili* nuts, small seedy oranges, wedges of pale *piña* dripping with juice arranged artistically on a piece of banana leaf. Another vendor was determined they should buy his squares of pressed rice. "*Pinipig, pinipig,*" he insisted, pushing his product under their noses.

But before anyone was allowed off the bus they must be given a cursory inspection for smuggled cigarets. None were found —or admitted. Luz tucked her feet under her as her seatmates crawled over her to get out for a stretch. Her mother held the baby out over the side to make a puddle in the dust. No one noticed and Luz didn't even care, she was fast losing her acquired city sensitivities as she slipped comfortably back into the land and customs of her ancestors. As they waited she looked down the street for the shop of the carver of light wood. On the way back she must get some of the figures for Laura. These she would like as she liked all the things she called "native crafts" or "folk art." Laura was as delighted as a child with the strings of thin-sliced capiz shells in the Manila shops. There were plenty of those shells here. The windows of the houses were made out of them. They filtered the blazing sunlight to a soft gray and closed tight against the dark at night. Why did we ever go to glass, wondered Luz.

The road from there on was gravel and dust. Women held handkerchiefs to their noses, Luz pulled her scarf tighter. The man beside her slept, his head against her shoulder. Somewhere in the back a guitar was strumming softly. She liked this part of the trip best, for miles in the shade of the lansones trees clusters of small green fruit hanging from the branches. Too bad they were not ripe. She would like to take back some of this for Laura, too. She got so excited over the fruits and vegetables that were new to her.

It was after four when they approached Pagsagan. The town looked smaller than she remembered it. The steeple of the church was not as tall and the shrine of the Blessed Virgin had been washed by rain and winds of its gilt and blue. There was something new and bright just before they reached the center of town, an imposing structure of pink stucco like a frosted cake. Must be an *Iglesia ni Kristo* church as in Manila. That would mean real competition for the parish priest. A cart pulled by carabao was ahead of them and would not make way so she had plenty of time to see the next new thing, a school. This lifted her spirits, a high school, maybe? Someone must have got to the congressman before he gave away all his slush fund. This was progress indeed. Luz's family all piled off at the next stop. They sorted out their bags and boxes. The adults and bigger boys loaded up and they began the walk to the barrio. A mile, two miles? Who knew, who cared? No one had ever measured it or timed it. It was just the distance from here to there. Only an American would ask how long, how far.

It was a pleasant walk, the air seemed cool after the muggy

(Laura's word) heat of Manila. The familiar feeling of home enveloped them. The younger boys who didn't remember it were full of questions but nobody answered them. They just walked.

Uncle Manuel's house came first. A paper star hung from the thatch roof above the open ladder steps. A child saw them from the window and with a shout the welcome began. The news of their arrival sped ahead of them, and by the time they reached Lola's house the clan had gathered. Aunts, uncles, cousins to the fourth place, and neighbors. The head of the clan sat stiffly in a bamboo chair. Deep wrinkles crisscrossed her face but her black eyes were sharp beneath crepe lids. She smiled through cracked lips unsupported by teeth. Her black hair had only a streaking of gray. Each one greeted her first by touching her hand to his forehead.

When Luz's turn came the thin hand twisted and gripped hers, pulling her down to a close look.

"City girl," she snorted and dropped her hand like a hot stone.

During the next few days Luz was not at all sure she was a city girl. Christmas eve midnight mass in the shabby chapel was so simple and warm. Father Guevarra called each member of the family by name. He was a father to them, not at all like the priest in Manila in his fancy robes and lace surplice. Luz slept at Aunt Maria's house on a mat in the *sala* beside the boys. The nights were thick dark without a street light to pierce the blackness or the flash of a passing car. And quiet. No late jeepney, no fire alarms, no raucous merrymakers coming by, not even the vendor of warm embryo duck eggs calling, *"Balut, balut."* The barrio closed down at nine o'clock. It began to wake up slowly as the first rooster crowed and the first pale light made gray slits between the shutters. The bread vendor called from the street, and the pump at the corner creaked, down-up, down-up. The splashing indicated an early bather.

Christmas day was a melee of relatives, talk, and food hour after hour. Crops, babies, death, illness, comings and goings were told and retold and chewed to shreds till the next relative came. The biggest news was that the water from the falls was to be piped down to a power plant. It was no dream. Contracts had been let, fat ones. (Too fat, some complained darkly.) What would it do to their barrio? Electricity in the houses, city people taking over? There was even wild talk —by the congressman —of a swimming pool. Luz took it all in and tucked it away to ask José about. She knew, better than these barrio folk, that life here would never be the same again.

Rual came once to call, a proper call to mama's satisfaction. Aunt Maria and mama, Luz and Rual sat in the *sala* in four straight chairs, one hastily borrowed from a neighbor. Rual looked so uncomfortable Luz laughed inside, unkindly. He did not know what to do with his legs since they were not being used to support him, walking or squatting. He did not know what to do with his hands since they were idle. Luz was no help at all, she said nothing. He said nothing. Mama and Aunt Maria carried on the conversation.

Suddenly, Luz began to chatter about Manila, school, buses, shops, Peace Corps, everything —except José. Rual crossed his feet, recrossed them, put one ankle over the other knee, took it down. Hung his hands between his knees, then at the side, clasped them over his stomach. In final desperation he clasped them behind his head, pushed his chair back on two legs. The chair legs couldn't take it, gave out a warning crack, and Rual and chair crashed to the floor. He scrambled up and fled.

Bubbling with unsuppressed laughter, Luz ran to the kitchen. Mama and Aunt Maria sat still in their chairs, too ashamed to speak. Rual did not appear again.

The trip home was longer and more tiring than the trip down. School would not begin for another week but papa must get back to keep his job. Mama wept quietly all the way, the boys quarreled. And Luz tried in vain to sort out her feelings. She wished she were two people instead of one torn between the old life and the new. José went with the new, no question about that. But the dam was new too and would surely transform the old secure, but restrictive ways of the barrio and that new high school —lights and books were all it took to open doors to change.

Maybe she would bring Laura down when progress began to show. Luz twisted on the hard seat to give her hips a rest. Yes, and what about José? Would he be kissing her again? Manila became more attractive as they drew near.

21

The Culture Clash
and Non-Values

The Peace Corps Volunteer gang had arrived at the house on the UP campus as expected. Actually they weren't a "gang" or even a "group" since they had scattered to different parts of the islands. The only bond that held them together was that they were strangers in a strange land and had shared experiences briefly in the U.S. As they chattered they looked each other over critically. Kathy and George sat on the settee, George with his legs stuck out, his hands behind his head. The girls observed that Kathy had "let herself go." The sun had been cruel to her blonde hair, it was dull and streaked and she had cut it short for comfort. Now she fitted herself close to George's side and purred.

"What a meal you kids put on, I can't get over it. Spaghetti out of a store instead of rice and canned tomatoes with real hamburger. My gosh, how civilized can you be?"

"Oh, we don't have it so bad in Laoag, hon," defended George.

"Well, you ate like it was going out of style. We don't starve, actually, with a hot plate that doesn't heat and an ice chest that leaks."

"But we got a landlady."

"We sure have. She lives upstairs and lets us make cakes in her oven and brings us down things, like *pancit*."

"How come you kids got way up there?" asked Gloria who lived with Mary Jo in Mindanao, the southernmost island.

George slapped Kathy's knee, making it jump. "Because my little woman asked to go north."

"Well, George, north does sound cooler. How was I to know it was so dry and dusty. Anyway it's not as hot as here," she picked at the front of her yellow shift where it stuck to her skin and blew down, fanning it in and out.

Mary Jo called from the kitchen where she and Martha were stacking dishes, "Hey, you lazy bums come out and do your bit for your country."

"Is the water boiled?" asked Kathy.

"Mart says they don't need to, they use it right out of the spout."

"This I gotta see." Kathy stood up and dragged George with her. Gloria joined them.

Martha was putting Tide in the dishpan.

"You mean you wash dishes in water right out of the pipe?"

"Sure, well, we heat it," said Martha feeling both proud and guilty. "Drink it, too."

"Drink it," the others chorused. "That's too much . . . the wonders of technocracy . . . what will that do to the Peace Corps image? , , , and a refrigerator and a stove that gets hot."

"Oh, stop it," commanded Martha. "We already argued all that out with Jacobs. We are supposed to live like our counterparts, we quoted to him out of the PC Manual and all of UP profs have refrigerators and stoves. And can we help it that Americans brought pure water to Manila fifty years ago?" Martha was glad they had sent Mona home for Christmas. It was a relief to say anything without thinking how it would sound to her.

While the dishes were being washed and dried they argued as to which was more important to a good life, pure water or refrigeration.

Mary Jo settled it, "You can't make ice but you can boil water."

"Wasn't that Jello a treat!" remembered Kathy.

"I could do without Jello, or milk, or anything, if I could just have a cold beer now and then," confessed George plaintively.

Isobel and Jimmy had remained on the floor in the *sala*. Jimmy traced out on the mat the layout of Mindanao Institute of Technology where he taught math.

"It's a big campus, see —room to grow. The government is trying to attract settlers from other parts of the country. It's hard to get teachers down there, see, Filipinos don't like to go to the provinces and besides they're afraid of living with Muslims in Mindanao.

"Why? I think they're darling. I've got one in my class, he's very quiet."

"Well, they're not always quiet, believe me. Knifings are common and there have been massacres of Christians in the past."

The guests and hosts returned to the *sala.* All the chairs in the house were brought in but Jimmy and Isobel preferred the floor. Everyone wanted to tell the others how they lived, what they did or didn't do. No one got the stage to himself or the attention of all, but the chance to talk to their own kind, to say what they wanted to as strongly as they felt it was an emotional release. It was as if a lid had been lifted from a steaming kettle.

Gloria had insisted she would work only where Mary Jo went. She didn't say so but it was plain to the others that the Philippines frightened her, and she had not yet found a groove in which she was comfortable. She was as beautiful as ever, "plenty of time to spend on herself" was the female reaction. Her hair was in a smooth flip, she had on the right shade of lipstick, and she even wore shoes, with a Bandaid where they rubbed on her bare heels.

"We live in a barrio, a real one like the pictures, in a hut of nipa matting, thatch roof that leaks . . ."

"But it's cool," put in Mary Jo.

" . . .right on the school grounds, built by PC."

"With a shower, don't forget the shower." The Peace Corps fellow in the next barrio had fixed it for them at the back of the house. The water —when it rained —ran off the roof into a tank on top of the shed. Inside it poured into a suspended bucket which could be tipped by pulling a string.

"Where do other people bathe —or do they?"

"Don't be insulting, Filipinos are very clean people. There's a stream, the women wash themselves and their clothes at the same time."

"And drink it?"

"No, mostly they get drinking water from the well. It has a pump, put in by U.S. aid. The men leave on their *malongs,* the kids go bare and pour water over themselves to bathe."

But they weren't going to stay there, insisted Gloria. There was nobody to talk to, English was spoken in class but volunteers' meager Tagalog was not very useful outside of school where people spoke Ilacano or Visayan. Gloria wanted to move into Davao and ride bicycles back to school. Mary Jo said it would hurt the people's feelings and they would stay and get used to it. Gloria said she only sat in the back of the class all day anyway, the teacher never asked her how to pronounce English.

"Of course not!" said Laura heatedly. "Why would she want you correcting her in front of her class?"

"But what are we supposed to be doing then? They told us in training . . ."

They had each asked that question many times since their arrival and each had answered it in her or his own way. The Normal School in Laoag had not known George and Kathy were coming till they appeared, and no one knew what to do with them.

"I get along better than Kath," said George, "because she has an old Puritan conscience that thinks she ought to be doing something useful all the time. She worries the Filipinos. Now I don't care." He stretched himself out in a more comfortable position. "Sometimes they let me mock up a biology experiment. We toss a few seeds in a can and watch 'em pop. The book says take a lice —louse —lice out of a pupil's hair and count its legs. They enjoy that. I even got them out of the building to catch frogs. That's good enough for me."

"You're lucky here at UP, they're set up for you."

"Well, not exactly, but I just love my language lab. The kids are darling, the fellows are so polite and the girls shy, and if we get on the jeepney together they always pay my fare," cooed Isobel.

"Well, I don't exactly work hard," admitted Laura, "but my conscience doesn't bother me, I think I am making progress with my co-teacher. We do kind of plan the work together."

Martha had been listening. The difference between her situation and those of these youngsters in the provinces interested her very much. Now they asked her directly what she did.

"Several things," she evaded and then said right out what had been forming in her mind. "I have an advantage over you. It's not just that I have had more experience, it's the Filipino respect for age. Even my gray hair helps. They don't resent my suggestions, they let me do things. I guess that's my trouble — they let me do things but I can't get them to do things."

"Like —what?" asked Kathy, really curious.

"Like getting articles into the magazine on time. A deadline is something to avoid, I really do believe. It isn't that they are too busy or don't intend to, and they love seeing themselves in print, but they just don't plan ahead."

"That's it," said Mary Jo, "nobody plans."

"No, no," corrected George, "they plan and plan, but don't do it." Several spoke at once giving their own versions of a common experience.

"You all push too hard," Jimmy spoke slowly and softly from the floor and they all listened. He had said very little up to now. "I wasn't raised in the South—just the south side of Chicago, but I got it in me—a kind of relaxin' spirit. And it's growin' in me here. They got my kind of easy speed. Now, Mart, who cares if your old magazine comes out in December or February? They don't read it when it comes, I'll bet."

"Only their own articles," Martha agreed.

"Kathy, just you learn to sit and look purty, that's enough for a hot day. George's got the right idea, don't fuss 'em. Stop pushin', you guys."

"How about you?" asked Isobel, leaning back on her elbows and giving Jimmy a long appraising look.

"Me? I'm supposed to teach math. They've had a lot of drill and they're faster than I am. So I make 'em slow down and ask why. How do you know two hundred goes into six hundred three times? We are getting slower and slower. More restful every day."

Isobel came out with something that was in most of their minds. "I bet being black helps you get along."

"No, ma'am!" Jimmy sat up straight and pounded his fist into his other palm. "That's worse than being white. They're kind of used to white invaders but they don't think anythin' a-tall of black ones. My students looked at me the first week as if I was something out of the zoo."

"You know that's funny—I don't mean funny funny, I mean odd," put in Laura. "I've noticed they are very color conscious, not race, color. Luz tells me about a student as 'the dark one in row two.'"

"Well, I know the girls won't go swimming till the sun is low but I thought that was modesty," said Gloria. "Is it because they don't want to get darker?"

"Oh, they can be cruel about it, about their own color, not even anything as way out as me. Light skin and beauty go together, here like everywhere else." There was an edge of bitterness in Jimmy's voice they had never heard before.

"They've got a favorite joke in Loaog, maybe down here too, about when God made man he mixed up the mud and put him in the oven and left him too long, and he came out black. So he made him again and took him out too soon and he was pasty white. So he tried again and got him just right—brown."

"That's our little brown brother for you." Isobel got up from the floor and stretched.

Martha wanted to dig deeper. "It's different here though than in our country. There's no discrimination really."

"Oh, I think there is, in jobs. I heard teachers discussing a new man, and one said that he must have very good references even though he was so dark."

"It's the Chinese who get the real dirty deal, legally." They each gave an example of that.

"Why didn't they tell us those things in training instead of so much junk like how many relatives help with the rice planting."

"And *Utang na loob*."

"That's not junk, that's true."

"Ye-ah," agreed Jimmy tentatively, "but try and put your finger on it. Just try and figure out who has to do something for who."

"And they don't like to have you let on you know about it, have you caught that?" Before anyone answered George, there was a running step on the gravel, and the door burst open. "Dick! Who blew you in?"—"Hiya fella"—"Gosh you look great."

Dick's exuberance flowed over all. He slapped backs, kissed the girls, and collapsed in the biggest chair. The out-of-town crowd knew he was in the country but had not seen him. The next few minutes were a tangle of questions and half-heard answers.

"So you're selling aspirin to the Huks!" Jimmy's drawl halted the gabble. "If I could," Dick replied firmly. "I haven't found one yet, but I will. One Huk that is. It's a funny business, everyone talks as if everyone else knew who and where they are, and nobody will say anything right out."

"Well, don't be mysterious, man, we hear about them, too, but you been in the mountains where they are—if any," prodded George.

"I know the Philippine government had better wake up, they're on the rebound. Laura, you remember that Filipino we met in the cemetery? His father's a constable in Pampanga. They say he bumped off three guys to get elected cuz the Huks were against him."

"Kill, you mean?" Gloria asked unhappily.

"Kill, I mean."

"There was a lot of that reported here in Manila. Newspapers were full of it. They kept the score like we do for traffic deaths."

"Aren't Huks just plain communists?" asked Mary Jo.

"That's what every government claims about its revolutionaries who want freedom for their people. The Huks have fought the establishment, just like the real Formosans on Taiwan."

"Tata, tata, ta-ta," Isobel made like a trumpet. "Here comes Richard on his white charger!"

"Whatever they are, they get little support from Filipinos, even students at U.P." Martha couldn't resist that jibe.

"Well, Mart, your friend José . . ."

"Not my friend, I don't even know him."

"OK, OK, somebody's friend José is on the same wave length as the Huks, and his old man in Pampanga is doggone mad about it."

"Did you sell any toothpaste?" Laura calmly interrupted.

"Huh?—Oh—you oughtta see those gold mines around Baguio. Gold, guys, pure gold. Do you know what it looks like pouring out of a furnace, at two thousand seven hundred degrees? First the slag, it's liquid fire. I thought that was the gold. Lots of slag and finally the gold. Before it cools it looks just like a small cone of gray metal."

"Not gold?"

"Not gold color, but *gold*, baby! And it all goes to the U. S. Except what disappears," he added darkly.

"Disappears?"

"Damn right. That's what they say, 'disappears.' And in the Philippines you know what that means."

"Smuggled?" ventured George.

"Right, man, miners are damned clever about hiding a bit of gold dust. There's a name for ones who get caught, 'highgraders,' and they're blacklisted, can't work in other mines, but it's worth it. The Chinese get it eventually."

"Well, you've dug up a lot of excitement in a month, fella, while PC sits around and acts friendly."

"Some of us work," snapped Martha crossly.

"Some of us teach —sort of," Laura defended lamely.

"And all of us are counting the days till we go home." Gloria shouldn't have said it. The words ripped through their masks of I-can-take-it. Suddenly they were just strangers in an alien land. The mat on the floor, the rattan furniture, the garish painted walls, the *clack-clack* of the lizards along the eaves, all were foreign. In the silence the sounds of the tropical night were loud.

Jimmy broke it. "I could use a bite of that cake if you have any left."

Laura jumped up, glad of something to do. "Turn on all the lights, it's on top of the fridge where ants usually don't get, but I won't guarantee it."

"Do you know what was the matter with training?" she began while picking at a bit of frosting.

"Yeah, a lot of things."

"Well," she went on quickly, "they told us all they knew about Filipinos, what they liked and did and thought, how they acted, but they didn't tell us the negatives. Now we have our values, you know—things we think are important . . ."

"Like hot water."

" . . . and they have theirs. So we just added theirs onto ours and thought we understood them, but what we didn't know was their *non*-values."

"You lost me, kid." Jimmy locked his hands around his knees and watched her face intently.

"Now look . . ." She had been thinking this out for a long time as she rode buses and jeepneys. "We think time is important. Filipinos don't. We knew that but we knew it within our own value, from our point of view. I mean, time really *is* important, Filipinos just haven't found it out yet, they will when they get industrialized or educated. But what we didn't know is that they aren't just careless, or slow. They *don't like* time schedules. They don't like the restrictions. They'd rather not know when something is going to begin so they don't have to get there. And they don't care if other people don't get there either. *Time is a non-value*," she finished triumphantly. This was her discovery, she wanted them to appreciate it.

But they didn't buy her idea immediately. They rolled it around in their thoughts and comments. That sounds kind of silly. For every value there is an opposite value. Maybe it can all be put positively. We value time, they value casualness. Not the same thing. They don't consciously think "we value casualness," they are just unattracted by our value, Time. It's a *non*-value to them. OK, let's try it on for size. Think of another.

"Quiet," offered Mary Jo. "Classrooms are noisy, audiences of all kinds never stop talking. Nobody keeps still, ever. I think they hate silence."

"Honesty."

"Oh, come off, that's going too far. We aren't so great at that ourselves."

"No, but we value it. We count on it, we think students *ought not* to cheat. But here, jeez, it's a way of life."

"But George," Kathy remonstrated, "it's not cheating to them, it's sharing what you know with a friend."

"Teachers all accept it. It's part of *utang*, I think."

"No, not all teachers, some fight it," said Laura remembering her discussions with Luz. "But I think that is because they have learned Americans think it is wrong . . . And I expect that is mostly among American trained teachers."

"So honesty, as we think of it, is a non-value," Dick had not entered into the conversation before. Now he leaned forward and spoke directly to Laura. "Maybe you got something here. Take smuggling. Now we think it's terrible, sneaking goods in and out to avoid tax or tariff. It violates a law, cuts government revenue so it adds to our taxes. It involves connivance by police and government officials—just nasty all along the line, so it horrifies us. But to a Filipino it's OK. Gets him cigarettes he likes cheaper, outsmarts the big guy who is gouging the little guy, reroutes profits from government—which doesn't do anything for him anyway—into his corner of influence, or to a friend who will share the booty with him. As for bribery, that's just fair payment for services rendered. Now they know the Chinese get that gold that disappears! But there will be little rake-offs all along the line because the Chinese know that they know. As for the Chinese they have had to learn how to get along in a country where everything possible is done to keep them from getting the breaks. The only big loser is the U. S. and he'll never miss it, he's so rich."

"So honesty is not a great shining virtue that everyone in the world ought to respect," Mary Jo said thoughtfully. "It's just something that has value if it is useful to you and in the Philippines it doesn't get them what they want."

Kathy had been wriggling her toes and rubbing the back of George's hand. Now she expressed her discomfort. "You are tearing down my system of ethics, Dick. You just can't run a country if most people aren't honest, everyone loses."

"But if the top guys are the only ones who benefit from the system, you gotta get yours by snatching the crumbs, or get next to someone on the *in* so he will share it with you—or get something *on* him so he has to."

Martha, sitting by the window, heard a car coming slowly down their street. Laura turned her head at the crunch of tires on the gravel. The closing of a car door stopped the conversation. Their American ears knew that that solid, muffled slam was not made by a jeepney or taxi. Who?

"Embassy car," growled Dick. "Who the hell asked him?" He shot an angry glance at Laura.

"I did!" The words popped out of Martha without her intending them. She wondered afterwards what made her say them, and then go on to back them up. "He's doing pictures of my class."

"Mart, you don't . . . "

"He doesn't bite," from Isobel.

"Who?" from the out-of-towners.

Heavy steps came to the door, hesitated, and began to recede softly. The slatted doors were no barrier to sound in or out.

"You don't have to act like barbarians," whispered Martha scathingly, "he's human." She opened the door and called to the man retreating to the car. "Come in, Mr. Thomas. We've got a Peace Corps confab going here, but we can talk about the pictures later."

Phil, amused to find he was as much afraid of them as they were of him, returned. Latent courtesy and curiosity triumphed over hostility, and the group accepted him. Dick gave up his chair and settled his long body close to Laura on the floor, offering as an opener, "We were talking about Filipino values, Mr. Thomas."

"Phil."

"Oh, Phil," he forced it out. "Laura has got an idea that there are such things as cultural *non*-values, anyway Filipinos just don't take to things we think are good."

"Like, time, silence, honesty," they explained. "Can you add any?"

"Tell me more, 'til I catch on." These were nice kids but they made him feel old.

"I know one, space," offered Kathy. "We have a demonstration school in Loaog, started by the U.S. (of course, oh, for sure), classrooms all the scientific right size for just so many kids and all that bit. Well, the Filipinos hate it. They're uncomfortable, it's too big. Space is a *non*-value.

"Sure, look how they live, eight and ten to a room —with all outdoors to expand to if they wanted to. We feel sorry for them, I swear they like it that way. You know how they told us in training about the acceptable distance between people and how the Filipino's was smaller than ours?"

"Have you had privacy?" Phil was ready to enter in. "A group of Filipinos was asked by some researcher to list the things Americans value most and privacy headed the list. I don't think that's the most important thing in the world to us but because Filipinos don't like it, are really uncomfortable by themselves, they are impressed by the value we put on it. So it's a *non*-value to them."

"That's the idea, man," said Jimmy. "Look how they never go any place alone."

"And if any of us goes alone some one asks, 'Where's your companion,' or says 'I will accompany you.'" Each one could add something from his own experience.

Laura was pleased. "You see, gang, that's the way they should teach it to us. The values they reject are more important than the ones they accept. When we catch onto that maybe we won't be so sure we can transfer our values to everyone in the world."

"What values?" said Dick in a put-down tone. "Materialism, imperialism, racism?"

"Knock it off," from George, "we know our faults, it's more fun to talk about other people's."

Martha could keep still no longer. "I, at least, happen to think that we have some virtues as well as faults. And I think some of our values are universal, I mean good for everyone."

"What?" they challenged.

"Well, honesty, democracy, rational thinking, concern for others . . ."

Soft laughter rippled through the room. "The good old American way," someone said.

"That's OK, Mart, we know you're one hundred percent American," said George. "But suppose it is good, why should we try to force it on others who see it differently. Now if Filipinos are happy in their rice paddies under the extended family system why can't we leave 'em be?"

"George, you're nuts," said his wife. "They're not happy, they're sick, they're hungry, they die young, they want all the things Americans have."

"They have no choice," cut in Phil firmly.

"What do you mean?"

"I mean all traditional, agrarian societies are changing, nations are modernizing, economies are industrializing—whether it's good or bad for them. They can't stop it. As long as they are open to the rest of the world, see how other people live, and their leaders want status and progress. In the twentieth century they can't choose to stay underdeveloped, their only choice is what kind of a modern economy—government— society they are going to grow into. The lines are drawn: they either take the way of the U. S. and go for capitalism and democracy, or a facsimile or they choose the communist way with economic determinism and dictatorship."

The volunteers would not let that stand. "Oh, now come off it, guy. How about a nice home-grown dictator? What about the nonaligned?"

"There's no such thing as a *nice* dictator, and every nation is aligned," Phil stated categorically. "No one can exist alone, we're all interdependent. Only some nations switch alignment frequently or divide it between major powers. The Philippines have decided—or history has decided it for them—that their best interests lie with the United States, so they want all the help they can get with as few controls as possible."

"Natch, aid without strings," agreed Jimmy.

"Natch," Phil echoed. "Try and tell that to our Congress when they are debating appropriations. Just try and explain that the Filipinos will spend our money according to our non-values!"

"But can't nations think up systems that suit *them* instead of having to choose between ones that other nations have de-veloped?" pleaded Laura.

"I wish to God they would." Phil stood up. He knew he should not have loosed such a hard-headed barrage on these neophytes to the non-Western world. Actually he envied them their cynicism and naivete, he could indulge in neither. It was definitely time for him to go. But they looked so bewildered he couldn't leave without tossing a line to them.

"Keep on groping like the rest of us. You may spin some lines between us and the Filipinos which will be stronger than any we now have." His car was waiting, Martha followed him to the door and said, too loudly, "I do want those pictures, classes start the eighth. Come on out then." She felt silly as she turned back and caught Laura's eye but it was some satisfaction to see Dick's arm around Laura even in a brotherly fashion.

Laura sighed, "I didn't know it would be so hard."

"What? Talking to the Embassy?"

"No, understanding another culture —I mean *really*."

Gloom was closing in, and they urged Mary Jo to get her guitar.

George teased Laura, "This is Grand Central Station, two American arrivals the same night."

Gently, Mary Jo strummed the Filipino favorite, *"Leron, leron,"* and they joined in. Then she changed the mood to, "Planting Rice Is Never Fun."

"Do you remember that parody we made up for the final banquet at San Francisco State?"

"You mean betel nut and Lola? Now that we've seen gramma chewing betel nut, we can really put our hearts in it." The old tune and silly words cheered them up.

Laura looked at her watch and gasped, "Dick, the last bus goes at ten."

"Gosh, Dick, I wish we could squeeze you into the jeep we borrowed from headquarters but five . . . "

"No, no, you don't go my way." He did not seem to be in a hurry as he unfolded himself and pulled Laura up with him. "Walk me to the bus, no Filipino would let me go without a companion."

The night was soft and warm around them. Laura looked up at the black velvet sky strewn with glittering sequins and whispered, "I love the nights. All the heat and noise gone, Filipinos asleep in their houses, so it's all ours."

"You're sweet," he whispered. They walked slowly, too slowly, the bus lumbered by before they reached the cross street.

"The last one!" Laura mourned. "What will you do?"

"I don't know, ride a star beam home. Don't spoil this."

She leaned against him in response. They walked along the edge of the quadrangle where the flame trees arched over the embankment and pulled back quickly as a couple in the shadows rolled over on the grass.

"So," Dick breathed in her ear, "Filipinos do know what to do on a dark night."

Laura pushed her face against the hollow of his shoulder to stifle her nervous giggle. Suddenly his arms were around her, crushing her warm body against his. For a moment she felt his taut muscles, his pounding heart. His lips possessed hers. Then he released her. "Sometime . . . " It was a promise.

The world stood still again. "There's a jeep, run," she commanded him. He didn't need to run, the jeepney slowed down, and she watched him hop on next to the driver. What was a jeepney doing out here this time of night? As it pulled away she thought she recognized the side of Diego's head.

As she walked happily back toward the house she smiled to think that no Filipina would walk alone even that half block in the dark.

22

Americano, Go Home!

Phil did not take pictures of Martha's class on January eighth for the good reason that he was barricaded inside the Embassy. From a window in the Cultural Affairs office he watched the crowd of Filipinos milling around in the square between the old Embassy building and the new. Mostly students from UP, he assumed. They ran around bumping into each other, some brandishing sticks, uncertain of what to do now that they had forced their way through the entrance gates. The marine guards had quickly barricaded the front entrance with whatever they could find, chairs, tables and boards and now about a dozen men stood at the foot of the steps, quiet but alert, facing the students.

A few of them carried hastily printed signs at casual angles over their shoulders, "Give us Peterson," "Kill the killer." The Embassy had been expecting trouble of some kind after Thompson, an enlisted man at Clark Air Force Base, had killed a Filipino in a drunken brawl. The main street in the town of Angeles was a festering sore in the side of the base, offering bright lights, open bars, and brothels. The U. S. maintained the right to try and punish its own military personnel, and every so often Filipino indignation would flare up protesting what they considered an "insult" to their sovereignty. Lately students at UP had held protest meetings on a number of issues and this one issue always drew a crowd. The killing had touched off their anger, but these protesters were amateurs, obviously. They seemed to have no leader inciting them to action, and they didn't know how far they wanted to go. For all their talk, the U.S. still seemed like family to most of them and Filipino youth just don't defy their elders without deep provocation. A murder was hardly worth it.

José would be down there, Phil was sure. Now he saw him.

One young man, more venturesome than the rest was fumbling at the ropes of the flag pole that stood in the center of the square.

"You'd better not!" Phil wanted to shout it.

José had seen the boy, too. He jumped him, knocking his hands away. Phil felt a wave of pride. That guy had sense as well as guts. It would be tested when these students learned the ways of rioting. Next time it would be bricks, as Phil knew from experience in other countries. After that would come Molotov cocktails, tear gas, and bashed heads.

A bright spot among the black heads caught his eye, and he muttered, "Oh, my God, that fool!" Dick was pushing his way up through the crowd toward the line of marines. Something —the pull of watching eyes made him look up.

"Get back from the window!" It was the harassed voice of the chief officer. "That's no picnic down there."

"Bricks come next time, Mr. Gladson," said Phil pleasantly. He turned from the window and left the room in leisurely strides. With the door shut behind him he looked in both directions and seeing no one, bolted down three flights of stairs to the truck entrance at the back. There was Ben as he had hoped. Ben, who had outlasted many ambassadors and colonial governors before them, was secure and honored as "maintenance."

"Ben," he gasped, "there's a dumb American out there who's got to be nabbed before he causes trouble. Will you get the word to the lieutenant?"

Ben needed no more. "Them big Peace Corps, they don't know from nothin'." Ignoring the command of the guard at the door to stop, he walked out and around the corner to the square.

Phil breathed in relief; it would not have done a bit of good to ask a private to tell a lieutenant but Ben owned the place. Phil walked to the front lobby from which the receptionist had fled. Through the glass doors, over the heads of the guards he saw Dick arguing with José, evidently trying to provoke him to action. Suddenly, José's foot shot out and tripped Dick. As he fell, a marine at the end of the line leaped to him, lifted him, and, pinning his arms behind his back, marched him toward the back of the building. The crowd watched in surprise. Then someone laughed, another shouted, "Americano, go home!" Nervous giggles rippled across the square. Students nearest the gate edged toward it —and the protest was over.

From the sidewalk on the other side of Dewey Boulevard, spectators had watched the whole thing. Now they relaxed, joked with each other, and moved off, leaving two girls still intently focusing on the Embassy. Laura and Isobel had come downtown to get their cholera booster shots at the Embassy clinic. But as they got to the AID offices across the street from the Embassy they were stopped by the Manila police.

The police had arrived soon after the students but seemed equally uncertain of their role. They discreetly stayed on the far side of the boulevard on the reasonable assumption that the United States of America was able to protect itself.

To her horror, Laura saw the flash of Dick's hair shortly before he accosted José. "Now what's he doing there?" she fumed.

"It's where the action is, honey. The people versus power, you know," Isobel mocked.

"Against his own government!"

"Who else?" They spoke too loudly, people turned to look at them curiously.

"Peace Corps," the word was passed around.

Laura clamped her lips shut even as she saw him fall. She watched the marine lead him away and now she waited, not knowing what for.

"Look!" Isobel grabbed her arm and pointed to the corner of the new building. Dick was walking rapidly toward the boulevard, unaccompanied. The girls walked toward him, and as he crossed the street they could see his face was bloody.

Laura ran to him. "Dick, you hurt?"

"What the hell are you doing here?"

"Watching you," Isobel supplied.

"Did he hit you?"

"Who? No, I . . . " He brushed his hand across his forehead and looked in surprise at the blood. " . . . fell. Crazy guys, wouldn't *do* anything. They ought to have broken in, got the ambassador —and that guy of yours watching," he ended bitterly.

"Our hero!" from Isobel.

"Shut up, he's hurt." Laura's instinct was to get him out of sight, wash him, slap him. They were in front of the Swiss Inn. She propelled him in the door, past curious diners to "Ladies."

He stopped, "I'm not going in there."

"Well, I'm not going in 'Men's'. Watch the door, Isobel." She pushed him in, announcing, "Man coming in."

23

Ring Ceremony

Whatever the political effects of the protest, it had a profound effect on Martha. During the vivid account by Laura and Isobel, she changed her matchmaking plans. She made up her mind firmly, as she made it up about most things. Dick was not to have Laura. Her Laura was not to spend her life washing his face after he had hurt himself in some fool cause for the downtrodden. This decision presented her with a titillating challenge because she had no one else in mind, and she would be working against nature and against Laura. But when you know you are right, even if you can't see far ahead, you take small steps, and try out what is at hand. Having already rejected all other PCVs for Laura, there seemed to be nothing more promising at hand than Mr. Thomas.

So Martha became enthusiastic about her inspired picture project. It seemed innocent enough. Get Phil to take some slides of her class in action. Tape their voices with pronunciation correction and then run it for them. She counted on their interest in seeing themselves to sharpen their awareness of their audio errors which now they simply did not hear. Anyway, since she had a double motive it was worth trying.

It took several weeks to complete the arrangements. Nothing was simple if it came under the heading of communications. What a wonderful invention the telephone is, especially if you don't have one. There was one in the dean's office in the College of Education but it was so hard to get a connection with Manila Martha didn't even ask to use it. The College of Business Administration had the best one for some reason but there was always a waiting line. The one closest to home was in the infirmary but Martha always felt she should have some medical reason to use it. However, she tried it.

This time, firmness of purpose made her bold. She asked casually, "May I call the American Embassy, please?" This was impressive enough. She got it on the first try.

"May I speak with Dr. Thomas, please?" (Mart made up the "Dr." on her own.) "Yes, hello, this is Miss Wagner at U.P. It's not exactly an emergency." She noticed the nurse at the desk was listening while she filed her nails.

"I wondered if you could come out rather soon and take those pictures?" ("X-ray," she whispered with a knowing smile at the nurse.) "Yes, you could come out and talk it over tonight— and take a chance. . . . No, I don't know exactly who will be home . . . If you are sure you have time. Yes, thank you, good-bye."

She thanked the nurse and left, very pleased with herself. She probably hadn't fooled the nurse, but she had made her think she thought she had so she could never question her as that would embarrass—"shame"—the American. So if she could get the same nurse next time she would have no trouble.

Phil did come out that evening, and they made arrangements for the next week. But the day before he was to come the president of the Philippines declared a holiday in honor of the death date of some general. Martha didn't know whether in these circumstances he followed U. S. schedule or Philippines so she went to class but he didn't come. He explained later that the Americans in the Embassy didn't observe the holiday but the Filipinos did, and he supposed the U. P. would be closed. Laura had had similar uncertainties. It was teachers' meeting day, and she thought teachers would come even if classes weren't held. So she had started down town only to find her regular bus didn't come, jeepneys did not follow their more-or-less regular rounds. When she got to school the doors were locked. One of the women Filipina teachers had come, too, not having heard the announcement on the radio.

"Aren't you angry?" Laura asked her.

"I feel silly," she replied shyly.

"Silly—you! It's your president should feel silly, declaring a holiday with no warning the day before. How can a whole country stop that fast?" The teacher lowered her eyes in embarrassment but Laura persisted. "Why don't you write to him and tell him?"

The brown eyes lifted in surprise and she laughed.

"She laughed," Laura reported at dinner that night. "She just laughed when I said, 'Why don't you . . .'"

"... 'write to your president,' " Martha finished for her. "That is exactly what I said, first thing."

"Oh, you Americans!" chided Isobel. "Always thinking you can manage things and trying to persuade the Filipinos to do it too. Why can't you just accept what comes, school or no school, what does it matter?"

"Yeah, yeah, you're so Filipinized, till your boy friend starts edging toward the door about ten P.M. hoping you'll let him go home —then you feel insulted, like an American."

"Now we won't go into that again," warned Martha like the classroom disciplinarian that she was.

So the arrangements for the picture-taking started all over again. This time they were successful, and produced some interesting by-products. Martha could hardly wait for dinner time the night after the picture taking. Even the sight of Isobel's habitual creamed tuna could not depress her. As she helped herself to the green beans from Baguio that Mona had found in the market that morning, she sent up her trial balloon.

"Is anyone interested in going to a military ball?"

Isobel dropped her fork. "A what?"

Laura choked on a swallow of water. "A real one?" she coughed out.

"A real, formal military ball with an escort who is getting inducted into the military fraternity. And don't say, 'How American.' " She flung the last at Isobel; nobody was going to rub the edge off this fun.

"Who? Where? When?"

"Now keep still and I'll tell you the whole thing." Martha took a large mouthful of tuna and rice and washed it down with tea. "Today Phil came to take pictures of my class."

"We know that, but . . ."

"And he brought with him José, because he is coaching him in photography."

"We know that, but . . ."

"So Phil would tell him what to take; long shot of the whole class, close-up of a girl writing, very close up of me demonstrating how my tongue touched the root of my mouth to make an 'l,' two girls . . ."

"Come on, Mart, the *ball*."

"Well, while Phil was doing some of them over —he's very particular—José sidles up to me and says, 'Mum, I have to be inducted into the military fraternity in the ring ceremony.' Well, I tried to show polite interest, but I was surprised, most

Filipinos don't begin a conversation so abruptly. 'We have the military ball next Saturday, mum.' 'That's nice,' I say. Then he blurted out, 'Mum, I have to take a girl.' He stopped and I thought we were stuck there for good. But Phil came up, and José got the courage to say, 'The military ball, sir.' "

"Phil was so casual and interested he put José right at ease. He said, 'Oh, yes, it was a great affair and that José was an officer in the PNT and that they select a few to be honored as members of a military fraternity.'

" 'Is that where you have the ring ceremony?' he asked José."

"Ring? Sounds like a wedding," said Isobel, losing interest.

"No, no wedding. I finally pieced it together from the two of them. The man has to take his girl to the middle of the ballroom and stand inside a kind of arch, she puts the fraternity ring on his finger, and she kisses him."

"Neat," approved Isobel. "It is American."

"Yes, that's where they got it and that's what causes the problem because she has to kiss him on the mouth—he was very explicit about that, and he hasn't got a girl to take."

"He's got Luz."

"She won't go."

"Won't kiss him, you mean."

"That's right. So I finally grasped the import of his distress and I said, 'So you want me to get you an American girl who will kiss you in public.' "

" 'Yes, mum!' He was so relieved to have got it across. So I said I thought I could oblige."

"Well, Isobel's willin'."

Laura kept still. She had never been to a military ball. They didn't have them in Paddington, Kentucky, or at Midland College. But she had read about them, heard about them, and they seemed to her that they must be the height of glamour and elegance, dress uniforms, courtly officers, beautiful women.

"How about you, Laura, Isobel may be too tall. He was particular about that."

"Oh, it would be fun." Then a dark thought struck her. "But, Luz, oh my, I don't think she would like it."

"She's turned down her chance," Isobel pointed out practically. "But of course, if you feel that way . . ."

"How tall are you, Isobel?"

"Five seven—in low heels."

"José is taller than most Filipinos, I'd have to ask him."

"I'll shrink, I'll bend my knees, I'll stop eating. What do I wear?"

"I asked him if girls wear *ternos*."

"I have one the Williamses gave me." Laura had not quite given up.

"I'll have one made."

"You don't need to. He was so cute. He said, 'Some do, mum, the older ones. Some men bring their aunts.'"

"Aunts! My God."

"But he said most girls wear them —and he cut a line about a foot below his chin and another about at his knees."

"The darling!"

Martha was sorry about Laura, she would love to see her go and she was looking sad, though virtuous. Now Laura closed the issue, "Well it's no use my thinking about it. You go, Iz. I just can't risk my relations with Luz, I know she wouldn't like it." She felt a bit of pleasure in being able to be sure of Luz's reaction —or was she? She would ask Phil. It was nice to know he would know and would tell her straight out. But the ball would have broken the dullness of the days. She had not seen Dick since he had stalked out of the ladies room at the Swiss Inn, face red but clean, and had left them without a word. She hoped he had put something on that small cut but probably he hadn't.

Martha delighted in her role as go-between, especially as she felt no personal concern for either party. If José wanted to defy Philippine social mores and the taboos of his girl, it wasn't her business. And Isobel would survive whatever happened and glory in it.

So she reported to José that Isobel was five-seven. He was five-eight and although he would have preferred a smaller model he took what he could get. To Isobel she reported that she was acceptable to José. "He said he would ask your parents or guardian. I told him I was your guardian. (A snort from Isobel.) He said he'd get you back at twelve o'clock," ("No kidding!") "that he was very careful who his sister went out with, and he'd be just as careful of you."

"How sweet, this gets less interesting every minute."

Laura gave an exaggerated, "Hear, hear."

But Isobel had a dress made by the woman next to the grocery co-op of red chiffon selected after hours of touring the markets. Martha contributed a pair of white gloves and Laura a small white purse. A hairdresser piled her golden hair in a high crown. They all agreed she would grace any ring ceremony.

She was ready to go at 7:45 and sat down stiffly to wait. "First time in my life I was ready ahead of time," she complained. "I never wait for a man. But it seems late for dinner, you're sure he said dinner, Mart? I haven't eaten a thing."

At 8:15 when he had not arrived Laura offered her a glass of reconstituted milk which she refused. "It'll show in this dress it's so tight."

None of them were prepared for the crisis created by the arrival at 8:30 of her escort. José was not alone. With him were two other men whom he introduced as his cousin and a friend whose car they were using.

"Are the other girls in the car?" asked Martha.

"No, mum, this is all."

Isobel excused herself and left the room. They waited, nobody sat down. Nobody said anything. She took so long at whatever last minute duties she had that Martha went to her room. She was sitting on her bed, saying over and over to Laura, "I won't go. Chaperones! Of all things. Three men, what kind of a date is that?"

Martha took her hands and jerked her to her feet. "Yes you will go—after all our fuss and all his trouble to see this through. You're the one who understands the Filipinos, now this is their way, and you get on out there." And she did.

They got a racy account the next morning.

"It was in this hotel ballroom, see, and first we ate, mountains of Filipino food, the fancy kind and good. Lots of old people there and more officers than women. Three to one I suppose is the custom. About ten o'clock they cleared the floor and started dancing to the combo that had been playing all evening. And he can dance! Where do you suppose he learned the twist and the mashed potato? Not from that prim schoolteacher of his, I bet. The high point was the ring ceremony. I was afraid we'd be the only ones but there were others but I think most of them were wives or mothers or aunts. Anyway they didn't cause much excitement, and no one went into hysterics over the kiss.

"But when José and I started down that aisle you could have heard a toothpick drop. You'd have thought we were going to the altar—or the guillotine."

Yes, Laura could see the picture. José, stiff and straight in his dress whites, Isobel a red flame beside him, her golden crown on a level with his black head. Her bold blue eyes flashing with excitement and no one in the crowd missing this moment of shattering custom.

"José was so scared his arm shook, and he muttered, 'on the lips . . .' They must have drilled that into him. So I muttered back, 'OK, OK, the roof isn't going to fall.'

"So we stood in the arch, I put the ring on his finger and the band crashed. I gave him a big smack. Everyone clapped and laughed and cameras snapped and it was over. Only the photographers had been so excited they missed it and asked me to do it again—the gall! I refused. I had fulfilled my contract, paid for my dinner, and I wasn't going to entertain them for free. The colonel came up and thanked me for upholding the tradition of the army, no less. If that's all it takes to uphold the Philippine army, Asia can relax and forget the Philippines."

"I wonder what José told Luz," mused Laura.

24

Anger

Luz sat at her desk in the empty classroom, a pile of themes in front of her. She had sent Laura home after class, saying she would grade them herself. "Sent" was the word. She didn't want her around. She didn't want anyone around. She was angry, so angry her breath came in short puffs off the top of her lungs. She ground her back teeth with a satisfying sound in her head. She had never been so angry in her whole life. In fact it was a new sensation and not an unpleasant one. Every piece of her body, mind, and feelings participated in it. If she had a knife she might kill someone, but she hadn't decided whom.

This was two days before the military ball and Laura had casually mentioned that Isobel was wearing a red dress. Luz froze —before anger took over. She felt herself freeze. Her mouth would not open, and her knees would not bend though she felt as if she had been knocked down. Did Laura know she didn't know that José was taking Isobel, or did she think José had told her? Laura seemed utterly guileless. Her eyes looked straight into Luz's, and then worry lines were drawn around them at the expressions on Luz's face. All she could do was to hand Laura a curt dismissal.

"I will correct the themes, you go on home."

Laura went, mystified, hurt. Luz didn't want to examine why she was stunned, then angry. Resolutely she began to read the first theme. It was Caesar Tenego and would be bad.

TO GET HUNGRY

My mother and father live in the province. My father work in the government ["s" added the red pencil]. We are poor because they do not get big salary [insert 'a']. My mother, he is old ["she"].

Same old mistakes, she noted with an under layer of her mind. She knew exactly what would happen at that ball. José had described it all to her and asked if she would do *it*. Of course she had said no, as he expected. She was sure he would have been disappointed if she had accepted.

I love my mother. I love my father less. She beat me very often, although they are giving me money afterwards [red pencil busy].

He had not mentioned it again, and she supposed of course he was not going. But he *was*. He was going to that ball with that American girl, and she would kiss him—*in public*!

Sometimes you cannot always depend upon your father's pocket. My mother do the cooking and he is also sewing and sewing my sisters' dresses.

A red dress, that girl would wear a red dress. Of course she and José weren't officially betrothed yet. Since their families were not arranging it they didn't know how to handle the situation but Luz knew he was hers and that somehow, sometime, they would be married. At least that is what she had known in her heart until now, even though it had not been put into words. Now her anger revealed how firmly she had counted on, had assumed, this relationship.

I need money so badly if I have no job. I'll just stand and wait for a miracles to arouse. But if I either have a job, which comes from my education I can easily bother this trouble.

Stupid boy! Her red pencil broke as she X'd out the last paragraph. She gave up the pretense of work and sat staring at the wall in the back of the room. In *public* —*in public* —kept drumming itself in her mind. In public, a man belonged to his wife, or his intended. What he did in private didn't matter. Many men had outside loves. Father's boss had two jobs and supported two families. It was better than that terrible American divorce system where now you had a man and now you didn't. If José needed —liked—that volunteer he should keep it secret. Luz could pretend she didn't know and everyone else would pretend, too. But now he was taking her to a dance and kissing her in public. And she would be wearing a red dress. Luz never wore red. And her hair was blond—anger that had dammed up the tears broke. Luz put her head on her arms and wept. There was not even the rat with the notched ear to comfort her.

She stopped with a gulp when someone knocked at the door. Before she had time to mop her face, the door opened and José came straight in.

"How did you get here?" she accused him.

"Janitor told me you were here. You didn't come to the Luneta."

True, she had forgotten their regular Thursday tryst in a certain bench under a certain tree in the large city park. And she was glad —glad!

"I didn't think you'd come," she lied.

"Why not?" Obviously she had been crying but he had learned early from his mother never to ask a woman why she was crying, she told you. It was better to sneak away till she got over it. But he couldn't do that now, he had come for a purpose. Anyway, he knew why.

Luz pushed back her chair, walked to the window, and stood looking at the brick wall opposite while she wiped her face and smoothed her hair.

"I thought you'd be getting ready for the ball."

"That's not till Saturday," he explained lamely, and then aggressively. "If you don't like my taking Isobel, I can't help it. I asked you first."

"First!" she wheeled on him. "First and last, that's the way it should be. You knew I wouldn't do —that thing. It's —it's American. You know it's American," she finished scathingly, glad to have hit upon something she thought would reach him.

"Yeah, I guess so."

"That whole business was brought in by the American army, you know it."

"OK."

"Then why don't you object to it? Why would you be going, why would you be doing —*it?*" Why wouldn't he get angry so she could fight him? "You're the one who leads protests to the Embassy and yells, 'Americans go home.' But you go to their ball and follow their silly —immoral —customs."

So that was it, not the kissing, José guessed wrongly. He strode over to her and stood close. God, she was beautiful! Anger flushed her skin with deep color. Her eyes, usually quiet pools, were bright with recent tears. Her small breasts moved with her quick breaths. He clenched his hands at his side to keep from crushing her to him. He did not know that would have settled everything. But it was daylight, in a schoolroom, and tradition was too strong. So he only looked down at her and said harshly, "Listen, don't be telling me how to act. Politics are my business. I need to belong to that fraternity. I need those officers as friends. You keep out of it."

His harshness was a slap. Luz stepped back. "You mean . . ."

"You don't have to know what I mean." The moment of intimacy was broken and he strode back to the desk. "Anyway, I didn't come to argue about a dance. There's something I want you to do."

Luz stood by the first desk in the outside row feeling uncomfortable and strangely like a rebuked pupil.

"You know Dick."

She didn't know him except second-hand through Laura.

"He's meddling," José went on without waiting for an answer. "He's been up in Mountain Province, nosing around the gold mines."

"Doesn't he sell drugs?"

"He doesn't sell anything. He talks. He asks question. He thinks he's a revolutionary, and he's looking for a revolution. Talks about Huks and Formosans and Chinese as if you could lump 'em all together. He's for the underdog."

"You don't like that?"

"No, I don't. We'll do things our own way in our own time without any help from him. But that's not the point. One of my father's men came down this week to find out what I was doing."

"Protesting?"

"Sure. But he let out that Dick was hanging around the mines trying to make connections."

"I thought you and your father didn't get along."

"We don't, but he's my father and he keeps me informed about things that might be useful to me."

Luz still stood by the desk. She hadn't any idea what he was talking about. She hated mysteries. Her anger had been drained off, and she felt cheated of a showdown, and she didn't like being diverted from her personal injuries. She couldn't stand up to him now, she had no strength for it and in this area he was in command, trying to tell her something she didn't want to know.

"Manila is the place to sell drugs."

"What has this to do with me? You just told me to stay out of your affairs."

"You're her friend."

"No." She didn't have to ask whose.

"What?"

"We're co-teachers."

"OK, whatever you are, you'll be talking to her." José evidently thought that settled the matter. Luz didn't ask, talk to her about what. She understood her role was to be a go-between, and she accepted the fact that she was obligated to play it because Laura was performing a service by being her co-teacher. His message had been delivered but according to custom it should be wrapped up in casual, oblique conversation so that it was not so obvious. But neither of them wanted to risk reopening the subject of the dance. José hesitated, shifted from one foot to the other and without a soothing word turned abruptly to leave.

José took the first jeep that came along to Quiapo. He was not happy. He folded himself onto the rear end of a seat and made everyone else climb over him. Why did Luz cry? He didn't want her to cry, he wanted to kiss her but he couldn't. He moved his shoulders impatiently as if to shake off some restraint. Unconscious of the physical expression of his inner turmoil, he almost rode past his stop.

On the bus to UP he dug into his own feelings again. To avoid irritation with himself, he worked up irritation with Luz. She was too soft, too old-fashioned. Why couldn't he latch onto one of the swinging coeds that sat near to him in the Lib. and who didn't live in a dorm that closed at 8:30? He was a new kind of Filipino he reminded himself, and he should have a new kind of woman. He had insisted on coming to UP to break out of the circle of his father's influence, his political wheeling and dealing.

In José's world knowledge would spell power, not your relatives. There would be no soft-soaping of Malacanang and certainly no licking of Uncle Sam's boots. José's white shirt was made of cotton grown in Texas, woven in Manila on machines from Japan, and washed in Tide. His watch came from Hong Kong. His textbooks were published in the U. S. He much preferred American movies to those coarse, stupid ones in Tagalog. But he told himself it was all temporary. Soon Filipinos would grow and weave and manufacture what they needed. One day they would be economically independent and truly Filipino culturally. To achieve this a lot of the old ways had to go —including the marriage system —Filipinos had to do it all themselves. That thought brought into sharp focus the other source of his unhappiness —that meddling American. His instincts told him to ignore any mess the guy was in. He was so ignorant he wouldn't know a Huk from an Igorot. But he had to pass on the warning from his father, although just why his father should be concerned he didn't know and didn't care. Luz would take care of the message. He knew she would even if she was mad at him. Now one of those hip UP girls might not have understood him, but Luz—by the time he swung off the bus at the entrance to his dorm he felt comfortable again and right with his world.

25

One of Those Days

Things had been going along fairly calmly at the PC cottage on the campus, no sickness, no fights. It was two weeks to pay day so food money was holding out and letters from home had been arriving as expected. Students at the Normal School were showing some improvement in the use of past tense. There was only one cloud in Laura's currently blue sky, Luz was being very cool to her. Ever since that day before the dance when she had frozen solid at the news of Isobel and José, her usual warm good morning and the discussions of lesson plans had been hung with icicles.

"I suppose she's mad at me because you went with José," Laura had said to Isobel.

"That's nuts, *you* didn't go."

"No but I connived to get him a date who would kiss him."

"Kiss him! Jeez, that was a public performance. She's got no gripe coming. It's not like we had been sneaky about it in *private*. In public it didn't mean a thing. Anyway it hurt him more than it did her."

Maybe that wasn't it, but something had happened to change their relationship, and it worried Laura. If she could just come out and ask her, "Hey, Luz, what gives? Did I do something wrong?" That's what she would have said to an American, but she couldn't to Luz. So whatever the trouble was, it would have to grow or disappear in silence as Laura maintained as nearly as she could her usual behavior.

About a week after the dance came "one of those days." It began innocently with the usual trip to school. Since this trip to and from occupied two hours out of her day Laura had meticulously studied the process and was quite proud of the skill she had acquired in the art of bus riding.

Buses came frequently in the morning and she could choose between red, green, yellow, DP or MD or CAM as long as the sign in the front read "Quiapo." The lady conductress stood on the steps of a CAM bus encouraging business, calling "*Kapo, Kapo.*" She waved to prospective customers with a down stroke, and Laura wondered whether she ever persuaded anyone to get on who hadn't intended to go to Quiapo. She helped up the steps the young, the old, and those carrying bags and baskets. Laura, not qualifying in those categories, got on unaided. The conductress banged twice on the side of the bus and they were off with a lurch that sent the unwary hurtling toward a seat. Being a veteran rider, Laura did not take the seat she was thrown toward, she was selective. From experience she knew that if she sat in the longitudinal seat at the front there was less wind, and it was not as bumpy as those in the back. But the jerks threw you from side to side with nothing to hang on to, it was very hard on the middle muscles. On the right side of the bus the seats were big enough for two but had to hold three, on the left side they were big enough for one but had to hold two. Not much choice there. Buses, seen from the inside, seemed to have more than the usual number of wheels, at least three seats on each side were built over them leaving no room for the feet. Laura avoided these as she didn't like resting her chin on her knees all the way to town. She took a seat next to the window on the right side, gambling on having only one seat mate. Getting on at the campus, the bus wasn't full, and she had some choice. Coming out from the city the bus would be nearly full. If she had to sit in the middle of a seat for three, she was expected to sit forward so that her hips were in line with the knees of her seat mates—making more room at the back for their hips. On the aisle seat one's sitting structure hung over, feet were stepped on, and one had to get up to let seat mates out. In fact, from experimentation, Laura had concluded that on a crowded bus there was no good place to sit so you might as well just sit down. Tying a scarf to keep her hair from being blown, as there was no glass in the windows, she settled herself firmly into a seat and hung on to the bar of the seat in front.

She observed the driver in his uniform of short sleeved khaki shirt with frayed collar and pants with neatly patched knees and recognized him as her "regular." The steering wheel was wrapped in tape, and he wiped it frequently with a rag to keep his sweaty hands from slipping as he confidently guided

the bus on a swaying course between and around other competing buses, jeepneys, pedestrians, and *calesa,* the little car-
riages drawn by small horses reminiscent of Spanish times. With
few stop lights, the right of way goes to him who dares. This
driver dared. But he kept a sharp eye for possible customers.
Laura had never been able to figure out the Filipino sign for
getting a bus to stop. There was no apparent motion, a person
could even be looking in another direction but somehow the
driver would know that here was a passenger, and he rarely
made a mistake. Laura felt she had to step out into the street
and wave to stop a bus.

The conductress, in her uniform of dark maroon skirt and
blouse, had a special relationship with the driver. They exchanged comments tantalizingly in Tagalog or some common
dialect. In her role as saleswoman, business manager, and public
relations representative for the enterprise she must be aggressive, helpful, and efficient. For your fare of ten centavos she gave
you a piece of paper torn from a pad with a quick twist of her
thumb.

Laura learned the first day to hang onto her ticket even
though it was not collected as passengers left the bus. Part way
downtown an inspector had come on board and examined each
person's slip. Laura didn't have hers, and a great argument en-
sued until she found it on the floor by her feet.

As they turned from Quezon Boulevard onto Espania the
middle stretch of pavement was elevated above the strips on
either side, and Laura began to concentrate on getting off, a
feat in itself. There was no rope to pull, you were supposed to
hiss or say *"Para!"* or whistle —this last usually came from helpful passengers. If all this failed she sometime futilely shouted,
"Stop, I want to get off!" An unfailing trick she had just
learned was to bang once on the side of the bus like the lady
conductor. But it did not make for popularity with the man-
agement. Yesterday, merely the first *"Ssssssssss"* caused a
screech from the brakes, and *wham* the bus came to a halt in the
middle of a block. Passengers hit the seats in front of them.
Feeling guilty at having caused this event, Laura got off and
walked to where she had intended to stop.

To avoid a repeat of this, she started her *"Sssssss–para"* a
little late. By the time someone whistled for her, the driver had
already swung the bus off the main pavement onto the side
street lined with textile stalls and choked with taxis. Sometimes
he would stop right there, or, stalled by the traffic, the con-

ductress would allow passengers off anywhere. But not this morning. Deaf to Laura's pleading he drove on down under the bridge to his turn-around place. There was nothing to do but walk back around and up to the main street and back to the place where jeepneys stopped.

Actually, jeepneys had no regular stopping places but about two blocks from the bridge they changed signs indicating their routes. Each driver took down the card for "Quiapo," reached into a box by the windshield and selected another sign. One never knew the basis for selection so every jeep must be watched till one read "Taft." If she stood near the bridge when the signs had all been changed, they were usually filled up; if she walked back to avoid the crowd, they had not changed the signs.

Jeepneys were originally U. S. Army jeeps abandoned at the end of World War II. The bodies had been extended to accommodate eight people on two seats facing inside. There was actually room on each seat for three and a half and it seemed to Laura that she was always the half. The drivers had expressed their personalities, theologies, and lifestyles in their vehicles. The old ones might be hung with a bunch of artificial flowers, a picture of St. Christopher in his boat—a most appropriate patron of jeepney drivers. A rabbit's foot might be added, or a painting of a peso from war times with "Victory" superimposed. The newer ones had bigger bodies and seated ten. The paint jobs were creative and gay, the metal parts polished. Love messages to Inez or Clara supplemented St. Christopher.

Laura didn't want to walk any farther than she had to on this hot morning so she took a chance on getting a seat and stood at the place just before the bridge. An old jeepney passed her up and a red and yellow one was next. The driver held up two fingers indicating the number of vacant seats and slowed down. Laura climbed the steps at the back holding tightly to the bar, knowing that before she was inside the jeep would be on its way, sure that some fine day she would be thrown into the street. Four people in a row moved a little closer to give her space. It was the knee hip arrangement again. Laura knew she would never be as good at jeepney travel as Filipinos. It must be something you were born with. The girls could climb the steps sideways in their tight skirts without holding on. They could give a swing of the hips and swish of the hand that arranged their starched skirts so that when they got up there was not a wrinkle. Laura could not overcome her dislike of being pressed by warm bodies. There was no space for her arm except touching the moist hot skin of the sleeveless arm next to her. The man facing her had longer legs than any Filipino should have, and there was no place for her knees except alternating with his. She endured the ride, and he got off at the post office. A block from the Normal School she opened her purse and found she had no centavos. In fact she had nothing less than a peso note. So she reached over the other passengers and handed the note to the driver over his shoulder. He took it but made no motion to give her change.

"My change?" she suggested. No answer.

"My change, please." This time more firmly. He gave no indication that he had heard her. Everyone in the bus looked at her. They were nearly at her corner.

"He haven't change," whispered the woman next to her. That was silly, this early in the morning with plenty of customers. Of course he has change. In a few seconds they would pass her stop.

"*Para!*" she commanded. The jeepney stopped, and the driver handed her back the peso. This was a crisis. She didn't want him to lose his fare; drivers made only four or five dollars a day, but she did not have the fare, and she had to get off. Everyone in the jeepney shared her embarrassment. The man closest to the driver offered him the ten centavos. No, no, others objected. Each one held out his own fare, which the driver collected, then counted out her change, dropping each coin with exaggerated care into her palm.

She left the jeepney feeling guilty. Had she misjudged him; didn't he really have change? Or was he trying to shame her, a rich American, into leaving the whole peso. The kindness of the other passengers added to her sense of inadequacy. It was a bad start to the day.

Being late, she ran across Taft Avenue and into the school building. Just past the office she slipped on the water that habitually oozed from the girls' toilet and fell on her left backside. Students passing looked the other way, suppressing giggles. This did not surprise her; by now she realized that if they didn't notice she too could ignore the incident and would not be shamed. She was not hurt but she had to place her hand in the puddle to get herself up, and the back of her dress was wet and dirty. In the teachers' washroom she managed to get in an awkward position and wash it out in the basin. There was no towel to dry with so she did what she could with the tissue in her purse. Her dress was print nylon and would soon dry.

Classes proceeded quietly with conferences on the themes Luz had corrected. Laura sat at the small table she had insisted be put at the back of the room after she found out Luz was quite unable to cope with the notion of team teaching. She found mistakes that Luz had missed, and worse yet she found some of Luz's corrections were in error. She wisely decided that in view of their present strained relations they should be overlooked. Four months ago she would have felt it was her job to call attention to them, but now her personal rapport was more important than improving the English language. I am being Filipinized, she thought, learning SIR: the Smooth Interpersonal Relations that they kept talking about in training. But prepositions seemed to be an insurmountable stumbling block. Before, after, in the middle of, next to, nearby—all of these were taken care of in Filipino by the word *sa*. This meant it was almost impossible to give or get directions. The inadequacies of that word were compensated for by, "I will accompany you." Luz was obviously shaky in this area, too, so between classes Laura suggested, "Do you think we might spend some time on prepositions of place, maybe like 'before,' and 'after,' and 'beyond.' "

"It would be all right," agreed Luz in a voice that meant: "Go ahead if you think it will do any good."

After an hour of illustrating, pointing, drill, Laura had to admit it had been a disaster session. She was thankful for the bell which rescued her from the intricacies of the English language.

Luz had been making excuses for a week for not going to lunch with Laura. Today she hesitated at the door as if waiting for Laura but Laura's nerves were frayed by the day's incidents, she didn't want to talk anything over. So she walked right by her and went on to join the cafeteria line. She could see on the tables ahead that *guinatan* was the main dish. It would be today, it fit. That was one Filipino dish Laura thoroughly disliked. The pieces of sweet potatoes, cassava, and *saba* floated in a sweet coconut gravy. It was always served lukewarm and tasted something like thin paste.

She left the line mumbling something about mailing a letter. She did have letters to mail as last night their household members had inspired each other to a writing stint and they were all out of stamps. Any post office business was always a trial. Someone pushed his way into the stamp window ahead of her. They were out of airgrams, out of seventy-centavo airmail stamps. The clerk slowly counted out for each letter two tens, one fifteen, one twenty, and three ones, which had been restamped to raise them to fives. Indignation bubbled nastily in Laura. *Can't they do anything right?* She applied the brakes. *Stop it, now just stop it. You are letting little things get to you.* On the way back she bought a banana from the fruit woman for two centavos and some boiled peanuts in the shell for four centavos. They were tasteless this way but nourishing.

The afternoon slid by. Consciously, she drew a comforter around herself, thinking, *Now nothing will touch you, you won't pay attention to mistakes—you won't even listen. English is a crazy language anyway, let them do what they can with it.* She shut out thoughts like, *then why did you come? If they are going to use English they should learn it right.*

Slowly the hands of the clock jerked toward three o'clock and the day was over. Gathering up her books and papers, Laura intended to slip out quickly, but Luz had other ideas. As Laura passed her desk with a perfunctory, "Good night" she said, "Shall we be talking about the themes?"

They had already talked about the themes but if Laura hadn't been in such an irritated mood she would have noticed that Luz was making an elaborate do about cleaning up her desk. Laura had learned that this meant she had something to say which had probably no connection with the opening topic. So they talked about the themes, they talked about chalk and how to get more. They talked about the weather, how it was getting hotter—which seemed to lead no place. Still Laura lingered. She knew by now that the importance of the subject Luz had on her mind could be measured by the length of the approach. But tonight she seemed to get no nearer to it until apropos of nothing she said, "Will your Dick be coming to Manila soon?"

"I don't know, he's taking orders for his drug company up around Baguio."

"Maybe business isn't too good."

"Well, he doesn't write, so I don't know." *Why this sudden interest in the drug business?*

"Manila is better for Americans."

"Oh, some like it out of the city."

"The mountains get cold at night."

Oh, for goodness sake, Luz, why can't you tell me what you're getting at? Nothing for it but to play along. "Some, I guess."

"And trouble up there."

"Around election time there was, I didn't know about any now, do you?" Maybe she could smoke her out.

"Many troubles in the mountains. Tomorrow we give the test."

"Yes," agreed Laura surprised. Evidently Luz thought she had conveyed her message, the conversation was closed, and they both started for home.

Now what was that all about, Laura wondered as she caught her jeepney. She scarcely noticed the crowding as she went over the conversation hunting for clues. Obviously, Luz thought Dick should not be wandering around Mountain Province. Did she want him here to amuse Laura, or Isobel? Or did she have a friend in a competing drug business? How little she knew about her co-teacher, actually, except school and José. She must have been acting as a go-between, but whom was she between?

Laura got off the jeepney to change for a bus in Quiapo. It was more crowded than usual because she was late. She had to step over the garbage at the curb and go out in the street to see her Balara bus as buses were two or three abreast here and would often go by without pulling over to the curb. There it was —behind the red one, she waved, and someone pushed her. As she turned, annoyed, she saw her handbag was open. She almost grabbed the hand that was withdrawing her billfold.

"Stop!" she cried as he ran.

"Stop him! Thief!" She stamped her foot and yelled helplessly. People looked at her curiously, let the man through, and continued to pile on the buses.

Balara was now in front of her, and she got on, not knowing whether she could pay her fare. But she didn't care. She just had to get out of this place. Taking the first vacant seat, she searched her bag. Only the billfold was gone. In her change purse she had enough for the bus. The conductress was waiting.

"Somebody stole my billfold," she informed her angrily. No comment, no flicker of interest even. Probably she was used to this.

Only her billfold. She tried to remember what was in it. Not much money, she had that much sense, her old ID card from college, no loss, snapshot of the family, her mother's charge plate she had brought by mistake, and, oh yes, Phil's telephone number. Well, she wouldn't call him anyway but it had been kind of nice to know she could in an emergency. She snapped her purse shut with as loud a noise as it would make. She had been lucky so far, almost every other volunteer had had something stolen, many with much greater loss. But today—it just had to happen today with everything else.

On the trip out she tried to analyze her intense reactions. It was the uncertainty, the not knowing what was happening, the inability to cope with ordinary things sometimes. Eight times a day she would get on and off public vehicles, never being sure how to stop them. Not knowing why the driver didn't give her her change, feeling stupid when the passengers helped. The leaks in the toilets, which nobody fixed; English rules she couldn't explain. Then Luz trying to convey a message vaguely. Purse snatching, that was understandable. No one helping—that happened in all cities. But there was the added feeling that all the onlookers were a little glad, an American would never miss it. If you want to steal, choose an American, by all means.

Luz took her jeepney to Buendia without incident. She had done it so often it took no thought although she was late and had missed the driver who knew her. She had no trouble stopping one, in fact, made no effort at all, just stood on the corner, and the right one held up one finger and stopped. She enjoyed this ride, snuggled comfortably between a large soft woman holding a bulging string bag on her lap and a thin young girl with smooth warm, moist skin. Living all day as a dignified teacher among white starched uniforms, this human contact was cozy.

She was pleased with herself for having transmitted José's message to Laura so smoothly. Now she could tell José she had done it, Laura would tell Dick, and he would know José had warned him, and if he was as smart as Americans were supposed to be he would stick to drug selling and leave Filipino business to Filipinos. In fact, Luz felt better than she had in weeks about her own affairs. As for Laura, well, she'd better tend to her Peace Corpsing. Hopping off the bus, she walked the short block from the corner to her home. The baby ran out to meet her and hugged her knees. Picking him up, she fondly spanked his smooth bottom and carried him on her hip into the house.

"Mama, I'm home," she called in Tagalog.

The bus from Quiapo did not go around the UP quad-

rangle as usual. It stopped at the city reservoir and the conductress called "Dansvair." Everyone was off the bus before
Laura figured out that was "Transfer." She changed busses and
got off at her corner. She scuffed the thick gray dust of Ap-
picible Steet that puffed around her feet and did not notice the
bougainvillea splashing rose and violet on the flaking paint of
the house walls. She was just going to stay miserable.

Mona met her at the door happily. "My seestir is coming,
mum."

"Oh? When?"

"Today already, mum. She say our house beauteeful."

Laura looked at the matting floor, the garish walls, and
sank down in a termite-riddled rattan chair. "That's nice."

"I tell heem, mum, you are the nicest mum I evair worked
for!"

"Oh, Mona-you're-I'm-*thank you*." It was salve for the
scratches and bumps of the day.

26

Smuggling

Breakfast was the best meal of the day, the most like home. The volunteers were like most Americans, ubiquitous eaters, adopting or adapting easily to the seasonings and recipes of various peoples and places with some exotic exceptions. But breakfast habits are distinctly American and whether one's origin is Kentucky, Ohio, or Maine, breakfast is supposed to begin with orange juice. "Start the day with sunshine," sing the advertisements, and Americans do—there is really no satisfactory substitute. The volunteers allowed that papaya was good, rather like melon; that pamelos resembled grapefruit, except they were dry, with skin an inch thick; that the greenish, loose-skinned oranges tasted fine when you spit out the thousands of seeds and got the pulp loose from the tough membrane. But you couldn't squeeze them for juice: it would have taken three to make a small glass. After pay day they splurged and bought a small jar of Tang, and that was the nearest they came to the orange juice institution.

Dry cereal, which Americans invented and have expanded by hundreds of ingenious variations on the original themes of corn flakes and shredded wheat, is another tradition. Certain imitations, imported from England, could be purchased in the Acme market in Manila, but they were expensive.

Toast is a perennial stand-by. Hot, buttered toast, not by any means to be confused with the cold, hard crustless rectangles the British call toast. And not the limp, white bread that Filipinos always think Americans have to have. The Peace Corps girls diverged slightly at this point. Isobel pointed out that English muffins are "kosher" in New York. Laura leaned toward doughnuts, cake, not raised. And Martha, usually Spartan in her tastes, extolled the mouth-watering qualities of pancakes with maple syrup from Geauga County, Ohio. They agreed that there were also French toast, Danish pastry, corn bread, and blueberry muffins.

Now it had never occurred to any of the volunteers that toast was a nationalized item or that it would be hard to come by. But in a variety of Peace Corps kitchens all over the Philippines inventive talent was being directed to the means for making toast. Bread held on a fork over a gas flame was most unsatisfactory. It wouldn't stay horizontal so one corner was soon in flames while the other was soft and white. A piece of tin supported on four corners by small stones over a burner worked fairly well, or bread could be fried in a pan. After a few weeks, most volunteers gave up with regret and cultivated a taste for substitutes.

Laura was very popular at the house on the campus because the Williamses had lent her an old electric toaster, the kind that was an inverted V shape with side doors which swung up and held the bread against red hot wires. It did come out toast if lovingly watched.

Bacon was very fat, thick-sliced, and expensive. Ham and sausage were unavailable, which left eggs. No one inquired as to their freshness, no one sniffed suspiciously as they ate them about twice a week at a peso a dozen.

"Mona, where's Diego these days? He hasn't been around," Isobel inquired as she peeled an orange.

Mona put the bowl of scrambled eggs on the table before she replied, "Hiss 'n jail, mum."

All eating stopped.

"In jail!"

"What for?"

"How long?"

Mona wiped her hands on her skirt and took her time. "Dey fine pessos een hiss jipney. PiCi say hi smuggles them to de sheep."

"P. C., what's Peace Corp got to do with . . ."

"Philippine Constabulary, Mart, for cripesake."

"Did he?"

"No, mum."

"Then why . . ."

"Dey fine dem unner da floorboards of hiss jipney."

"Did he put them there?"

"No, mum, he rent hiss jip."

"Then why?"

"Hi eess knowing who deed."

"But what do you gain by smuggling pesos, they're only worth what they're worth."

"Dey seelvair, mum."

It took some time and digging to get the story straight. Mona's explanations seemed unusually confusing. But finally the main outlines came clear. Before 1953 ten, twenty-five, and fifty centavo pieces were minted out of silver. Now they were alloy. So the old coins could be sold in Hong Kong for more than they were worth as currency. One night when Diego was driving late, two men had boarded his jeepney and told him to go to the wharf, Pier 5. This was not his usual route but he was willing to go anywhere for a few extra pesos. As they approached the wharf, four uniformed men came from behind piles of steel girders and ordered him at gun point to stop. Before the men surrounded the jeep his passengers had melted into the jungle of crates and steel. The policemen ripped up the floor boards and there to Diego's astonishment (according to Mona) were boxes of "seelvair" coins, bound for a Norwegian freighter, so they said.

"Norwegian freighter!" exclaimed Martha, "I read about it in the *Manila Times* last night."

"About Diego?"

"About a freighter smuggling coins. I'll get it."

They all huddled over the columns headed

RP COINS SEIZED FROM SHIP

Customs authorities intercepted an estimated P70,000 worth of Philippine silver coins on board the Norwegian freighter which docked shortly after 10 A.M. yesterday at Pier 5, from Cebu.

Packed in 10 wooden cases lined with tin plates, the coins were in 10-20 and 50 centavo denominations.

"But that ship was bringing them in not out," Laura objected.

"I didn't say it was the same ship," Martha defended her find, "but if they could pick them up in Cebu, they could pick them up in Manila. Read on."

The ship's officers admitted before the customs authorities that the ten cases were not manifested. They said the cases were loaded in Cebu by four unidentified men who, the officers said, claimed the cases contained seashells.

"It's probably a ring. They're collecting them from all over the country."

Mona had lost the stage. She retrieved it by going to her room and coming out with her clipping of three days earlier. The girls were surprised. Mona never taxed her sixth-grade reading skill by reading the paper. She must have been looking for this. Laura read aloud,

Philippine silver coins worth P5 million were smuggled out of the country last year by a syndicate headed by a Chinese national in connivance with government personnel. Silver coins are collected by members of the syndicate called "collectors" made up of aliens and Filipinos in the Luzon area.

The coins are shipped on certain inter-island vessels bound for the south, like Cebu. Members of the syndicate escort the coins.

From the south, the coins are then put secretly on foreign vessels bound for Hong Kong, the report stated. Philippine coins demand a high rate of exchange in the crown colony.

The collectors are paid a bonus of from P15 to P30 depending on the amount of coins collected. The report stated that at least four gasoline stations and five transportation firms had sold to the syndicate P500 worth of coins.

Skipping over the rest, Mona was corroborated; it was all there.

"Have you been to see him?"

"No, mum."

"How did you know about it, from the paper?"

"Oh, no, mum."

"How, then?"

Mona disdained to answer. Anyone should know that when your man was in jail someone would tell someone who would tell someone who would tell you. And it wouldn't take twenty-four hours to do it.

"Can't you raise bail?"

"No, mum," scornfully.

"But, Mona, you don't seem to be worried," observed Laura.

"No, mum, hi get out."

"Get out —escape?" hopefully suggested Isobel.

"Hi ees knowing who did eet, dey get heem off."

"Well, if he knows who did it and he's getting the blame he should report them." Martha spoke like the law-abiding citizen that she was.

Mona sadly shook her head at how difficult it was to explain things to these teachers.

"Now hi work for de hold-uppers at de dock."

"But they were police."

"One PC, mum, tree dressed like."

"Jeepers, this gets better and better, highjacking, huh? In police uniforms. Who arrested him then?"

"The one."

"What a set-up!"

"Gosh, I'm late." Laura ran for the door, a piece of toast in her hand.

Smuggling became a consuming interest at the PCV house. It was not only its novelty as a common crime, it was the attitude of the Filipinos toward it which they could not grasp. It was rather like watching a kaleidoscopic sporting event at which you selected sides you rooted for at random. They found themselves joining in the fun. Newspapers daily provided fuel to feed the flames of their interest.

Martha followed the cigaret smuggling most avidly. As she did not smoke herself, she took a kind of righteous satisfaction in seeing people make money out of other people's weakness. The fact that that put her on the side of the law breakers didn't seem to matter. Bold headline flashed in the *Manila Times*,

SMUGGLING LOSS IN TAGBILARAN REVEALED

Tagbilaran, Bohol - The alleged suspicious loss of ten cases of assorted blue seal cigarets for sale at public auction has been revealed by a ranking Bohol revenue official.

He disclosed that of the sixty-four cases of smuggled cigarets turned over by Camp Dagohoy only fifty-four cases were accounted for during the auction sale.

This was marvelous, everyone who had handled them was involved some way, but no one to really pin it on. Martha read

on and reread but could not figure out what actually happened.
Another, bigger headline had Isobel reading every word.

CLARK BASE USED FOR SMUGGLING

Philippine and American authorities have begun a crackdown on smuggling through U. S. bases, it was learned, as the first concrete case came to light yesterday.

A large shipment of watches was brought into the country aboard a U.S. 13th Air Force plane that landed at Clark Air Force Base highly placed sources said yesterday.

WATCHES HELD

The shipment, consisting of more than 2,500 men's and ladies' watches, was impounded by Filipino and American authorities at the base.

The shipment was discovered in various hiding places inside the C-47 which was used by ten JUSMAG officers, headed by a lieutenant colonel, who came from Hong Kong.

Goods are smuggled from U. S. base post exchanges or are brought in by planes which touch at foreign places like Hong Kong, Tokyo, Bangkok, and the United States.

In the case of the watches, it was not immediately known whether it was the plane crew or the passengers who brought in the shipment.

"We're all in it," Isobel gloated, "U.S. pilots, JUSMAG, and Filipinos."

"What's JUSMAG?" asked Martha.

"U. S. Military Advisory Group, I forget what the 'J' is for."

Laura let those things slide by, but the coin smuggling stuck with her. She noticed things that had seemed like insignificant isolated events before. The woman at the *sari-sari* store carefully looked over the change she was about to give her and once took a ten centavo piece out and substituted another. Diego was out of jail in a week, and Mona asked if she could have her pay in coins. This they indignantly, firmly, or laughingly refused, each reacting in character. One of her students said he was collecting old coins and asked her to save any before 1953. Also, it seemed to Laura that coin smuggling should be connected with the gold smuggling Dick seemed to know about.

Probably only because they were both metals, she scoffed at herself. Gold was not in the headlines anyway. She wanted to find out what José knew about it but her only way was through Luz, and Luz was all school business these days. She never referred again to Dick's whereabouts, and Laura was still mystified by her sudden interest and disinterest. Dick had not returned to Manila, at least he had not come to see her.

Besides the regular smuggling stories there was the lurid Stonehill, an American, and Peter Lim case to keep the news exciting. That was a grand mixture of graft, bribery, politics, big business, deals, and murder.

"Crime, you name it, it's got it," Isobel summed it up. Under a headline: MORE ON STONEHILL "BLUE BOOK" LIST there was a list of prominent people, supposedly implicated.

Glancing down the list, Isobel exclaimed, "Wong! Isn't that the name of that Chinese family we met in the cemetery?"

"Yeah, but every third Chinese is named Wong," said Laura. Nevertheless she added the item to the other little worries that were collecting around Dick.

The frustrating part of smuggle-watching was that they never knew how any particular case came out. There might be arrests, bail would be supplied, trial set, a great many indignant words spread over the incident, then it vanished from the news, replaced by the latest crime. Were smugglers ever really tried and convicted, they wondered.

When the *Free Press* came out with a long expose headed, WHO WILL POLICE THE POLICE it was good for an evening's rap session with other PCVs in Manila. They picked it to pieces.

It's the same in the U. S. . . . who here hasn't had a parking ticket fixed? You know it's not that bad at home . . . We've all been robbed of something . . . Nobody reports purse-snatching in New York either.

"Listen, this is really different,"

All over the country Policemen have been charged with attempted rape, theft, swindling and perjury. Some have been accused of physical injuries, abuse of authority, maltreatment, violation of domicile and threats.

"It's the pattern not the exception."

"But where would you stop the circle? Criminals pay police, police pay politicians, politicans pay for votes, voters expect favors, politicians get funds from Chinese . . . "

"There, you see it all ends up with Chinese."

"Now you're talking like Filipinos, using Chinese for scapegoats."

"Well, look at the Lims and the Wongs and . . . the Garcias, and the Lopezes and the Castellos . . . and the Stonehills and the Brooks and the U. S. bases."

And that's where they left it. Deep inside, Laura kept asking, "Where is Dick?"

27

Chinese Food and the
President Cleveland

Across the small red lacquer table, Laura and Phil smiled at each other. Laura smiled because of this blessed relief from Peace Corps talk and because a relaxed, safe sensation was gradually enveloping her. It was as if she had been swimming in deep water and had come upon a raft, a temporary respite, but welcomed. Phil smiled because he had left the affairs of state in the Embassy and was fast losing his tensions in the depths of the gray-flecked eyes opposite him.

He had sent Laura an invitation by mail for dinner and to watch the sailing of a President liner. Undaunted by having received no reply, he had thoughtfully taken a taxi to the campus and called for her. She was ready in a state-side sleeveless dress of mint green that gave the illusion of coolness —and illusion was all that she could offer in that line. She might have phoned a reply from the hospital to his office, having heard of Mart's tricks, but it didn't seem necessary. He would come. She was a little surprised at the form of entertainment he had suggested. Her father used to tell about going to the station as a boy to watch the Chesapeake and Ohio trains come in, and told of the thrill a train whistle always gave him. No one she knew watched airplanes take off unless there was a friend aboard, and certainly there was no excited audience for the departure of a bus. So why for a ship? As a land-locked Kentuckian she had never seen an ocean liner come, go or stay, but if it was worth a written invitation it must be worth seeing.

The Dragon House was enchanting. Of course she had eaten in Chinese restaurants in the States but they were without atmosphere. Perhaps a square lantern with gilt paper and tassels hung over the cashier's desk but that was about all. The tables often had once-white cloths now spotted beyond detergent salvation with soy sauce and tea. The menus were greasy and bent. But if one got a peek into the kitchen it was always immaculate, at least that was the way it was in the places frequented by students in Midland College. But the bowls of chicken chow mein, sweet-sour pork, shrimp chop suey were delicious and cheap. She assumed they were authentic Chinese but tonight she learned better.

The waiter was at her elbow handing out a steaming washcloth held in tongs. At her astonishment Phil laughed, "Wash before you eat."

"Ouch!" She took a corner and dropped it on her plate. Phil took his warily and began to rub his hands as if they were really dirty. The man at the next table was wiping his arms, face, and neck. Laura could hold hers now. "How refreshing," she exclaimed, "after hot, dusty Manila. Who thought this up?"

"These Chinese, vely crever people." Phil and the waiter shared the joke. "We'll start with shark's fin soup, that's a sign it is going to be a banquet."

The dinner consumed two hours of gastronomical pleasure, suspicion, exploration, and delight. When Laura could get her mind off the food, she told Phil about their new interest in smuggling brought on by Diego's arrest.

"Doesn't anybody try to stop it? Really stop it, I mean."

"Oh, yes, everyone is against the smuggling other people do. Haven't you seen the postage cancel 'Stamp Out Smuggling'? But as long as it is profitable, it simply cannot be policed. These seven thousand islands, you know, all with beaches on which boats can land."

"Why, it's like a game."

"Right—the favorite outdoor sport, next to cock fighting which is also illegal, except on Sunday."

"I'm glad you didn't ask me to go to that."

"Couldn't, too many American tourists there and I can't risk my reputation being seen with Peace Corps."

"Wretch!"

"That's the way you talk about me."

"I do not — I'm *here*."

"Well, your friends do."

"No, honestly, the PC gang thought you were quite decent for a diplomat—atypical, of course," she teased.

"By the way," he picked carefully at the bones of a stuffed fish, "is he still up north?"

"Yes, selling drugs," replied Laura firmly, not noticing that no name had been used.

"I just thought of him—don't look now—because over to your right against the wall is Mr. Valera, whom we met at the cemetery."

A moment later Laura casually glanced that way and was embarrassed to find the man looking at her. He half rose and nodded in a courtly way.

"He remembered me," she exclaimed in a whisper.

"Of course, that's part of his talent."

"Does he smuggle?"

"Oh, not personally. Smoothes the way for the rest of the family probably. But he's really a great guy. I asked some old Philippine hands about him. His grandparents left China about the time of the great migration to Formosa in the eighties. One branch of their clan came to the Philippines. Almost everything they owned had been sold or stolen during a famine. They started new, as so many thousands have in the countries around the rim of China. First a tiny shop in front of the shack where they lived. Every member of the family working from dawn—before dawn to dark, living on rice and bits of fish or half rotten vegetables they could salvage. But slowly expanding, a few more goods for sale, another shop, lending money to a Filipino who wanted to have a fiesta and when he couldn't repay, taking his shop.

"The next generation built on what the first had established. They had learned the tricks Chinese have to learn to make a go of it. Valera's mother was chosen by the family to step up to a new level of influence by marrying a promising Filipino. The family made him rich, his sons are Filipino citizens and now are in solid both politically and financially. This Valera is educated—Harvard Business School—sharp, and a Catholic. But more than that. He has been brought up on tales of the glories of old China in the days of the emperors. He dreams, so they say, the old imperialist China dream of hegemony over Southeast Asia."

"Does that make him sympathize with Communist China or Nationalist?"

"That's where information stops and rumor takes over. The family of Wong had banking interest in Formosa long before Chiang and his crowd made it in Taiwan. Rumor says he supports the old-line Formosans who are just waiting for a chance to overthrow Chiang. The farmers have prospered under the new regime and are buying the land from the former landholders. But the city Formosans have been shouldered out of control. But rumor also says that his family took over a profitable business when the Japanese were defeated, that he hates Japanese and is helping the Huks in the Philippines."

"You lost me, I thought Huks were communist."

"Not originally. Another angle is that his ships carry on a thriving trade between Shanghai, Hong Kong, Taipei, and San Fernando."

"Isn't that up near Baguio? Does it have a port?"

"A good one and not many alert customs inspectors." That took them back to coin smuggling. "Small potatoes," Phil dismissed it. "Serves to sort people out for the big jobs—he's coming over, don't mention Dick."

Laura looked up when Mr. Valera paused by their table and said, "Good evening, Miss Mathews, and Mr. Thomas. Are you enjoying your dinner?"

She smiled at him. "Oh, very much indeed, so many things new to me."

"Passable Chinese food," he conceded, "slightly westernized. Perhaps sometime you would do me the honor of serving you North China food in my home."

"Oh —well —I —thank you," she stammered.

"It would be better than in the cemetery." He laughed easily, Phil and Laura joined in and with a bow he moved on.

After he was out the door Laura said, "Now why on earth would he ask me to his house, I'd be scared to death. Did he mean it?"

"I expect so, just being nice to a foreigner, I think." But that was not what Phil really thought. In fact, he did not like the idea at all, so he shut it out of his mind.

"We've had the last course, shall we go? The ship doesn't sail till midnight with the high tide, but it's fun to watch the people."

"No fortune cookies?"

"Oh, you midwesterner! I'll see if they have any." He called the waiter by snapping his fingers and asked about the cookies. The waiter smiled, spoke to another waiter who went to the kitchen and in a few moments returned triumphantly with a plateful of the three-cornered confections.

"They keep them specially for little girls from Kentucky," Phil teased her.

"I don't care, I think it's fun." She broke open one and read from the little slip of paper, " 'Long life and happiness.' Oh, they all say that."

"No, mine says, 'Be careful whom you eat with and don't

be seduced by a southern accent.' "

Laura flushed, broke open another cookie, " 'You will take a long journey,' that's better."

"OK, let's go watch other people go on a long journey." He called the waiter, and they had the hot towel treatment again and went out into the night, luminous from the moon bathing the earth in its second-hand light.

It was a short taxi ride to the pier where the *President Cleveland* was docked. They walked slowly along its white side. Laura's eyes followed the graceful curve of the prow up and up. "Enormous!" she exclaimed. "They don't look that big in the movies. And it's alive."

Phil was pleased with her surprise, and it was alive with lights in every cabin, the decks floodlighted and crowds of people on the dock, the gangplank, and the decks.

"Do you want to go on?"

"Can we? I'd love to."

As they walked up the gangplank her excitement mounted. Ships were different from buses, trains, and airplanes. They had dignity and grace, too. On board, she absorbed impressions of thick carpets, rich mahogany, gleaming white wood, and polished brass. It seemed like what she thought a luxurious nineteenth-century hotel would be—but compressed. The staterooms were compact, convenient. She would love to have stowed away in an upper berth. Phil picked up a menu in one of the dining rooms. There was only time for her to gasp at the array of courses and gourmet titles of the dishes. They took the elevator to the top deck and promenaded arm in arm.

"I've read about this," she said.

"This is how you start a shipboard romance," Phil explained.

As they returned to wharfside, Laura said, "That's a fun way to travel, I'll do it sometime. Next to going yourself it would be fun to be seeing someone else off. I'll tell you, you see me off."

"*No*," Phil said with more vehemence than seemed necessary. Then with a quick change he said brightly, "OK, we'll do it." He picked up an imaginary handbag, grasped her elbow, and steered her back to the gangplank, chatting, "Now, Aunt Tilly, the first thing you do when you get aboard is to go to the purser's office and reserve a deck chair, there are never enough to go around. Have you got your steamer rug? OK. Then sign up for the first table sitting, the second would be past your bedtime. Have you got your hot water bottle? Have a good trip." He handed her the "bag," took her chin in his hand, turned her face up, and touched her lips lightly with his. "Good-bye."

Before she could reply he was gone, and she was being moved up the gangplank by the on-coming crowd. At the top she stopped and turned to look back at the wharf. She was somehow shaken by the performance. He was suddenly so different, she didn't have time to play her part. Now he was nowhere to be seen. She felt very much alone. Maybe being "seen off" wasn't much fun if you were going alone.

The ship's bell clanged, over a loud speaker a voice announced, "All visitors please go ashore." People began streaming off, and she went with them. At landside she didn't know which way to turn and hesitated.

Behind her a deep voice exclaimed, "Cousin Jane!" Strong hands gripped her shoulders and swung her around into a breathtaking bear hug and a hearty smack on the mouth.

"Imagine seeing you here," Phil exulted with gusto. "Don't look so startled at your own kissin' cousin."

She pushed him away. "You play games hard."

"It's your game, you suggested it, I'm just a realist." He was very gay, effervescent, even. She had never seen him this way.

"Look, gangplank going up." Suddenly paper streamers were thrown by passengers on deck to those on the wharf, red, blue, yellow, pink.

"Oh!" she gasped in delight, "where did they come from?"

"The stewards pass them out. Grab one."

She picked up the end of a pink one dangling in front of her and waved excitedly.

"Whom are you waving at?"

"That nice old man with the cap and red coat; he doesn't have anyone to say good-bye to." The man changed a scowl to a smile and she threw him a kiss.

Phil picked up a roll of paper that had landed unopened at his feet and threw it up to second deck. Hands reached for it, and it was caught with shrieks of delight by a comely Filipina in a yellow suit. Phil waved with both arms.

"Who is she?"

"Just last year's Miss Universe. You can have your old man."

The stately liner was moving slowly away from the pilings. The strip of water between land and ship widened, the streamers broke. "Good-bye —*bon voyage*—so long —" voices rose and fell. The short throaty blasts of the hardworking tugs were joined by high whistle of the ship.

As they watched the slow glide of the majestic vessel headed for the high seas, Laura gave a long satisfied sigh. "Beautiful. I wish I'd stayed on it."

"*No*." There was the same vehemence in Phil's voice close to her ear. She moved away slightly.

"Phil, I want to go to Pier Five."

"Why?"

"Just curious."

"Those piers for freighters are no place to be at night," he said firmly.

"Smugglers, you mean?"

"I mean everything. All the underlife of the city comes alive and gathers at the waterfront at night."

"Then I'll . . .

"No, you won't. You're a sensible grown woman who doesn't run around doing ridiculous things and worrying people just for curiosity."

She wasn't sure whether that was a compliment or a put-down, but she melted because she knew she would never go by herself. It was kind of nice to be told off so firmly.

"Some day, in broad daylight, I'll take you to North Harbor where things really happen, the unscheduled vessels load. Now I'll take you home, like a good PCV."

28

Smugglers' Threats
and Church Sanctity

It was fortunate that Phil and Laura did not explore the North Harbor docks that night, although the thought rankled in Laura's mind for months, what if they had? What if they had seen a man wildly running from the water's edge? Probably run themselves to a main street and a taxi and home. What if they had arrived sooner? Things would surely have turned out differently, maybe for the worse, though for a time she thought there could be no worse.

Beyond the freight piers where the harbor was shallow and even small ships could come in only at high tide, a boat rode at anchor. It was small with only one funnel and no gleaming white paint, one of the hundreds of nondescript inter-island boats.

It settled low in the water as it was already loaded except for a pile of small wooden boxes on the wharf close to the hold. A man was bending over them examining shipping labels in the light of the moon.

At the sound of a step behind him, Dick straightened up and spoke as he recognized the man in a cap and turtleneck sweater. "Oh, it's you, Mr. Vergo."

"What the hell are you doing here?" was the harsh greeting.

"I just wanted to see a loading," said Dick. "But I don't understand, these boxes were to go to Taipei, I was told, on a Liberian freighter. Now they are marked for Hong Kong, and this ship isn't Liberian, I can't tell what it is."

"None of your damned bus . . . ." the man began and then changed his tone. "The Liberian ship didn't come in and we were able to get this one."

"But Hong Kong."

"Yes, yes, that's where the boat goes first, then they will be rerouted. Nothing for you to worry about, nothing at all." He took Dick's arm chummily and eased him nearer to the side of the ship.

"They're my boxes," Dick said stubbornly. "I have a right to know where they go."

"Yes, your boxes and we're grateful. Boxes are hard to get. We appreciate your cooperation, but that's *all* you have to do, my boy."

Dick stiffened at the patronizing tone and jerked his arm away. "You know what I'm in this for, and I'll not . . . "

A sound made him look up to see a shadow moving along the deck above them. It jumped, carrying Dick down to the planks of the wharf. With a swift twist, which he had learned on the football field, Dick was on top, but he did not get a firm grip. The man slid between his legs and dragged him down. Dick was taller and heavier but the man was slippery like an eel. They rolled near to the edge of the dock before Dick wrenched himself free. He saw the knife as it lunged at him. With a quick dodge he was behind his boxes, but the knife caught him on the shoulder.

Now he ran. Ran as he had never run for a touchdown. Both men had disappeared, and no one followed him. He didn't know where he was running to except away from the waterfront toward the squatters' shacks.

Dashing around and between the hovels, he stumbled over cans, dodged a yapping dog, scarcely realizing that he was heading for the spire of a small chapel. When he reached it, the double wooden doors were locked. He followed the wall around the corner, and a shaft of moonlight showed him another door, a rickety one that could not withstand his desperate shove.

In the dark he sank into a bench and felt his shoulder for the first time. It was wet. He touched his fingers with his tongue. He had not tasted blood since that time he fell on a can in the alley behind the apartment house in New York and cut his lip. Now he was conscious of pain. Stabs, reaching out from his shoulder, down his arm up into his neck. As his eyes adjusted to the dark he looked around. Moonlight filtered through the stained glass window high above the altar.

It had been a long time since he had been in a Catholic church, or any other kind. Some frayed remnant of his mother's early training had brought him to this perfect refuge.

That was what people always used churches for. To keep alert,
he looked at the side walls and followed the images of the stations of the cross he knew must be there, a touch of dim light
on a face, a hand. Back to the window. It was dimmer now —
blurred —he couldn't focus on the panes —black.

29

Why?

Pale light in an oblong shape —deep set in a frame of thick gray wall. No altar. A fly crawling slowly across murky glass. Streaks of dirt that ran down the wall to a concrete floor. The floor grew spikes in pairs of two —and two —and two. Follow the spikes up —slowly —beds!

Beds! Dick opened his eyes wider and turned his head slightly. The movement connected with a groan. His own voice? He felt a hand laid lightly on his forehead and a warm breath near his face. The face blurred, wavered, stood still, became straight nose, light smooth cheek, a mouth, nice mouth, lips parted. That's where the breath came from. Ears, little ears, brown hair scooped around them. He was beginning to know as he carefully moved his gaze to the eyes. Eyes that had two drops forming at the corners. It was!

"Dick, Dick," the lips whispered, "it's Laura."

She didn't have to tell him. He took a deep breath, and it hurt so he shut his eyes and let himself float, suspended in some place, some time, between then and when he would have to know *now*.

Actually it was some days before Dick was able to put together the then, the now, and the in between. Pieces of the puzzle were supplied by the priest who had found him and taken him to the Manila General Hospital, the nurse and the doctor who had received him, Laura, who had word of his whereabouts by means of a circuitous route she was never able to trace. But some pieces would always be missing. His stab wound was not deep but it had become infected, and the loss of blood while he ran had left him weak and unresponsive to treatment. He was in a charity ward of eight beds in the fifty-year-old hospital built at the beginning of the American occupation. All attempts at cleanliness by modern standards failed under the weight of relentless time, accumulation of dust and mold, inadequate scrubbings, peeling paint, and timid whitewash.

That first day, when Laura got the message by way of a jeepney driver (not Diego) to come to the hospital, she had found José waiting in the front lobby. Signs read, "Visiting Hours, 2-4 P.M., 7-8." This being four o'clock, she hesitated. But José, with a nod to the girl at the desk, led the way around an open court, down a hall. At the door of a ward a man squatted. José dismissed him with a word in Ilocano, explaining casually, "I hire him to watch, mum." Just inside the door Laura stopped. Dick lay in the first bed, pale and still, his red hair a tangled mass on the gray pillow. She had never seen him quiet, certainly never helpless. The whole room felt like a soiled army blanket smelling of urine and Lysol, and Laura's first impulse was to get him out.

"Can't we get him moved? The bed—I mean the sheets, well, the . . ."

"We see the head, mum," said José competently.

So down the hall he had taken her, opened the door marked "Superintendent" and ignoring a roomful of waiting people had knocked at the door of the inner office and entered. To the gentlemen seated at the desk he had introduced Laura and waited for her to carry it from there. Much embarrassed at having barged in obviously expecting special treatment, she explained the situation and apologized for bothering him about a patient's room problem.

But the superintendent seemed not at all surprised nor offended at the request and apparently knew all about Dick's case. He explained at length the policies of the hospital, the doctors, and the services, which to Laura seemed to have no bearing on the point at issue. The only part that came clear was "Who pays?" She couldn't answer so he graciously bowed them out. The door closed behind them and Laura stood still.

"I don't understand, José. I am sure Dick's family will pay when we inform them, but I can't."

"Mum," began José. In his earnestness, his Ilocano accent increased, demanding Laura's concentrated effort to cut through to what he was saying. "Di doktor triting heem pree, kase no-pay patient. Mum don' moob sir to pay room den doktor not trit heem. Free patient not having pay doktor. De doktor my ninong, mum. He not gib me present por Chreesmus so I say, 'You triting sir pree!' So sir stay in pree ruum, mum."

Laura was completely vanquished by the flow of words. She was used to Luz's accent and had long ago ceased consciously translating it. But José's cadence and rhythm were different.

"Thank you —a —could you say it slower for me?"

This time she gathered that free doctoring went with a free room. Dick had already had free treatment from José's godfather so he should stay where he was. She stumbled over her thanks, overwhelmed by the care and thoughtfulness at the hands of José who did not even approve of Dick. Things began to fit together.

"The man you hired to stay at the door?"

"From my province, mum."

She knew by now that was supposed to explain everything.

The days of recovery passed quickly but mysteries multiplied. A huge basket of flowers was delivered to Dick's room, yellow gladioli, pink roses, blue delphinium. They laughed at how they overshadowed the bunch of mixed painted daisies Laura had bought from a street vendor for fifteen centavos and stuck in a jelly glass. But Dick would not allow them to be removed even when their heads hung limp in the heat.

"Who from?" was Laura's natural question when she saw the flowers.

"No card."

"You must know, don't be so mysterious."

"No card," was all he could say.

"I get clean pj's every day," he announced happily the third day as he sat cross-legged on his cot. "Others don't."

"That's discrimination," Laura reproved firmly.

"I know it, but I didn't ask for them," which obviously absolved him from blame. The next day, "A nurse from another floor brings me extra food," he confided.

"Why, for goodness sake?"

"It took a while to find out. Seems the nurses can buy food at the canteen, and the head nurse on that floor is a cousin of Mona's aunt."

It was another thread in the web they both felt drawing around them, protectively, inexplainably. Laura rather resented it at first with her rugged pay-your-own-way take-the-consequences-of-your-own-acts kind of Puritanism. But Dick happily accepted any special service that came his way.

"It's the system, don't knock it. I can't figure out why I'm in it but they must have their reasons. So once you're *in* the thing begins to work. There's a pattern to the web but we can't see it."

"I suppose it's a substitute for social security."

"Oh, sure." Dick had figured that out long ago. "In some ways it's better. But hampering, too. Now I suppose if any one of these people ever asks me for a favor or needs help, I am bound to give it come hell or high water."

"Yeah, only you have to give more on account of you're a rich Americano."

As his wound healed and his strength returned they had long talks. But Laura's many questions were never fully answered to her satisfaction. What was he doing on the pier? Who was Mr. Vergo, also on the pier? Who had it in for him, and what was he going to do about it? Finally she cut right through protective wrappings to the dark suspicion she had been keeping under cover for months.

"Are you involved in smuggling?"

Dick turned on his side toward her, folded his hand firmly over hers as it lay on the bed. "Laura, my dear, I want you to understand —at least as much as I can tell you. I don't know it all myself, less than I thought, I guess, since I don't know who jumped me that night nor why. You know my concern for the Formosans." He felt her hand stiffen within his. "No, I'm not being sentimental about the downtrodden and oppressed. Now try and really listen and don't close your mind. I love my country. Oh, I beef a lot as we all do, and I complain and belittle. But I know, deep down inside, that we've got something, something precious that most people want. Even maybe if they don't know they want it —a country of our own and the chance to manage it. Now Filipinos know the value and security of a family, of a tribe, of a barrio. There's even the larger more impersonal unity of a province even though they don't really control it. But a nation! That's a whole big piece of real estate with different kinds of country in it and people, some of them don't even know each other. But all together they own that land, that is a nation, that has an identity. Now José and other students are beginning to realize this, they want more power to run their own country, without the paternalism of Big Uncle.

"When I was in high school the history teacher harped on the idea that the day of nationalism had passed —or should.

"Its time has passed in Europe—only they don't know it. But it's just beginning in most of the world. So OK, it doesn't make sense for every little group of Africans to get together, design a flag, think up a name, call themselves a nation, and get admitted to the UN. That's how the U. S. felt about the Filipinos when we bestowed upon them the honor of our good government! Now that's just what Nationalist Chinese have done for the Formosans."

"Who are also Chinese."

"Yeah, sure, but they had the feeling of being a people — that's what they told me in New York. Then came Chiang Kai-shek and his crowd and now they don't have a country."

"Weren't they under Japanese rule before that?"

"Yeah, yeah, always under someone."

Laura controlled her impatience with the circuitous route he was taking to answer her question because she sensed he was showing her himself, not the bantering, preaching, grand-standing Dick but the boy-man with a purpose. He closed his eyes for a few minutes and then went on.

"So I joined the Peace Corps. Maybe it didn't lead directly to Formosa but I was sure there were Filipinos, too, who felt as I did. Then the PC wouldn't have me. So I came anyway." Long pause this time.

"There are things going on here, a restless undercurrent below the layer of Americanization. Below the radios blaring rock, the English-speaking press and school, the democratic-styled government, rotten to the core. Beneath the protective, maternal system, the neat white shirts, the painted toenails, the blue seal cigarettes and the whole crust of imported sophistica-tion and privilege, there's something yeasty. And I'm in touch with that underneathness, only I'm not sure what or who it is."

"Mr. Valera?"

"He's above it all but holds the ends of a lot of strings which he pulls and accomplishes what he wants. He has never asked me to do a single thing —but he's here."

Dick glanced at the flowers and back to Laura; yes, she knew.

"Mr. Vergo, the man I saw at the dock, was in the hotel in Baguio when I was there canvassing the company store at the gold mines to see if they'd carry my line. He spoke to me —as all Filipinos do to Americans —and took me to dinner. His son's at UP and he knows all about Peace Corps, and he knew I wasn't. Only later did it seem strange that he knew so much about me. I did get some orders; the stores have Chinese man-agers."

"Oh."

"Connection maybe? Maybe not. You get to imagining everybody knows everybody. You know, like that Chinese furniture store on Pin-a-Pin Street. I went in there to get a table for my apartment last week, and he asked about you and remembered we had seen him at the cemetery."

"Now the Great Drug Company sends me shipments of small quantities of things so I have some on hand for customers. Then when I get big orders —if I ever do —they'll come by freight, of course. The stores up around Baguio and further north always insist that I leave the box the things come in. They are good and strong, and you know how hard it is to get anything like that here so I didn't think too much about it except that it was good business to please my customers. Then it got to me that they were more interested in the boxes than in the contents. They kept ordering cough syrup, rubbing alcohol, heavy things like that, but only a few at a time. So I got curious and asked questions, and they were evasive. Just lately they made me feel by some comments they dropped that I was in on something and let me 'guess' they were using my boxes to ship something out of the country."

"Silver pesos maybe?"

"No, they make fun of that."

"Gold?" she whispered it.

"Could be, I don't know. That's what I went to the wharf for, to see if I could find out what they were shipping in my boxes and where. And I'll find out yet!"

"Even after . . ."

"Even after."

As he talked, a conversation she had had with Luz a long time ago came back to mind, Luz's questions about his being in the north and that Manila was better. She realized now that Luz had been giving her a warning that she was supposed to pass on to Dick. She never had. At that time she was too new, too unperceptive to identify the go-between function and the oblique way of conferring important messages.

A nurse glided in, noiseless on rubber soles, slipped a thermometer into his mouth, and took his pulse. Dick smiled at her lopsidedly. She blushed and tightened her lips.

While the nurse finished her duties in the ward, Laura tried to get the situation in focus but only one thing was clear to her.

"Dick," she tried to sound casual as she poured him a glass

of water. "You know you are being used."

"I know."

"But you don't care."

"Sure, I care, everyone cares about himself. But I want to help. I want to be a part of what is happening. Here, Formosa, anywhere people are stirring, are grasping for power that should be theirs —are searching for . . ."

"For what?"

"Don't make me say it, it sounds too corny, and it is so abused and smeared with greed and blood."

She said it for him, softly, "Freedom."

Swifly he pulled her down with his good arm and pressed his lips to hers, hard.

"Ready for supper?" sang a cheery voice with a tray.

30

Dick's Dilemma

Laura sat in a large chair of woven rattan in the Williamses' *sala* with her feet tucked under her. She had gone straight to them after her conversation with Dick, and by some miracle they were home for the evening. She had told them all she knew, counting on their discretion and counsel.

"Somebody's got to stop him," she finished, "he's in danger."

"Yes, he is," agreed Mr. Williams and then was silent for a long time while Laura waited impatiently for him to pledge help.

"Well, you know this country, you know the people, you could tell him to cut and run."

"No, I can't."

"Why not?"

"Because I wouldn't cut and run myself."

"But you're a missionary, you are —legitimate."

"Yes, I came to spread the gospel, by one means or another."

"Well, that makes it different, you have a recognized, respectable mission. You have support from people you can trust —I mean of course you don't cut and run —I mean . . ." Her voice trailed off helplessly.

"Once I would have if I could," he laughed sheepishly. "Maybe you didn't know that our family was interned in Santo Tomas by the Japanese, two thousand of us from all over Asia for three years. Strange things happen to people when they are confined and food gets short. I'll tell you the long story some time but the short one is what it did to me at sixteen. At first we kids thought it was an adventure, we played with a basketball we'd found in a closet. Then one day a kid kicked it and it began to leak. We nearly killed that kid before our fathers dragged us off.

"The Japanese had never taken prisoners before. They were amazed that we allowed ourselves to be taken alive, and they really didn't know what to do with us. They made no provisions for our needs so they let the Filipinos sell food to us.

"That was not too bad as long as our money and their food lasted. But as the occupation stretched out food was scarce for all. The Japanese provided a little but we never could have survived without what the Filipinos shared with us.

"The men had a strict system of distribution but we boys made a game of trying to get bits of extra for ourselves. We were victims of someone else's crime. We were being punished for something we didn't do, and I hated the Japanese. Maybe you can love your enemy if you can fight him but it's harder when you are totally within his power. I turned against the Filipinos, too, because they couldn't protect us from the Japanese. Only I loved those thin brown hands that shoved a kerchief full of rice under the gate. I'll never forget one old woman who would come with her blouse bulging with bananas. We boys would move along inside the fence till she was close enough to see her face. It was a funny face kind of shrunk up on one side with small eyes. She would stop, face the fence and call us names—and bananas would drop inside.

"But I was never going to come back to Asia, and I would have cut and run right then if I could have. I would stay in the U. S. which was rich and strong and could whip the Japanese or anyone else. But here I am. It was those hands, bringing what they had. So I've brought the only gift I have, the message of a loving saviour.

"Now Dick didn't need to be interned to appreciate giving and he has brought what is precious to him —himself—to be used for political freedom. His gift may be misused. He may lose, they may lose, they probably don't understand his gift. Does it matter? He, we, *you* have thrown in our lot with people we don't understand, some who don't want us, some who will take advantage of us. That's the chance we all take."

Mr. Williams's story and the sharing of his faith made Laura uncomfortable. No one she knew talked like that—out of the pulpit. She could not claim to have "thrown in her lot" with the Filipinos. She had no intention of risking her life for them, and she thought Dick was crazy to play fast and loose with his. She had to be honest.

"But, Mr. Williams, I'm just not—well—that dedicated. Peace Corps volunteers are a pretty hard-headed selfish lot, we make fun of the starry-eyed ones who say, 'We have a lot to give.' "

"Oh, sure, but if that was all there was to it you would be home enjoying the affluent life." He stopped her protest. "Anyway, the Filipinos have taken you to their hearts as they have not with any other Americans."

"Really?" Laura didn't feel that Luz had "taken her to her heart." They couldn't even talk together like friends. She had reduced all her great goals of increasing international understanding and the like to just that one thing, but she was failing and it hurt.

Mr. Williams was continuing. "Obviously you're different from other Americans. You live in houses like theirs, you ride public transportation, you know a little language."

"You speak better Tagalog than any of us."

"But I've been here a long time, so it doesn't surprise them. Short termers in church, diplomacy, or business seldom do, though the Embassy encourages it. But I honestly think," he laughed in a teasing kind of way, "that the reason they like you is because you don't expect anything of them. The Spanish came and changed their lives, religion, government, names. The Americans came and insisted the Filipinos learn representative government. That was great sport and they took to politics like ducks to water and colored it to suit themselves. The American army forced military discipline on them; businessmen came and made them work hard at regular hours and be on time; missionaries were helpful and kind but they took a lot of fun out of life by forbidding gambling, drinking, and fornication. But then came the Peace Corps, lively, young, singing, dancing, drinking, whoring—some of them—and they love you. You don't criticize."

"Well, I'm not so sure. We gripe a lot when we are by ourselves. We want to help but they never ask us, and a lot of us don't really know what to do."

"Oh, well, they haven't taken you in to be one of them because that would give you a right to change them. But they display you, you amuse them and give them prestige. And you will influence them too, though you may never see it yourselves. You, my dear, are fast replacing us as examples of good will and person-to-person concern."

"Do you mind—I mean—is that bad?"

"No, no, no, of course not. We old timers know our function better than that. How could there be too much goodwill spread around this aching world?"

Laura wanted to talk with him about Luz and a lot of other things, but it must be another time, they had come a long way from her present purpose.

"And Dick—he's different?"

"Yes, he's different. The selectors were right, he doesn't fit the Peace Corps. Anyone who goes to another country under government sponsorship, or any organization for that matter, has restrictions on his actions, certain areas he must stay out of, certain things he can't say. He is not a free agent."

"We volunteers resent that, and pretend it isn't so."

"I know, and you are freer than Embassy or army or even the church and just because of that PC will—has—made some bad mistakes until you learn to accept the fact that you are a foreigner and you can't speak to Filipinos as frankly as you do sometimes. But Dick is his own agent, will take his own risks, will make his own mistakes, and must take the consequences."

Laura left the Williamses quieted but as unhappy as when she went.

The next day Dick was dismissed from the hospital and returned to his apartment. Laura was glad there was less opportunity for intimate conversation. She didn't want to see inside of him anymore just now and longed for the return of a surface relationship. But she could not throw off the feeling of walking in a fog with no signpost to point directions and no one to ask. Isobel considered the whole thing an exciting drama, and she had pestered Dick for details until he told her to stay away.

Mart had a what-can-you-expect-in-a-country-like-this attitude, and she did everything she could to persuade Laura to avoid entanglement in Dick's troubles. Laura didn't want to talk to either one of them so she ate her meals in silence and felt uncomfortable under Martha's watchful eyes. With Luz she stuck strictly to school business. Luz gave no indication of how much she knew after her first apparently sincere expression of sympathy.

So there was no one, no one to talk to who might help her make some sense out of the situation. Except Phil. She had been avoiding him because she couldn't face a possible put down or belittling of Dick. But the need to get down to solid earth, to get her head out of the clouds of idealism, dedication, mission emanating from the Williamses and Dick overcame her reluctance. She needed some hard thinking on this, and it had occurred to her that Phil had access to a means for stopping Dick. So she made a point of seeing him.

They walked in the Lunetta, stopping in the thin shade of each little tree valiantly trying to cover the wounds the war had inflicted on the big public park.

"You could tell the Embassy he is here illegally," she suggested.

"They already know."

"You told them!" she exclaimed angrily, forgetting that that is just what she had suggested.

"I didn't need to. That is not in my department."

"Who then?"

"My dear girl . . . "

"Don't patronize me!"

"Then stop acting like a 'dear girl' and use your head. It is the business of Political Affairs to know everything Americans do in the Philippines which might affect relations between our governments."

"Which means?"

"Dick didn't come with the Peace Corps, he's an unregistered alien. The Philippine government has no record of issuing a visa, so . . . "

"*So* they deport him!" she supplied triumphantly.

"No, they keep him and watch him."

"The Philippine government? That's disgusting."

"The U. S. government, too."

"U. S., that's outrageous! You mean to stand there and tell me the U. S. government would stand by and watch him get himself into trouble? I thought it was the business of a government to protect its citizens."

"Protect! When he violated a law so he could get into trouble? My God, how sentimental can you be?"

"So you are not going to help, you are going to lecture me. You are worse than the Williamses. They wouldn't stop him because he had chosen to risk his life for a cause. You won't stop him because he chose to disobey a law for something he thought was more important, and the government thinks—I don't know what it thinks—if at all."

"Well, if you'll calm down a minute I'll try to tell you." He pulled her down on a bench under a tree. "Now listen."

"That's what everyone asks me to do, 'Listen,' and I do and it just gets worse."

Ignoring her petulance Phil began slowly. "The government of the Philippines is worried about a rise in terrorism in the north. They don't know how much is a resurgence of Huks with encouragement from the outside or how much is just local politics or bandits. José's dad among others insists it is the beginning of a real revolution. Anyway they are getting something valuable out of the country that provides them with funds. It's not just the ordinary kind of smuggling—cigarettes or silver coins. I told you about the gold that gets 'lost.' Well, a small amount they don't bother with but this is on the increase. OK, now Filipinos are very clever—with Chinese help—in evading the net of their own government. But a big dumb (pardon me) American full of good will, making friends and stamping around the gold mines just might get tangled up and lead the government to something. Now is that so indefensible?"

"Yes! Well, no, not for Filipinos but our government shouldn't let an American be used by a foreign government."

"Oh, no? What do you think you are being used for?"

"Nothing, absolutely *nothing*, we're non-political." Even as she said it she didn't believe it.

"Well, think again. The U. S. offered you to the Philippines to change the image of Americans. The Philippine government took you for window dressing and to counteract any swing to communism, especially on the campuses."

"They have no right . . . "

"Oh, yes they have. A government's whole duty is to protect the nation and promote well-being. It can draft men to fight for that, and it can train them to spy. In Dick they get a free and willing tool."

"How can you say such a terrible thing? No government has a right to make a person do what is against his conscience, and Dick is here to liberate men from the oppression of government—he says—in some way, anyway he's working against oppressive government and it's subversive, it's—it's wicked of government to try and get an advantage out of it."

She had been twisting her head scarf into a knot, now she gave it a jerk that ripped the flimsy fabric. "I came to you for help, I wanted . . . "

"Bread, and I gave you a stone."

"Now there's nobody to help him. Nobody cares a thing about him."

Phil picked up her hands, smoothed her fingers flat over the mangled scarf, and said softly, "You care, and that should be enough for him." He got up. "Come on, I'll take you to the bus."

She didn't want to go to the bus, she was not ready to go home. Angry and disappointed as she was, she knew when he left her she would be adrift again on her own troubled sea. But his face was set. He didn't look at all like the gay young man who had played games with her on the wharf. He was already two steps ahead and even his back looked stern. There was nothing for it but to go.

It was very lonely on the bus. She almost wished he had offered her a ride in that hated Embassy car.

31

Heat

April approached with a heavy breath that sapped energy and smothered purpose until about 9:00 in the evening when its weight lifted. Dust from the street coated shoes, sifted through the cracks along the window frames or blew in through the screens.

"I never heard of needing to brush window screens every week so you could see out of them," complained Martha, as she sat directly in front of the electric fan lent to them by the Williamses. "Somebody'd better whisk this fan out of sight if Lawrence drops in, it's a luxury."

"I'd bet he doesn't say a word, he's a good egg," Isobel soothed.

"Boiled or fried?" The heat was really getting to Mart.

"Come to the pool, it does help," Laura urged Martha.

"It's so hot walking over and back I can't see what good it would do."

"Well, just try it."

So she did. The university pool was open to non-students only on Sunday mornings. Mart came home after eight o'clock mass, put on her bathing suit with a dress over it and walked back past the chapel to the walled-in pool. The water didn't look very clean but she eased herself into it. It was a warm tub bath! She should have known. How could it be otherwise with the sun boiling it day after day. Still, it was enjoyable. How long it had been since she was wet all over at once with warm water. She moved around with a languid side-stroke. *Could you perspire under water,* she wondered. Floating about, she became the temperature of the water. Getting out, she laid a bath towel on the hot cement rim and stretched out. The slightly moving air on wet skin felt almost cool. When it was no longer cool she slipped back in the water, which now felt cool to her hot skin. Pleased with herself for having discovered the trick, she alternated, wet —warm —dry —hot —wet until she felt as limp as her towel. Isobel spent most of her time on the rim. For weeks she had been frying her carefully oiled skin until she was as brown as any Filipina. There were no Filipinas at the pool, Mart noticed. Some Filipino men and a few Thai students were making waves with a stroke she had never seen before, butterfly, Isobel explained. But apparently swimming was not a favorite sport of Filipinos with their thousands of miles of glistening beaches.

Martha wore her wet bathing suit home under her dress, thus extending the evaporation period. Mona looked at her disapprovingly when she came in.

"Weeman don sweem in de daytime any more ahctually," she pronounced firmly.

"Did they ever?" Then remembering that "any more" did not have the implication of a change of habit, "Why not?"

Mona would not answer. If mum didn't know that she shouldn't expose herself in public it wasn't up to Mona to tell her, and if she wanted to brown her precious white skin—let her.

Public schools would close April tenth. With the end in sight, Mart was pushing to get out one more magazine, Laura was anxiously preparing exams, but Isobel had already relaxed. She let her students get by with sloppy pronunciation as she was sure they would all slip back to normal anyway over vacation. Ramon would go to the province for vacation so he came almost every night, to Mart's keen annoyance.

Vacation itself was a subject of national controversy. The Secretary of Education had announced that the school year would be shifted so that eventually vacation would come in June and July. But since the law said it could be changed only a month in any one year, the next term would begin in July this year. The other month change would come the following year. The reason given was that it better fitted the Filipino climate and culture. Anyway, the school year had been set by the Americans who didn't like the hot weather, according to the *Manila Times.* Since Filipinos didn't mind it, it would be better to have vacation during the rainy season so the children would not get wet walking to school. This had obviously been decided by men who had never had a houseful of children underfoot confined by rain in a small house.

No one knew how this affected UP which was not exactly

under the Bureau of Education but reported directly to the President of the Philippines.

Peace Corps didn't much care one way or the other. The directive had gone out that volunteers were to plan special projects for themselves as they were allowed only one month vacation. This called for all of their ingenuity and creative ability: to think up something they wanted to do, that would be different from whatever they had been doing, that would not be overtasking and still get the approval of Director Jacobs.

Martha described all the work it was going to take to finish the set of slides Phil and José had taken although she knew by now they would never be put in usable form. She hated unfinished projects and it had really been a good idea. But Phil dismissed it with a short laugh.

"Now you know what happens to most of our assistance projects. We have a bright idea, the Filipinos agree, we furnish the material, the skills, and really try to teach them but somehow a whole lot of it just frazzles out. U. S. Congress gets mad, we can't explain it. They'd just have to live here awhile to understand it.

"Then what's the use?" queried Martha, who liked to see results.

"Oh, something comes of some of it —think of what this has done for José. That boy's got ability and a brain, and he'll use every skill he can grab."

"But he's a protester."

"Sure, aren't you? I've just been listening to you."

Mart liked his teasing and she wished he'd be more aggressive with Laura. Her plans in that direction weren't going very well.

Laura had worked up a lovely scheme for a project in Laguna. If Luz would just ask her down she could start some recreation for children. She had only the haziest idea of what it could be, and Luz looked perfectly blank when she talked about Daily Vacation Bible School without the Bible or day camps. And she did not respond to Laura's hints about going to the province for vacation. She was as deaf to it as she had been at Christmas. This had become almost an obsession with Laura, an obstacle to friendship which she was bent on overcoming. The two of them taught together, discussed all manner of things amicably, and were still worlds apart. Laura could do nothing to shorten the distance.

"If I just knew what to do, I'd do it," she repeated till her housemates were tired. "Something about me annoys her, and I don't know what I'm doing wrong."

"Well, you can't get anywhere by pushing head-on, that's for sure," said Isobel in the way she had of indicating full understanding of Filipinos. "Do you want me to be a go-between?"

"My gosh, no, heaven forbid." So that settled that, for a while.

Laura's daily trips to Taft Avenue became more tiring as Manila steamed like an unsavory pudding, emitting the stench of man, his beasts, and his machines.

The day finally came to the Normal School when all exams had been given and graded. Laura and Luz sat side by side at the desk going over records, attempting to arrive at an agreement on grades. Most of them were not difficult. Laura did not try to push her own judgment between a 1 or a 2, a 2 or a 3. As they went along they put aside the lowest group on which they had strong disagreement. Now they had to be faced.

"Luz, I don't see how you can avoid failing Angeles. She just hasn't done passing work all year."

"She will be married in May, actually."

"What difference does that make in her grade?"

"Not any, so why not pass her?"

"Because she did failing work, that's why."

"But it would be nice to give her her diploma before her wedding already."

Laura took firm hold on herself. Actually it would not lower the reputation of the school because Angeles would never enter another educational institution. She would never crack a book again, but she could show her diploma to her ten or fourteen children. Let it pass, there were more important ones to come.

"Caesar Francisco. Now I have him down for a 4."

Luz poised her pencil above the scratch pad. "He did get a 3 in the exam."

"You know how he did that. You told me yourself about the paper in the toe of Manuel's shoe."

"But he has tried."

"A 3.5?" Laura compromised.

When they came to Domingo Laura felt her determination stiffen. "Now there can be no doubt about him. He can't write, read or speak English and he doesn't care. He failed!"

The blood rose in Luz's face, turning her skin a rosy brown to the hairline. This she had foreseen. She had taken the precaution of preparing a line of defense. But now that she was right here, facing the facts with Laura beside her she was embarrassed about what she had to do.

"He's passing in all his other classes." She tried to make it sound final, and failed.

"So —"

She shouldn't have to answer that question. It was silly, so —? Of course one teacher couldn't be different. Laura was waiting, her clear hazel eyes searching Luz's face. Still Luz couldn't answer. It went so deep. It meant shame to her. A teacher would be ashamed to fail a student others had passed. But shame was something that Laura couldn't or wouldn't understand. Luz had tried before to explain it. So she remained silent.

Laura felt the barrier between them rising like a wall. She pushed the bricks down. The two of them must communicate.

"He's a relative of Mr. Lopez, isn't he?" She offered to make it easy for Luz.

"Yes, but . . . " That was part of it but it didn't stand alone. She knew Laura was scornful of special treatment of relatives, but she could just label it "cultural," and it would be better than to know that Luz was afraid of shame.

"Yes!" she stated firmly and then in defense. "That happens in the States, too, I know it does."

Laura's indignation cooled. Of course it did. She thought of how she and her friends had lamented that they were not daughters of a college trustee, like Elizabeth. But they were never sure she got special treatment. Oh well, she and Luz had at least talked across the wall. That was as much as she could expect.

Luz was the one that was unhappy. She felt smaller, somehow. She wanted so much to have Laura's respect and she didn't want to dissemble to get it. Domingo's card was marked "4."

Laura should have left it at that, but curiosity forced the question, "Does anyone ever fail in a Filipino school?"

"Oh, yes!" quickly and then on reflection. "I'm sure somebody does."

"I really don't see how schools expect to maintain standards if everyone passes no matter what they do. In some schools in the U. S. they grade on a curve."

"A curve?"

"Yes, it's been established that in an average group there

will be so many 'A's' and so many 'D's' and the others falling between on a curve of a graph, you know, and some fail."

"That's terrible. Like for example if eight students did very good work they would not all get 'A' or '1'?"

"No, but . . . " She gave up. Why try and defend the curve system, which she had never liked herself?

Laura stood up, pulled her green print shift away from her body where it clung with perspiration, and admired Luz's crisp neatness, for the hundredth time wondering how she did it. At times like this she was acutely conscious of the cultural note they had been given in training that the body odor of Caucasians is offensive to Filipinos. She moved away from the desk.

"What time should I drop by your house, mum —Laura?" The "Laura" was added quickly.

Laura remembered with a start that this was the night Luz was coming to dinner.

32

Luz Comes to Dinner

It had been Martha's suggestion to invite Luz to dinner. Laura had reluctantly agreed. Yes, it was a natural thing to do, for an American, but even Americanized Filipinos seldom invited a few friends in to a sit-down dinner and she was not at all sure it wouldn't be a fiasco.

"Nonsense," Mart had said. "It is natural for us so we will do it. What better way to get acquainted on an off-work basis. Filipinos had better learn to do it. They all have help so it's not much trouble. If she doesn't want to come she can say no."

"Oh, no, of course she can't say no!"

"She can say yes and not come," suggested Isobel. "They do it all the time."

"I'd hate that, we'd get ready and wait and not know . . ."

"Then we'd eat it ourselves," Martha said practically. "What shall we have for dinner?"

There was a long discussion on this. Should it be Filipino food or American? Maybe she wouldn't like American but it was timid to serve her Filipino. It should be something that didn't spoil if she were late.

"We'll just plan on that," said Martha.

"She gets to school before I do," Laura defended.

"Of course, they can do it if they want to."

"We could start to cook after she gets here like they do in the province."

It was finally decided they would compromise on a combined Filipino-American menu. Mona was consulted.

"What is a very special Filipino dish—that you can cook, Mona?"

"Deess, mum?"

"Food. Something you have at a feast."

"Not too fancy a feast," put in Isobel. "I don't want to starve the rest of the month."

"*Adobo*, mum?"

"No, something you don't have often."

"*Pancit*, mum?"

"You make?"

"You buy, mum."

"Oh, that's the rice noodles with all those things in it, shrimp, pork, onion, tomatoes. That's good."

"*Lapu lapu*, mum." The way she said it they knew Mona had been working up to a climax.

"What's that!" Isobel was suspicious.

"Feess, mum, stuffeded."

"*Lapu, lapu*, wasn't that the name of the *datu* who defeated Magellan? That would be a nice historical touch."

"This is food, not ancient history," Martha reminded her, "and I think that sounds great. Will you get all the fish in the market?"

"Yes, mum."

"And rice. Now for a vegetable."

"Onions?"

"Enn fees, mum."

"Carrots?"

"Enn fees, mum."

"Tomatoes?"

"In fish, mum," they all chimed in and laughed together, Mona the hardest of all.

"I'll make a pudding out of that can of corn we have been hoarding. That's as American as apple pie, and Filipinos eat corn, too. Now for dessert." Laura was getting in the spirit of the thing.

"No cheekin, mum?"

"Not with fish."

"Let's not get that Filipino, one main dish is enough. Besides, it's all we can afford," reminded Isobel.

Mona looked disappointed; they had said "feast."

Dessert must be American. Jello, that pleased the volunteers so much? Better not risk it. Ice cream? Everyone liked that.

"Cake, mum." Mona was so sure of it, they agreed. That was Mart's specialty. Isobel generously offered to buy rolls.

Luz had accepted the invitation so calmly, with a lift of the eyebrows and a slight tilt of the chin, that Laura was uncertain whether she had understood. But she hated to risk insulting her by asking for a more definite reply. Today, a week later, the hassle over grades had driven everything else from her mind. Luz's question as to the time of dinner came as a confirmation of the event.

"Oh, about 6:30." At the surprise in Luz's face she explained, "We can't get over our American habit of an early dinner." Now Luz looked really distressed so Laura made a quick revision. "Seven o'clock would be fine since it is four-thirty now." She realized Luz would have to go home first and traffic must be figured in. "OK?"

"Yes, m . . . OK."

Surprise, consternation were mild words to describe the panic Luz felt at hearing dinner was so early. Her new dress would not be finished 'til 5:30. Then she must get home, wait 'til dark to take her bath in the lean-to, wash her hair and make the jeepney and bus trip out to UP. She'd never accomplish all that in time. Maybe she'd better not go at all. She had considered this many times since Laura's invitation but she was compelled to go, not by the Peace Corps girls, by herself. She had worked out every detail so carefully she could not give up now.

From the tiny hoard of money she saved out of her salary for herself, she had extracted fifteen pesos. Two evenings after school she had toured Paco, Quipo, and Central markets looking for the perfect dress material. Remnants, imported from the States, were stacked to the ceilings of the little stalls, colors, patterns, fabrics to stimulate desire in the heart of any female, but they were more expensive than those made in the Philippines. Philippine fabrics were just as good, she tried to persuade herself, just as bright, just as soft, just as fine —well, almost. She looked, she fingered, she spread out, she held up to herself, but she kept going back to the American fabrics. There was something, just something that made them different, and she had never had a piece. To go to dinner with Americans she should have an American dress, she rationalized. And there it was! She knew it the minute she saw it, pulled it out of the pile and spread it on top of the other pieces. It was yellow, no pink, no, about the color of ripe mango. It was a shaft of late afternoon sunshine laid across her brown arm. Wide open white blossoms had been tossed across it at random. It was two yards, just enough for her slim figure —if it was short. She'd have to get out of the house without her mother seeing her.

"Ten peso?"

"No, too much, seven."

"No, mum, nine?"

"What's your best price?"

"Eight, last price, mum."

So she counted it out and left, hugging the precious package to her. A dressmaker around the corner from home agreed to make it for six pesos. Her school shoes would have to do. She bought some good smelling shampoo with the last peso.

After Laura had gone Luz swept the grading books into her desk drawer, ran out to the street and squeezed onto the first jeepney. It wasn't just the new dress and the excitement of dinner that gave her this feeling of exhilaration, it was a piece of news she had been saving for two days, waiting till just the right moment and setting to tell Laura. Telling her would complete the good feeling she had just from knowing it herself. She did not bother to figure out why. Tonight was the perfect time. The news acted as a shield for her shyness. What kind of a house they lived in, whether she would be dressed properly, or what strange food she would be expected to eat was not as important as it had been two days ago —before the news. She now had a secret sense of personal importance.

It was seven o'clock, and dinner was almost ready at the Peace Corps cottage. The *lapu lapu* was in the oven, the corn pudding was turning brown on top, rolls were warming, and the rice was almost fluffed. Cucumbers and raw sliced *sincamas* swam in vinegar and salt.

"It's too soon, I told you not to plan dinner till seven thirty," said Isobel.

"Laura gave her an extra half hour," Martha said. "Anyone should be able to get dressed and get here in two and a half hours."

"Traffic is bad," Laura reminded them.

7:15 —7:30 —7:45 —no Luz.

Laura stopped pretending to read the paper.

"Maybe she forgot. I'm going to eat a sandwich," fussed Isobel.

"How could she forget, we just talked about it at four thirty. This gives you time to put on something decent, Iz. I do think those shorts are lousy."

"It's hot, and I'm going to be comfortable in my own home, thank you."

"I just don't see how you can run a country where people have no sense of time," a remark Martha made frequently.

"She's probably decided not to come at all, like I told you in the first place."

Martha could not stay out of the kitchen. "Fish is getting dry."

"You guys can do as you please, but at eight sharp I'm going to cut myself a piece of it," Isobel said peevishly.

Seven-fifty-five, steps on the gravel road. They all fell silent and listened. The steps turned toward the house.

"Just in time," grunted Isobel.

Laura drew a relieved breath, smiled at Martha, and went to the door. She was so surprised at the girl she saw there she hesitated before asking her in. This smartly dressed young woman in a skirt above her knees did not look like the shy circumspect young woman she taught school with. She managed to greet her graciously and introduce her to Martha. Martha was more blunt.

"She's lovely! Laura why didn't you tell us how pretty she is?" Luz blushed and liked Martha instantly.

Isobel caught in a flash a trim figure with hair piled high, all bronze and gold like an autumn picture, and sneaked to her room to emerge in a dress and heels.

The *lapu lapu* was served grandly with his head on a bed of shredded lettuce, his eye shining, his insides stuffed, and a creamy sauce running down his sleek sides.

Mona whispered in Martha's ear, "Give mum dee eye, mum." Martha looked horrified and poised the knife above his middle.

"De eye, mum." They could all hear her, and suddenly Luz giggled and explained.

"The eye is considered the best piece."

"You eat it?" gasped Martha.

"Yes, mum, it is very tasty."

Mart stared at the eye. It stared back. "How do I get it?" she asked helplessly.

Mona, emboldened by the presence of a fellow country-man, brought a sharp knife and deftly dug it out in one stroke and put it on Luz's plate. That broke them up, they laughed and choked, and after that conversation was easy. The corn pudding was rather shriveled, and Luz merely nibbled at it. She asked for sugar on the cucumbers. There was no big spoon at her plate so she managed very well with a fork until the last bits of rice and fish. These she chased around on her plate until she saw Mart use a piece of bread to push it on her fork, and Isobel used her finger. Luz used her knife. The cake was a fitting climax, and Luz ate two pieces.

They talked about schools, avoiding grades, about food and eating habits. Luz was full of questions of the kind they were now accustomed to but had resented at first. They tossed them right back. How old was she, how many brothers and sisters? Did her father work, did the boys go to school? Isobel asked where she got the material for her dress and how much she paid for it—to Mart's embarrassment but not Luz's. It was a girls' fun evening.

By the second piece of cake the conversation got around to José, and Luz made her momentous announcement as quietly and casually as if it were ordinary news.

"José will be having a job on the dam in my province."

It fell flat. "That's nice," commented Mart, who saw nothing startling in the news. "What will he do?"

"He's an engineer, mum." How great that word sounded, not a student after next week, not a farmer, not a tenant, not a laborer, but an engineer. She even knew the kind, "civil." But that was about the limit of her knowledge of an engineer.

Laura caught the glint in her eyes and noticed that her breath came in short puffs.

"Luz, that's wonderful. Will you be going back to the province?"

"I . . . no . . . I will teach." It was an anticlimax but how could she explain that she and José had not yet agreed on a method for a non-arranged marriage. José had said flatly, "Elope." But she couldn't do that—yet.

Isobel was practical. "You better go back, Luz, and hang around, he's a handsome guy."

Luz shot a pitying glance at the blonde who had kissed José, but did not reply. That girl had no power to hurt her now, she was sure of her man.

Another idea occurred to Martha. "Will he be working for the government?"

"Yes, mum."

"But I thought he was kind of a revolutionary."

"He says, mum, revolution is for students. He is over being a student already. He will get a good position and go into politics maybe and revolt from the inside."

"Like his father?" suggested Isobel.

"Not like his father, he will not be in the same province." Oh dear, she might have known they would not understand what an enormous step this was for him—and for her. To leave his home base and strike out for himself in a strange place. She was so proud of him, and now they were picking her glorious news to bits.

Involuntarily she looked to Laura for help, and Laura responded. "I think he is very smart to do it, Luz. If he went back to the Laoag he'd always be in the shadow of his father."

"Even he is Liberal Party, his father is Nationalista." If that wasn't revolution enough there was no use talking about it any more. Besides, her eyes had been busy from the moment she had entered this house, and now she felt at home enough to let her curiosity surface. She had never been in a house occupied by Americans before, and pictures in magazines had not prepared her for this—this display of familiar Philippine things put to strange uses.

"Clam shells?" she asked pointing to the arrangement on colorful San Francisco leaves in the center of the table.

"Yes, our Peace Corps friends in Cebu picked them up on the beach and cleaned them in muriatic acid." Decorations were Isobel's speciality.

"Very big mat," Luz nodded to the *sala* floor.

"We have such awful cement floors, so we sewed four small mats together. They aren't very straight," Laura apologized. She couldn't tell whether Luz liked them or not.

Luz's eyes moved to the curtains. Fancy white lace curtains, tied back, were common enough, but these were plain net and hung straight, covering the windows. They must filter the light almost like capiz shells.

Mart followed her gaze and was embarrassed. "They're dirty and the sun rots them but we are going to make more, the net is very cheap in the market."

Luz continued to ask about each item strange to her, or seemingly misplaced. The mat on the wall, woven like a sunburst, came from Poco market and covered a crack. The painted red tables had been cracked brown varnish. Luz marveled at the window screens. No flies? How could that be?

"Well, they don't keep out gnats, lizards, or cockroaches," said Laura. "Or mosquitoes. The university sends a truck down the street spraying a cloud to kill mosquitoes, and it just drives them into our closets for refuge."

Amused and complimented, now the girls gave Luz a tour of the house, telling where they had scrounged for each item. Luz sat on a mattress on a bamboo bed and made a resolve to cast aside a life-long ambition. She would not crochet a lace coverlet to spread over satiny blue rayon on her bed—if she ever had one—she would have a cover of plaid *patajong*, red, yellow, and blue. That bedspread threw an entirely new light on Laura. It wasn't state-side, it was Filipino woven, what they made skirts out of in Mindanao. Just two lengths basted together and not even hemmed.

Laura took Luz to the last bus, ran home, and went straight to bed and worried. Had the dinner been a success or had it widened the gap between them? Why did Americans just naturally, inevitably fix things, use what was at hand but change it? They had spent practically nothing on their second- or third-hand furnishings, a little paint, some sewing, some cheap mats, why had it amazed Luz so? She hadn't missed a thing. She had laughed. but not as if they were silly but as if she liked it.

The moonlight slanted in through the window, and Laura put herself to sleep sliding down the beam and then slowly climbing back up. She hoped she was on the way up with Luz.

33

Letters Home

FROM MARTHA

Dear Alice:

This is not going to be a letter for students to hear and it's not going to be a do-your-best-to-understand type. I'm disgusted, fed up, had it—or whatever the current slang is. I've been here eight months and I might just as well have stayed in Mt. Vernon as far as having any effect on the Philippines is concerned. And nobody needs to tell me that you can't change a culture in eight months. I know that but I did think I could do a little something in my small corner (humility is a virtue, I would remind you). Well, I've just got to describe what it's like to try to get a project done in this country. My PC housemates are so absorbed in their own experiences I don't get much sympathy for my affairs. (When have I ever asked for sympathy!) It's not sympathy-pity I need it's sympathy-how-can-it-be-like-that.

So—this is the way it is and I won't be able to convey the harassment that results from the pile up of little things. Peace Corps even has a term for it—culture fatigue.

Martha wrote on, rapidly, compulsively. It was as if her control dam had broken down. Her efforts to get along, to excuse, to work around, to be tolerant, to look beyond the immediate situation, to see things from the Filipino angle—all had washed downstream by her forty-five years of inherent Americanism. She allowed it all to pour from the point of her pen onto the pages.

I do all the work on this magazine the College of Education publishes. I found the July issue had not gone out till September . . . the contents is determined by articles the faculty members want published, result—dull . . . Sympathy with overworked faculty . . . make

about $2,000 a year . . . the major problem is to get the articles *in*
after they have been promised . . . editing a major job, how much do I
change? Spelling better than mine . . . they like big words with obscure
meaning. I sit with a dictionary beside me. . . . Manuscript to the
printers . . . half-day's travel by bus and jeepney . . . page proof late of
course . . . proofread . . . return to printer . . . another page proof,
new errors . . . typesetter positively creative in changing good English
to bad. We did get the October issue out in November. . . . In December I discovered the issues were stacked under the secretary's
desk . . . something about a postal permit . . . secretary now my enemy
for life.

Enough about the magazine. My private pet project is the set of
slides with a tape on teaching English. Phil and José, Laura's co-
teacher's boy friend, took the pictures and made the recording at no
cost to the university, but I have to get approval before it can be used
in class. And something has stalled. I can't find out what. Nobody will
say it isn't good but no one will OK it. Somehow, somewhere I have
stepped on somebody's toes, but I guess I'll never know whose or why.
This is so exasperating. Why can't they come out with it so it can be
fixed up to suit them?

I'm not doing well either on my muddling meddling matchmaking, to which you know I am addicted. Laura is certainly muddling
along obviously devoted to Dick, the ex-PCV—I was going to say
"scamp" but he's too serious for that about his revolutionary leanings.
At the same time she's leaning—and that is the right word—on this
very right man, Phil at the Embassy. There doesn't seem to be anything I can do about it, strange to say, and anyway I am going to
Cebu tomorrow with another middle-aged volunteer.

So, my friend, "thanks for listening,"
Martha

Dear Mom and Dad:

My letters to you lately have been full of difficulties and irritations and I have made a resolve to stop thinking that way. It can
become a habit—a typical Peace Corps habit, I must admit. So I am
turning over a new leaf and beginning with you. I'll tell you about a
charming member of our household I have not mentioned before because she has a long story. She's a cat. If this letter has more form
and "style" than usual it is because I may polish this tale up, deper-
sonalize it and submit it to *The Boluntario* which is the PC Philippines

227

newspaper. I think I'll call it, "Cats Isn't Cats" (with apologies to "Pigs Is Pigs." Remember how we used to laugh over that?).

To begin with, all we wanted was a kitten. Not a personality, not an invasion, not any international incident. Just a small, ordinary cat to have around the house for company. Male preferred. He wouldn't even have to catch mice, we don't have any. We have cockroaches, twenty-nine varieties of insects, frogs, snakes, but no mice. We didn't know we all wanted a cat until the Williamses came to call one day with a kitten in a box.

It was a little wild, full of fleas, yellow, white, and black, which, on Mart's authority, means it is a she. But we thought we could handle that. She was so little, we'd keep her in the house. So she became part of our household and we revamped our lives to accommodate her.

Laura stopped writing and looked intently at the cat curled up in their best chair with its head tucked under a paw. She could well imagine her mother's disappointment with a letter about a cat. But she didn't feel like writing about anything personal. She was tired—tired thinking about human relationships, especially her own. It was easier to think about cats, cats vs. people. And Tiza had revealed so many cultural differences that her mother really should know, if she were ever to get any insight into her daughter's life here. So with pen poised she tried to get into focus the major crises which life with Tiza had encompassed.

That name first. It was short for *mestiza*, the word for mixed Spanish and Filipinos. The cat was obviously mixed and fortunately Mona had thought it was funny, too. Discipline caused more trouble. Tiza had to be trained —to a box, to stop that awful yowling, to stay out from under people's feet. Mona disapproved at every step.

"Filipinos don't train anything," Isobel had airily announced. "You tell them or you fire them."

"So you can't tell Tiza or fire her. She has to learn gradually from experience how to behave." But if anyone slapped Tiza, Mona went weeping to her room.

After receiving a name, some training, and a bath with expensive flea soap —which Mona protested—Tiza flourished under the lavish outpouring of affection from four lonesome females. She pulled them all together, made them laugh and relaxed them with her antics. This alone was worth defying the Peace Corps rules about no pets.

With their door open to cats others came. Mart with that

half-dead ball of fur she had found in a tuna fish can in a
garbage can. They could not restrain their horror at people
who abandoned but would not "put to sleep" unwanted animals. This precipitated another crisis with Mona. "Iss too many
cats," she insisted. All their loving care had not saved the kitten.
Mona made no effort to conceal her disgust at the ceremonial
burial they gave it.

The next cross-cultural problem had been initiated by
Isobel's Thai students. Hearing she liked cats, they presented
her with a mangy gray monster with a chewed-off tail. Tiza
scolded and hissed from inside the screen. Isobel sneaked food
to it. Mart said darkly that the Zoology Lab paid fifty cents
apiece for stray cats. Iz had howled in protest that she could
never admit to her Buddhist Thai that Christian Americans
killed a cat. Mona threw stones at it. The unwelcome intruder
disappeared one day, and no one asked any questions.

Then came spring, or some kind of seasonal cat cycle and
neighborhood cats came to call. Mart said the Veterinary Department spayed cats free for the practice. "And you a Catholic,"
Isobel had teased. *Cats are cats,* Mart reasoned. But a side
glance at Mona's horrified face had stopped that idea.

Laura had sighed, "Well, Tiza, if you must, take the black
one. He's the prettiest." She had.

Laura finally got it all written down, making it as interesting and amusing as possible. But it was an exercise in futility.
She closed abruptly.

Well, Tiza had two kittens, black. Three cats are more fun than one
but we sensibly gave the kittens away, realizing they would soon be
replaced. One went to the Lawrences, PC deputy director. They have
seven children so it won't last long. I gave the other to Phil Thomas
because Mart found out he was a cat rescuer.

Conclusion: So—cats aren't cats in the Peace Corp. They are
emotional compensators and symbols of international, intercultural,
interreligious differences.

So that's our cat tale!

All my love to you both,
Laura

Laura slowly folded the letter and put it in an envelope. It
would take a lot of postage. She wasn't happy about what she
had written —all that cat business so she would not have to write
about what was really important. Circumlocution was not com-

229

fortable to her; concealng things might get to be a habit.

But no one had a right to know how she felt when Phil took the tiny kitten into the hollow of his big square hand. He held it near his face and with a finger gently traced the white line that ran from the nose around the ear. A sensation of loving care flowed over her as she watched it encompass the kitten. She consciously shook it off. The man from the United States Embassy was hard, hard, don't forget. He had refused to help Dick, how could he be so tender with a kitten. It didn't fit.

She had laughed sharply, "You're an odd man, but I see our kitten at least has found a friend."

He had frowned at the tone of her voice but had made no reply. She knew he knew what she meant, and now as she sealed the envelope she wished she had not goaded him.

FROM ISOBEL

Sharon Darling:

As far as the university is concerned this is summer vacation, but dear Peace Corps says we have to cook up a project to occupy us, so U. S. Congress will be impressed. I had some swell ideas that didn't work out but now I have thought up a doozy—teaching horseback riding at the country club in Baguio. As I always say, it just takes a little imagination to get along in this world. I figure I'll find a new "companion" or two or three up there, I'm pretty tired of what I've had around here.

Last night we had what was supposed to be a bust to appropriately wind things up. Like most events around here it started simply enough, to be a double date. Dick, the ex-PC guy came to town and expected Laura to be waiting around for him, but she wasn't eating her heart out waiting, she had a date with that fellow at the Embassy I told you about and she wouldn't break it. Seems that's part of her ethical code—don't break a date. So Dickey-boy was stood up, which pleased me. He's more my type than hers but neither of them seem to know it. I opened my big mouth and suggested Ramon (my attachment) might get him a date with a Filipina and we'd double.

"Big deal," he muttered in his beard but he couldn't think of anything better to do. So I told Ramon to get a sharp date for Dick. He said (to make it short) he'd get Nina (say that like it had a "Y"). But Nina couldn't go unless her friend Rosa went. So good boy Ramon got his friend Baby for Rosa. Go ahead and laugh, I did, but that's his *name* not a nickname or an insult. When Dick heard it he

blew his top and refused to go but changed his mind when he saw this
big (for Filipino) hulking basketball player. But I'm getting ahead of
my story.

Isobel was having trouble with her letter, too. She wanted
one of her old buddies to laugh with her about an evening so
Filipino, so utterly fantastically alien to their way of doing
things that she still giggled to herself every time she thought of
it. But it just couldn't be made as funny written down to someone who hadn't any background on it.

To make it real she had to include details.

You won't believe this, but Dick and Baby had to call on Nina's
parents. A girl can blind date apparently but her parents have to *see*.
So Tuesday Dick and Baby and Ramon, of course, to introduce them
took a bus and a walk to Fil-Am Life Homes (pronounce that "Fel-
lum"). Ramon finally found the house and papa came to the door. You
ought to hear Dick tell this. Papa didn't know what they were there
for and Ramon didn't tell him. But seeing an American he began to
tell World War II stories. Various females kept going in and out and
Dick kept his eye on the prettiest, hoping she was Nina. They thought
they were invited to dinner but were never sure, anyway they stayed
as papa was on the Bataan march and they couldn't leave him there.
Ramon said they had passed inspection though he wouldn't tell them
how he knew.

Well, Wednesday came, Rosa could go and the date was on for
7:30. It would take more paper than I've got to tell you the complica-
tions of getting three fellows and three girls to a restaurant when each
one was in a different part of the city. No couple could go alone, of
course, and the girls could not go unaccompanied.

After it had been hashed out by the fellows and both sets of parents, Dick solved it by saying the three girls and Ramon—because he
was the best known—would take one taxi and the two other guys
would go together. The first taxi had been waiting all this time, the
meter clicking like crazy and I knew each click hurt Ramon where he
lives.

Well, we got there and I will spare you the details of the dinner.
When you go out to dinner in the Philippines you have either American food or Chinese. This was American, so they claimed. The steak
was warm leather, potatoes "home fried" like no home would claim
them, the drinks too strong even for me but that made you forget the
food. The ice cream was mostly reconstituted coconut milk, I'm sure,
although usually that is one thing you can get good. The girls mostly

giggled and said nothing. Dick and Baby argued American professional football. Ramon was too much interested in Nina and it was a lousy evening. Since we didn't eat till 9:30, by the time we were through it was time to go home, unwinding ourselves the way we had come.

Dick said no more Filipinas for him. It was like dating a gorgeous flower that turned out to be a cactus. I told him there were other kinds available. If you ask me that boy is ripe for the picking and Laura-girl had better get cracking.

"It's good-bye Manila for me for a month. Baguio, here I come.

Iz

34

I'm Free, I'm Me

Laura and Dick walked through the gateway into Balara. It was early evening but already dark. Families and picnickers had left the park, and they met only a few couples on their way out. They circled the dry fountain and Laura laughed.

"Isn't it funny for modest Filipinos to put a nude lady pouring non-water out of a jar in a family park?"

"She has a drape," observed Dick, "and besides she is Greek, or Roman, so that makes her art." He took Laura's hand and steered her across the street, around a service shed to a grassy slope overlooking a valley. The lights in small houses on the opposite hill seemed very far away. They stretched out on the grass and talked in whispers although there was no one to hear but a small goat tethered to a tree. The heavy heat of the day had passed, leaving a soft light warmth and a thick stillness that sopped up all sound except for the singing of the locusts. Stars hung from the black satin canopy.

"If I half shut my eyes they look like those tiny white Christmas tree lights that twinkle," said Laura. But the illusion quickly vanished, the stars were not twinkling and merry to-night, they were watching. And Dick was in no mood for fanciful conversation. She tried to keep a light chatter going to postpone the event she felt approaching. For many months she had imagined this night, had placed it, staged it, and rehearsed it. She knew the "sometime" Dick had promised would come, and she thought she knew what she would do. But not yet. Her blood and her nerves felt him touching her, a purposeful, intimate touch; with her ears and a part of her mind she heard him talk in tense tones.

"It's tonight, this it it, Laura. I am going to meet them."

"Them?" She didn't want any "thems" or any other "this is it" to distract from the total physical climax toward which they were moving. Politics, intrigue—what did they matter. This was their night, hers and Dick's. But Dick went on.

"I am sailing tonight on the *President Cleveland* with Mr. Valera for Taiwan. A pleasure trip, he said, but I am sure it is because I have asked in a roundabout way to go with some of the—a—goods being sent to Formosa Freedom Party. But I never get any response, no recognition of my request. But I think this is it."

"But who, why?" Laura turned down her pulse to examine the apprehension she felt in another part of herself.

"I thought I knew, but this morning a strange thing happened. I got a message. It's that network, I don't know how they do it. But a little bamboo table was delivered by a jeepney to my apartment. It was just like one I had bought last fall from that Chinese furniture store. But I haven't been back on Pin-a-pin Street for a long time, so I said it wasn't for me. But the driver pointed to a sticker with my name on it taped to the leg, and he left. I was mad—and curious, too—so I tore off the sticker, and under it was a tiny folded piece of paper and on it was printed in pencil, 'Tonight at eleven, Pier Twelve.' "

Now Laura was thoroughly alarmed. "Dick, you can't mean to go, you don't know what you are walking into!"

"I've already walked," he said flatly. "I know I don't know, I told you that in the hospital. But I'm inside in some small way, and that's where I want to be." He pulled at the grass near him, tearing it to shreds. "I don't know what connection there is between Mr. Valera and the note. The *President Cleveland* sails at midnight so I'll go to Pier Twelve first and can still make the ship. I've got to find out whether I'm in contact with two groups or one. I have to make sure now whom I'm helping."

Laura lay back on the grass fixing her attention on the stars again. This was a part of Dick she could not share and did not want to. She would wait for him to come back to her.

He came quickly. "So this may be our last night—for a long time—who knows." He bent over her, shutting out the stars. "Our last, and first."

His lips softly nuzzled her face, ears, and throat and finally pressed hard on her lips. Sensation she had never known before swept over her. All feelings seemed to dissolve into one. She welcomed his weight upon her, and the pounding of his heart met the beat of the blood in her body. Slowly, gently, his hand found the way beneath her skirt and stroked her thigh, fingers probing. Time and place were no more, the only reality was their two bodies yearning for completion. All her feelings, physical and emotional were concentrated in that part of her that was readying for intrusion. She felt his muscles harden.

Suddenly, without any conscious decision there came revulsion. It was as if her private, personal door slammed shut. Consciousness returned, she opened her eyes, pushed her hands against his chest, and shoved him roughly aside and stood up— all in one motion.

"I can't!" she gasped in a quivering breath.

"Damn you, you will!" Dick jumped to his feet and grabbed her. "You can't do this to me." His face was hot with anger and frustration. Laura went limp in his grasp, and with a shake he released her.

"You're a cheat, a hell of a cheat! For months you've been telling me by every way a girl has that you wanted me."

"I know, I thought I did." She said it calmly, wonderingly. "But I can't. I don't know why." She didn't feel like adding, "I'm sorry."

The fire of his desire began to cool, he tried to regain his nonchalance as he tucked in his shirt and said with a short dry laugh, "I should have known right from the beginning. You're a kitten —a cat —" an edge of bitterness in his voice. "A cat that walks away, that doesn't belong to anyone."

"Well, I don't belong to you." She was surprised to hear herself saying it. "But I'm not a kitten, not a cat." Her voice rose and she flung out the words, "I'm me, myself, just myself! And whoever takes me, takes me whole, *all of me!*"

She tossed her head back and looked up, her face pale in the starlight. Dick watched her, amazed. She was happy! So quickly, so easily she could toss him off. He turned away, disgusted with himself. He rarely made mistakes about girls.

"So it's over," he said, "I'll catch a bus." He strode off, and Laura came down to earth. She didn't want to be left alone in Balara at night so she ran after him.

He got on a waiting bus and she followed him in. It was an awkward moment. They were the only passengers, it would be silly not to sit with him, but he had so completely removed himself. Anyway he was taking up a whole seat so she sat in front of him. The awkward moment became an embarrassed one when the conductress came by for the fare. Laura had brought no money. She shook her head. The woman went to Dick who gave her one fare, and she returned to Laura. Laura, both annoyed and amused, turned to Dick. "Mister, can you spare a dime?" Without a change of expression he fished out another ten-centavo coin.

The funny side got the better of her. How life's great climax can be cut down to size by a thing like ten centavos. She heard a sympathetic rumbling chuckle behind her. It was a short ride to Apacible Street. "*Para!*" she called.

She stood up and felt a big arm around her shoulders and a brotherly smack on her cheek.

"You might wish me luck, anyway."

"Oh, I do, I do! And please be careful."

She stepped down from the bus, and in the street light he saw her start off on a run and skip.

A skip! She had not skipped since she had long braids. But it went well with the song in her heart, "I'm free, I'm me."

In another level of consciousness she was wrestling with *why*. What had stabbed her awake from that all-encompassing fog in which she rushed to the pinnacle of physical pleasure? Her Dutch Reformed ancestors turning in their graves?

("I'm free, I'm me.") Or the innate value she placed on personal privacy? ("I'm free, I'm me.") Or resistance to shattering her whole-ness? ("Free-me.")

In her new-found release her concern over Dick's entanglement faded.

35

Omega to Alpha

Laura woke with the sun shining on her face. No "UP Beloved" rang out this morning. Classes were over, and there was no schedule to keep.

Laura stretched her legs till her toes touched bamboo and stretched her arms above her head with a deep breath. Then she slowly moved her hands down her thighs as far as she could reach. She was all in one piece, she belonged to herself. A human relationship which had given joy and pain had been terminated. In gratitude she pledged herself to do better with other personal relationships. She would make new efforts to work through to a satisfactory understanding with Luz. She would not allow a termination or deterioration of what little progress toward understanding they had achieved. Little irritations would be ignored like ants (which are only ants, she told herself) and deep differences recognized and accepted if not resolved. Filled with all this noble purpose, Laura rose and dressed.

There was no one to get breakfast for or eat with except Mona. Mart had taken off for Cebu with the only other middle-aged volunteer. Isobel had gone to Baguio and its coolness several days before on her summer project. Since Luz had not responded to Laura's suggestions for a barrio vacation school, Laura had trumped up a research project on the contribution of Filipina women to the economy. There was plenty of live material at hand. Any Filipina with an education was teaching, all the women professors at UP were married, the woman owner of the *sari-sari* store at the corner was typical of hundreds of thousands of small women entrepreneurs. Today she would start properly for any research, at the library. She was sure PC Director Jacobs couldn't care less what she did. He had already retreated to his nipa hut on the shore near Zamboanga where he could wiggle his toes in the sand, drink his imported Scotch, smoke blue seals, and get the volunteers and Washington off his back.

Still in a euphoric state of mind, she returned about 4:30 from a day with books. The house was empty. No one around to relate the day's events to. No one to argue with. The three volunteers had become a sort of family, she realized, different as they were. And Mona, too, although they still didn't know how to regard her and fit her as a servant into their egalitarian ethic. She, not being bothered by notions of an unstratified society, was quite happy with her status and understood it perfectly.

So, rather at a loss without the family, Laura took a cooling bath, dressed in as next to nothing as she possessed and turned on the fan in the *sala*. The *Manila Times* lay on the table, something struck her as unusual. Oh—it was open. Not that that was important, just strange. No housemates here and Mona never read it, though she could. Curious, but not apprehensive, Laura settled herself in the rattan butterfly chair and glanced at the pages which were before her. The usual headlines, "PRESIDENT PRESENTS AWARDS"; "SMUGGLING RING SMASHED"; "BODY WASHED ASHORE." She stopped, reread that headline, and read on.

The naked body of an unidentified man was discovered this morning by fishermen on the south shore of Corregidor. Constabulary and police are investigating, as foul play is suspected. The man was allegedly American, judging by the appearance of the body, which is about 6 feet 1 with red hair. There is a partially healed scar on the left shoulder which could not have been the cause of death according to Coroner de Gusman, who set the time of death at about one A.M.

Laura's hands gripped the paper, her breath came in shallow gulps.

Corregidor police stated that no one answering that description had been seen on the island. Port officials and ticket agents at the hydrofoil docks said no passengers had been reported missing. There has been no reaction nor inquiry by the U. S. Embassy or business community. Captain Miguel Cullo advanced the conjecture that the body might have been thrown overboard from one of the interisland boats

that left North Harbor last evening. Also some sloops commonly en-
gaged in nefarious enterprises were known to have passed Corregidor
in the night.

There was more. The newspaper report made the most of the
gruesome mystery. Laura read it all but before she finished she
was numb except for the pain which sank deep, deeper into her
being —a knife slowly thrust through her.

She crushed the pages fiercely in both hands but she could
still see the terrible print, "BODY WASHED ASHORE."

A body —just a body —not a person, no name, no reason,
no explanation. Nobody to say he tried, he wanted to help, he
believed. He was just a body. She bit her lip to keep from
screaming, "He's a person, a living, thinking, doing, happy person, not a body, a naked body, a nobody. Somebody killed him
because he cared."

What did they do with an "unidentified body"? There was
no one to claim him, no one to say, "He's mine." "Oh, God!"
she whispered. "God, he was important to you and you know I
did love him."

Laura sat motionless, gripping the paper. Questions like
stones rolled around in her mind unanswered. Could anyone
have stopped him? Had there been any way to divert him from
his purpose? Protect him from his ignorance? Her anger
burned out now, leaving only ashes of helplessness.

Pictures dissolved into other pictures in a mist that seemed
to fill the room. Their first meeting, his gay impulsivenesss that
had swept her off her feet —and started her in a new direction.
Pleasure she had had in her life; fun, laughter, but not the
geyser-like bubbling up from the inside to overflow on
whoever was near which he had brought her. It had broken
through layers of restraint from being a minister's daughter to
an answering spring of taking life at its fullest. She was grateful
to him. Then there was the night she had walked away from
the Glowing Coals, asserting her right to be herself—and he
knew and called her a kitten who yawned. On and on through
the past months he had shown her himself and herself till she
felt bound to him, needing him, though there had been no
promises. Then had come the change. She had refused to look
at it straight until now. After their talks in the hospital she felt
as if he needed her. She wanted to guide him, protect him,
divert him or find someone who could. The love she thought
she had for him she tried to use as a force to pull him away

from himself, she could not accept him as he was.

Her stiff lips silently formed the words "I never could have done it." And then last night—when suddenly she was free. Dusk had crept in through the windows and filled the room with tangible fuzzy gray. It enveloped her soothingly, softening lines of reality, and she sat on without moving. Quiet came to her; cold as ice, hard as stone, the fact of death settled on her heart, numbing it.

Sam Wong sat in the back room of his shop, alone. Spread out before him on an old carved chest, not the cheap modern junk he sold out front, was the *Manila Times*. Sam was happy with a deep healing happiness of having eliminated an old, old hurt. He had several pages of the paper from different sections laid out together. By the light of a single bulb he traced the words again in order.

"SMUGGLING RING SMASHED." Over and over he read every word of the story, savoring each. Filipinos were so easy to use it was hardly a challenge. They would smuggle anything for crumbs. They were even happy with the silver coins play and the smell of gold made them putty. Getting gold out of the mines was not difficult. Highgraders made a practice of it, and there was always an inspector who could be cut in. Everyone knew the Chinese were the buyers, and a nice profit there was in that since there was no other market, except the U. S. government who very virtuously insisted on trading above board. But getting any quantity shipped out was more difficult. The boxes for drugs had helped there, they even had U. S. shipping labels which could be rerouted. It had been working very smoothly. So now the stupid Philippine Customs Commissioner had decided to play hero. "Customs Commissioner Ramon Eslabon said, 'Heads will roll in this case, I promise you.'" Not Sam's head, only Filipino heads. In a few weeks it would blow over, and the boxes could be shipped again on President liners instead of being sneaked out on the interisland boats. But the American had got too nosy. He even had ideas about where the gold should go, and no offer of a cut would keep him out. Then first uncle had interfered, and that was the beginning of the end.

Sam had saved the best item to the last.

"*President Cleveland* SAILED AT MIDNIGHT." Among the VIPs on the passenger list was Mr. Raphael Valera. The reporter had kept an eye on him as he was always news and noted,

Mr. Valera was last passenger on board. In fact, this reporter learned on good authority that he had persuaded the captain to delay the sailing for five minutes. He was obviously expecting a companion who did not appear although he stood by the rail watching until after the gangplank had been raised. To all appearances Mr. Valera sailed without his friend, whose identity has not been ascertained.

So he sailed without his friend! Alone! No admiring young American to listen to his tales of old China, of the escape to Formosa. The silly American wanted to help the Formosans throw off the yoke of aging Chiang Kai-shek, and Uncle had let him think he was doing it. But Sam knew, oh, how he knew the net that Uncle was weaving. By the time they reached Taipei the American would have been charmed by the heroism of Chiang, impressed by the success story of land reform on Formosa, the happiness of landed peasants, and would be beginning to doubt his own cause. By the time he had been introduced to gentle-seeming Chiang and fallen under the mysterious spell of Mai Ling and had been pumped full of anti-Mao propaganda he wouldn't know which side of the line he was on. Oh, Uncle was clever, he could make believers out of anyone he wanted from flame-throwing revolutionaries to U. S. Ambassadors. He wouldn't soil his long-nailed hands with smuggling, but he stole people. By the time Uncle got through with him, the American would be of no use to Sam. So he had to be disposed of.

Sam Wong ran the point of his tongue slowly along the line of his wrinkled lips grown thin with the years he had plotted his revenge on the family which had chosen Uncle for the top family position instead of Sam. As for the gold, Sam didn't care who got that as long as he made his share of profit—and a little more. It could be consigned to Formosans, Chiang, or Mao. It brought a better price on Taiwan than in Shanghai. But this time, just for once, he chose Shanghai for the pure satisfaction of taking both gold and Uncle's boy out from under his nose.

Sam frugally turned off the light bulb and closed his eyes. He stroked the three lucky hairs in his mole and amused himself with visions of black-sailed sloops slinking past Corregidor out to the South China Sea.

The *Manila Times* did not publish all the news. Phil had stayed late at his office reading the same items as Sam. Now he reread an official memo marked "Confidential," that lay on his desk. The memo should have given him pleasure as it recorded a case successfully completed. In ponderous diplomatic language it notified the persons whose names were listed that the Philippine government with some assistance from the U. S. Embassy (modestly) had stopped a major leak in gold from the mines to the U. S. market. As a result it was expected that the sale of gold to U. S. would increase slightly. The case was closed.

Phil brushed a hand across his damp forehead. Was gold that important? A little more gold and one "body" to pay for it. This case had not been Phil's assignment but he had been in on it. Could he have stopped it? Or maybe just flubbed it? He placed the memo in a folder and slipped it into a file drawer marked "Classified" which he locked.

He walked to the window restlessly and looked down into the empty square inside the fence. Dissatisfaction with himself filled his being. Why had he not taken more aggressive direct action to win the girl he wanted? It had not been in tune with his normal nature. He usually fought for what he wanted, what he believed was important. His eyes picked out the dark line of the flagpole and followed it to the top, now empty. Certainly he was not a "flag waver" but he would fight for the country it represented. He worked doggedly within the department for policies which respected the dignity of other nations. And as for smaller things—he wandered to his desk and sat down regarding curiously his strong square hands—a kitten left in a trash can could make him angry.

But Laura—he had yearned for her with his whole being, as he wanted her now. His fists clenched against his forehead, his throat ached. But he had wooed her gently, lightly, never showing the intensity of his need for her. Why? He knew why in the depths of him, and now he laid his hands open before him as if looking at the truth. She must come to him. He would not destroy the image she had of another man in order to turn her to himself. He had counted on time, persistence, the ultimate rightness of it, the power of the love she must feel in him to draw her to him. If she had been in any danger he would have fought for her, but he had been so sure he could ultimately win her in fair contest with a living man. But now —one could not contend with the dead . . . One could not win against a memory.

The office had long since been dark. Phil rose slowly, his muscles stiff from tension, and went out, passing the guards with an indifferent goodnight. On the Boulevard several taxis slowed down, hopeful of a fare but he motioned them on. Finally he hailed one, got in, shut the door. The driver started out before he received directions, and after about a block he asked, "Where to, sir?"

Silence. Then in a voice louder than necessary and contrary to all his careful reasoning, Phil commanded, "U.P. Campus, Diliman."

Mona had hid in her room when she heard Laura come in. She had made sure she wouldn't miss the news but she did not know how Mum would take it and she was too timid to be present at the crisis. Now dusk had come and there was still no sound nor movement from the *sala,* and Mona was thoroughly frightened. But curiosity was stronger. She tiptoed out and saw Laura sitting, rigid as stone, looking at nothing. Not daring to speak to her, she slipped by into the kitchen and began noisily getting out pots and pans. Something ought to wake Mum up.

There was a knock at the door and, thankful for the interruption, Mona ran to admit Luz. Laura looked up. She was not surprised to see Luz, somehow she would know and would come. But she wasn't up to making it easy for her.

"Have a seat, mum." Mona supplied the amenities, which included the inevitable next question, "What will you have?" Neither girl answered her so she retired to the kitchen.

"I'm sorry," just plain, straight, and sincere. Luz had tried all the way out on the bus to compose something appropriate to say. But fancy words seemed useless, facing Laura. Laura nodded. She didn't think she had any voice.

"I . . . well . . . I'm sorry." There didn't seem to be anything else to say. To see Laura silent, shorn of her bright, capable, everyday self, was a shock. Luz's mind reeled with questions. Filipinos never took death quietly, and mysterious death was pulled apart to the last quivering shred of emotion shared by everyone.

She had come just because that is what one did, and she knew now because she really wanted to. But she had never expected to see Laura—or any American for that matter—defenseless, unable to cope with events. She wanted to put her arms around her. She wantd to cry with her, but Laura was not crying, she was so terribly quiet. So Luz and Laura just sat side by side and strangely Laura felt herself relaxing in the outgoing warmth of Luz's concern.

Mona's solution for any situation was food. She brought in

slices of last night's cake and tea and started to turn on the light, Mum never ate without looking to see if it was clean.

"No, please." Laura was not yet ready to come to life.

Without her will, her healthy hunger took over. She nibbled at the cake, and the liquid relieved the ache in her throat.

Yearning to share Laura's sorrow but not knowing how, Luz offered her own joy for Laura to share. A warm human comfort flowed softly between them as Luz began to talk,.

At first, Laura scarcely heard what she was saying, being still so immersed in her own sadness. But gradually the words came through, and she began to grasp their significance as she forced herself to think outside of herself.

"Where did you go?" she aroused herself to ask.

"To Cavite, one of those little hotels out near Sangley Point." Laura knew them, nasty places known to Peace Corps and the Navy by names other than hotels. She couldn't imagine Luz in one.

"With . . . ?"

"Yes, with José, of course." Luz's voice had a lilt.

"But, Luz, you're so —a—your family —I mean, how could you?"

"So that now we can get married," Luz explained again patiently.

Laura turned and looked at Luz as though she had never seen her before. The street light sent a pale shaft through the window that caressed the soft curve of Luz's face. *She is beautiful,* Laura thought. There was a glow through the delicate blending of rich creams and browns of hair, skin, and eyes. Laura must understand what had happened to her, and Luz was eager to have her understand.

"You see, now that we already," she chose the word carefully, "*belong* to each other, the priest will have to marry us, our families will have to approve, we will have a regular wedding, and it will be all right!" she finished triumphantly.

Laura fumbled with these ideas and the sequence of events which seemed so upsidedown to her, so logical to Luz. Luz, the traditional protected Filipina woman, had taken her love in violation of her code and so secured her marriage. Laura, the modern, liberated American, had refused her lover, and there would be no wedding.

Luz could not follow her thoughts, even with her sensitive Filipina antenna of interpersonal relations. But without a complete knowledge of the situation she sensed that the tragedy

on Corregidor did not write the end of everything for Laura—
not as it would have if she herself had lost José. She was grateful for the fact that she had been able to open to Laura her
deepest feelings, and Laura had listened and really seemed to
hear her. Luz's cup of happiness was full, and now she could let
it overflow to include Laura. She talked on softly.

"We will have a house. José says he will not live with my
family," proudly. "We will build a house just for us and
Laura—Laura," the name came naturally but she must be sure
Laura was taking it in. "I want you to come and help me deco-
rate it, make it pretty—like yours," she added with a sudden
shyness.

Laura heard the words. The invitation she had craved, had
tried to achieve by devious and obvious means was now offered
freely. The months of groping for each other, the mistakes, the
hurts, the moments of rapport all fused into a natural request
for a friend to help a friend. Laura did not need to pick her
words carefully. Just a simple "Yes" melted the last barrier between them.

Tears are close to laughter when pain and joy mingle and
no explanations are needed. So absorbed was Laura in the in-
tertwined emotions of the last few hours she did not hear the
crunch of tires on the road. But she did hear a familiar firm
purposeful step on the gravel walk. A wave of yearning for the
strength and love she knew were there swept over her.

She rose with a long shuddering sigh, turned on the light,
and opened the door wide.